W9-BXH-285

Congress
and the Court

The Supreme Court, a stormy petrel
in the politics of the country

CHIEF JUSTICE WILLIAM HOWARD TAFT

Walter F. Murphy

Congress and the Court

A CASE STUDY IN THE
AMERICAN POLITICAL PROCESS

THE UNIVERSITY OF CHICAGO PRESS
CHICAGO AND LONDON

Library of Congress Catalog Card Number: 62-9739

THE UNIVERSITY OF CHICAGO PRESS, CHICAGO & LONDON
The University of Toronto Press, Toronto 5, Canada

 Published 1962. Second Impression 1964. Composed and printed by THE UNIVERSITY OF CHICAGO PRESS, *Chicago, Illinois, U.S.A.*

To my Mother

and to

the memory of my Father

PREFACE

The observation that Supreme Court decisions are political in effect is commonplace, yet there is relatively little literature which actually explores the reactions of other branches of government to Court decisions. This book is an effort to contribute toward the filling of this gap. My purpose is the limited one of examining the decisions of the Warren Court and the resulting response of Congress, both to the decisions themselves and to the stimuli of interest groups whose goals were affected by judicial action. I hope that this case study will shed some light on Court-congressional relationships and will serve as one of the empirical steppingstones to a more complete theory of American politics than we now possess.

Like all studies which focus on a single period, this one has inherent limitations. It investigates the Court's relations with Congress during a time of crisis. Much can be learned about the Court and Congress during periods of relative quiet, but there is also a great deal to be gained from observing the behavior of members of these two institutions under the stress of conflict. There is another difficulty, perhaps an insuperable one, which every case study must face, that of generalizing from a single instance. I have met this difficulty—though I do not claim to have completely overcome it—by beginning the book with a brief survey of previous clashes between Congress and the Court. I have not attempted a full history of Court-congressional relations; rather, I have tried to put the political struggle over the Warren Court into historical perspective, and then, after analyzing the attacks on the Court during the years 1954–59, to utilize the historical material to aid in drawing some conclusions about Congress and the Court.

My research methods have been quite simple. For the historical chapters I have relied heavily on published works, though I have also done a considerable amount of investigating of original sources. Throughout the book I have depended for data on the Court on analyses of judicial opinions, although sometimes I have not accepted at face value the explanations offered by the judges. As a check on my own deductions, I have also resorted to some of the statistical methods developed by C. Herman Pritchett[1] and elaborated by Glendon A. Schubert, Jr.[2] None of the apparatus of this form of analysis and little of its results will appear in the text.

In studying the more contemporary reaction of Congress, I modeled my research as far as practicable on the methods of Stephen K. Bailey, in his book *Congress Makes a Law,* rather than on some of the more statistically oriented works. While I make obvious use of speeches in the *Congressional Record,* committee hearings and reports, as well as roll-call votes, these sources seldom reveal the pressures to which legislators are exposed or the bargaining and trading which lie behind a speech or a vote. And these factors are as crucial to understanding the relationships between Congress and the Court as they are to understanding the legislative process itself.

Thanks to the generosity of the Brookings Institution, I was in Washington during the final month of the first session of the Eighty-fifth Congress and for all of the second session. I was thus able to observe at first hand some of the events which I describe. I have relied far more heavily, however, on interviews with senators, representatives, congressional staff members, executive officers, party officials, lobbyists, and newspapermen.

Without exception, these interviews were "off the record," and as much as it pains an academician, my sources cannot be cited or even listed. I am aware of the pitfalls of depending on interviews—memory lapses probably being as dangerous to accuracy as efforts at self-justification. Realizing this, I have used no information which I was not able to verify, at least in large part, either through my own observations or through the testimony of another informant who, if possible, was hostile to my first source. In several places I use dialogue between senators, dialogue which I did not hear. In each case this dialogue is printed as it was reported to me by reliable witnesses. It is not likely, of course, that my informants could have had total recall of these conversations. Even so, I believe that the material in direct quotes represents a substantial reproduction of what was said; and I have used dialogue as a literary device to avoid the tedious stringing out of indirect quotations.

There is a perennial problem of the proper nomenclature to be applied to groupings along the political spectrum, and this difficulty is even more apparent when discussing judicial alignments. "Liberal" and "conservative" are terms as slippery as "left" and "right," and putting them within quotation marks does not infuse them with the quality of precise, objective meaning. I have frequently used these words in their general, but widely understood, sense. I make no apology other than to repeat what Bailey has said about this problem: "It is a distressing fact that the most meaningful words in the lexicon of government are those least capable of clear definition."[3]

One final point needs to be mentioned. Decisions of the Warren Court aroused emotions as much as they stirred thoughtful reflection, and my own position should be stated. While not agreeing with every pronouncement of Warren, Black, Douglas, or Brennan, I concur in C. Herman Pritchett's evaluation of the decisions of the Court's controversial 1956 Term:

> No court can preserve liberty in a country whose people are bent on losing it. But the judgment of a Court, which accepts its responsibility under the Constitution to judge, can give a nation the chance to see how its actions look in the long perspective of history. . . . It can give a community the opportunity to measure its conduct alongside the yardstick of constitutional liberty. The Warren Court is performing this highest of judicial functions.[4]

Recognizing my own prejudices, I have tried to be as objective as possible and to look at the struggle from all points of view; but I put forth no claim to absolute neutrality.

The Princeton University Research Fund generously supported the later stages of this research, just as the Brookings Institution supported the initial stages. Stanley Kelley, Jr., of Princeton University, read the manuscript in two different drafts. Alpheus T. Mason and William M. Beaney, both of Princeton University, C. Herman Pritchett, of the University of Chicago, Jack W. Peltason, of the University of Illinois, and Alan F. Westin, of Columbia University, each read the manuscript in full. Anthony Lewis, of the *New York Times,* and C. Aubrey Gasque, of the Administrative Office of United States Courts, read portions of the book. To all of these people I am deeply grateful for thoughtful criticism and encouragement. I, of course, assume full responsibility for all errors.

My research assistant, Louis K. Werner, of the Princeton Class of 1961, helped check the documentation and did some of the newspaper and periodical research. Mrs. Alise Malone and Mrs. Jean Frost typed portions of earlier drafts. Mrs. Helen Wright carried on the main burden of typing, aided in the proofreading, and made valuable editorial suggestions. I am indebted to Mr. F. Brandon Carlon, of the Department of Defense, and to Mrs. Carlon for their hospitality during all of my visits to Washington in 1959 for follow-up interviews. I would also like to take this occasion to thank collectively the government officials, lobbyists, and newspapermen who gave so freely of their time and information to assist in researching this book. My wife and children performed the most difficult service of all—cheerfully sharing three years of their lives with the friends and foes of the Warren Court.

CONTENTS

1. INTRODUCTION

The casual visitor who wanders through the white marble temple which houses the Supreme Court of the United States comes away with a dominant, almost overwhelming impression of serenity. This tranquillity can be dimly perceived even on the huge stone patio that opens onto the street and the small park in front of the Capitol. Once the tourist climbs the thirty-six steps which extend the width of the building and enters the long, high-columned corridor leading to the courtroom itself, his faint perceptions have turned to unmistakable, however unconscious, recognition. His voice drops to a hushed whisper. Awe gets the better of curiosity, and he looks straight ahead as he walks. When a guard allows him to pass through maroon velvet draperies into the small courtroom, the visitor's awe turns to reverence, and he has to check himself to keep from kneeling as he takes a seat on one of the red-cushioned benches.

Some people, turned sour and cynical from overlong contact with politics, have been less inspired by the Court's working space. One pair of reporters has likened it to "a classical icebox decorated by an insane upholsterer,"[1] but even sophisticated newsmen who cover the

Court with the same air of ennui they would affect in a morgue cannot escape the feeling of peace which pervades the atmosphere.

This air of serenity reinforces the myth that the Supreme Court has traditionally and normally enjoyed the respect and confidence of the American people, that the Court's history has been a chronicle of puzzled citizenry seeking guidance from Jove-like judges and returning from Olympus grateful for divine revelations of constitutional panaceas. Like Daniel Webster's physical appearance, then, that of the Supreme Court building is a living lie. The path of the development of judicial power has been neither straight nor smooth. The Justices have at times been praised as demigods, but they have also been damned as despots. Their hold on the psychology of the American people has sometimes seemed unshakable, but at other times the Justices have had to endure loud jeers of popular disapproval. Occasionally the Justices have taken no part in the political conflicts that divided the nation. More generally, however, the Court, despite its frequent disclaimers, has been, as Chief Justice Taft once observed, "a stormy petrel in the politics of the country."[2] Even more, the Justices have often been active participants in the processes through which national policies are formulated. "We are quiet here," Oliver Wendell Holmes said, "but it is the quiet of a storm centre as we all know."[3]

Claiming authority to interpret the Constitution as well as federal statutes and executive orders, the Supreme Court wields great power. But this power is not unlimited. First, there are the ideological restraints which the Justices impose on themselves; next come the internal restrictions of the Court's being a collegial body and having to act largely through lower court judges. Third, the Supreme Court is also subject to restraints from the other branches of government. Congress can increase the number of Justices, enlarge or restrict the Court's appellate jurisdiction, impeach and remove its members, or propose constitutional amendments either to reverse specific decisions or drastically alter the traditional judicial role in American government. In addition, Congress can strike at judicial power by simply abolishing one tier of federal courts; and conceivably it might try such a tactic against the Supreme Court, as indeed was suggested by one of the Radical Republicans during the Civil War. Reinforcing these theoretical possibilities is congressional control of the purse. Judges are utterly dependent on Congress for appropriations to pay their salaries and to meet the costs of operating their tribunals and executing their decisions.

The President in nominating and the Senate in confirming judicial appointments can also help shape the role which the judiciary will play. As Chief Executive, the President commands the marshals who enforce court decisions. He can instruct them not to execute a court order and pardon them if they are convicted of contempt, just as he can pardon any person convicted of a federal crime. And as chief legislator and head of his party, the President can use his influence to persuade Congress to impeach the Justices, to increase the size of the Court, or to employ any of the other legislative checks on judicial authority.

State officials, except judges, have little direct means of checking federal judicial power. They do, however, have two weapons. The first is nullification, a doctrine which, though tainted by time as running against the grain of American constitutional development, has nevertheless been successfully used to frustrate several federal decisions. Second, and perhaps more important, is the influence which state leaders exercise on Congress, the party organization, and the Presidency. Of necessity, congressmen must operate from bases in local politics and are therefore usually sympathetic to the problems of state officials. While this is less true in the executive department, no President can afford to ignore for long widespread discontent among his local party chieftains.

Perhaps the most significant weapon to counter judicial power which political officials hold is that of their own prestige and their direct access to mass media of communication. A President to whom the nation looks for leadership can throw the moral authority of his office against that of the Court, just as can a senator, congressman, or governor. Whether such an attack will undercut the Court's power or boomerang to the detriment of the attacker depends on the facts of the individual situation.

Given a political system with such powers and counterpowers, it would be expected that there would be constant friction and frequent clashes among the people who share the power to govern. This book is an effort to analyze in detail the causes, the course, and the effects of one important conflict between Congress and the Court, that which began in May, 1954, and reached its climax in August, 1958. But this clash between Congress and the Warren Court cannot be seen in proper perspective without some understanding that this was only one of many similar conflicts in American history. Part I, therefore, consists of a brief summary of several of the more important Court-congressional battles. It is an effort to establish a background rather than to constitute a full history. With this background established, the remainder of the book concentrates on the Warren Court and its relations with Congress.

I THE HISTORICAL PERSPECTIVE

2. MARSHALL, TANEY, AND THE DEMOCRACY

By the time of Thomas Jefferson's inauguration in 1801, the federal judiciary had already become deeply involved in American politics.[1] In 1793, in *Chisholm* v. *Georgia,* the Supreme Court had held that a state could be sued in a federal court. This decision provoked the wrath of Georgia, and the state legislature gave serious consideration to a bill making any effort to comply with the Chisholm case punishable by hanging, "without benefit of clergy."[2] *Chisholm* v. *Georgia* was reversed, but by the adoption of the Eleventh Amendment rather than by violence.

Later in the decade, Supreme Court Justices intimated in several cases[3] that they had authority to declare acts of Congress unconstitutional, though there was no specific use of such power before John Marshall. In 1797, however, the Court declared a Virginia statute regulating rights of British creditors to be in conflict with a federal treaty and therefore invalid.[4] Probably the most conspicuous judicial involvement in politics during the period 1790–1801 can be found in the fact that federal judges not only did not declare the Alien and Sedition Acts unconstitutional but often acted as good Federalists rather than as impartial "jurists" and applied these statutes against Jeffersonians with aggressiveness and, at times, with almost gleeful political partisanship.

PACKING AND UNPACKING THE COURTS

The Federalist defeat in the election of 1800 meant that Jefferson's party would capture the Presidency and would dominate Congress. Nevertheless, the Federalists could still retain a foothold in the national government by continued control of the judiciary. Both parties recognized this potential; and less than a month before Jefferson took office, the Lame Duck Federalist Congress passed the Judiciary Act of 1801. This statute made needed reforms in the existing court system, the most important of which were the elimination of "circuit-riding" by Supreme Court Justices and the creation instead of sixteen circuit judgeships to handle trial responsibilities. But coming as it did during the final weeks of the Adams administration and creating new offices with life tenure to which deserving Federalists were appointed, the Act of 1801 was condemned by the Republicans as a piece of political jobbery. This charge was lent credence by the fact that the Federalists had tried to deprive the incoming President of a Supreme Court appointment by providing that when the next vacancy on the Court occurred, the number of Justices was to be permanently reduced from six to five.

In his inaugural address, Jefferson was conciliatory: "We are all republicans: we are all federalists," he had said. But the new President was aware of the potential conflict with the judiciary. William Giles of Virginia had warned Jefferson that "the revolution [of 1800] is incomplete so long as that strong fortress is in possession of the enemy." Giles urged "the absolute repeal of the whole judiciary system."[5] Jefferson was less inclined to immediate or drastic action. He told Archibald Stuart in April, 1801, that the repeal of the Act of 1801 was to be the work of the next Congress.[6] Meanwhile, acting out of fear of judicial power as well as under party pressure for patronage,[7] Jefferson went about the task of replacing Federalist prosecutors and marshals with Republican appointees. "The only shield for our Republican citizens against the federalism of the courts," he wrote, "is to have the Attornies & Marshals republicans."[8]

But doubts were quickly raised about the efficacy of this shield. Denied the opportunity to preside over prosecutions of Republicans under the Alien and Sedition Acts, some Federalist judges found other ways of harassing the Jeffersonians. Grand juries, compelled to listen to judicial instructions on matters of jurisprudence, made excellent captive audiences for attacks against the evils of democracy. There was even one occasion on which Federalist judges ordered a district attorney to begin a criminal libel action against the editor of the administration's official newspaper for criticizing the courts.[9]

Even more threatening was the suit which one William Marbury was bringing against James Madison, Jefferson's Secretary of State. Marbury had been appointed a justice of the peace in the District of Columbia by Adams; but John Marshall, then Secretary of State, had not delivered the commission. And now Madison refused to do so. Marbury brought suit in the Supreme Court, invoking section 13 of the Judiciary Act of 1789, which he claimed gave the Supreme Court original jurisdiction to issue a writ of mandamus in such cases.

On December 21, 1801, the Supreme Court granted Marbury's request that the Secretary of State be ordered to show cause why the writ of mandamus should not be granted. The prospect of Federalist judges issuing direct orders to a member of his cabinet was, to say the very least, distasteful to Jefferson. Senator Breckinridge of Kentucky told the President that this was "the most daring attack which the annals of Federalism have yet exhibited."[10] Two weeks later the Kentucky senator introduced a resolution to repeal the Judiciary Act of 1801 and, by abolishing the new circuit courts, to turn the sixteen recently appointed judges out of office.

This proposal brought on a great debate on the necessity of an independent judiciary as well as on the question of judicial review. Gouverneur Morris asked the Senate: Would not repeal be "a declaration to the remaining judges that they hold their offices subject to your will and pleasure?"[11] Senator Jackson of Georgia replied, "I am more afraid of an army of judges . . . than an army of soldiers. . . . Have we not seen sedition laws?"[12] Senator Stevens T. Mason of Virginia stated that he was in favor of an independent judiciary but not of judges who were "independent of the nation itself."

The pending case of *Marbury* v. *Madison* was a live issue in the debate, and Mason denied that Courts should "control the other departments of the Government. . . . Have we not heard this doctrine supported in the memorable case of the Mandamus lately before the Supreme Court?" The real danger, Mason asserted, was that "independence of the judiciary" would become "something like supremacy." Judges might, the senator said prophetically, "hold the Constitution in one hand, and the law in the other, and say to the departments of Government, so far shall you go and no farther."[13]

Senator Breckinridge categorically denied any judicial authority to void laws of Congress. "Is it not extraordinary," he asked, "that if this high power was intended, it should nowhere appear [in the Constitution]?" Such a tenet would make the judges, responsible to no electorate, virtual despots. Rather, the true arrangement was that "the Legislature have the exclusive right to interpret the Constitution, in what regards the law-making power, and the judges are bound to execute the laws they make."[14]

In rebuttal, Morris asked: "If this doctrine be sustained, (and it is the fair logical deduction from the premises laid down) what possible mode is there to avoid the conclusion that the moment the Legislature of the Union declare themselves supreme, they become so? . . . The sovereignty of America will no longer reside in the people, but in the Congress, and the Constitution is whatever they choose to make it."[15]

With party lines drawn taut, the bill passed both houses and was signed by the President in March, 1802, and the circuit judges found themselves without offices. To strike an additional blow at judicial power, the Republicans pushed through a second bill, one which provided that the Supreme Court should not meet again until February, 1803. The Federalists protested that since the Court had adjourned shortly after issuing the "show cause" rule in *Marbury* v. *Madison* in December, 1801, this new legislation meant that the Supreme Court would, for all practical purposes, be abolished for fourteen months. This argument did not deter the Jeffersonians, and the bill became law in 1802.

After the passage of the repeal, John Marshall wrote to the other Justices asking their views on whether or not they should resume circuit-riding. Although he personally believed "that the Constitution requires distinct appointments and commissions for the judges of the inferior courts from those of the Supreme Court," he said he would be willing to abide by the sentiments of the majority of his colleagues. And the majority preferred the safer course.[16] That spring the members of the Supreme Court resumed their trial duties.

JUDICIAL REVIEW AND IMPEACHMENT

The basic conflict was only approaching its climax. In February, 1803, *Marbury* v. *Madison* was argued and decided. Jefferson, expecting the Court to issue the mandamus, was prepared to disregard the order, but Marshall was too astute to allow his authority to be flaunted. After a biting, 9,000-word indictment of the administration for failing to deliver the commission, the Chief Justice held that the Court was without jurisdiction. Section 13 of the Judiciary Act of 1789 was unconstitutional in that it had added to the Court's original jurisdiction as specified in Article III of the Constitution.

While Marshall's biographer has called this exercise of the disputed authority to declare acts of Congress invalid "a judicial *coup d'état*,"[17] Charles Warren has pointed out[18] that contemporary opposition focused on Marshall's attack against Jefferson rather than on what has become the lasting importance of the case, the first explicit use of judicial review. And, at that, the hold on public attention of the Marbury case was short. Events in Europe, the question of the disposition of Louisiana and control of the Mississippi, preparations for the campaign of 1804, and alarming reports of secession sentiment in New England, all diverted attention from the Court. Then, within a week, the Justices somewhat mollified the administration by refusing in *Stuart* v. *Laird* to hold the repeal unconstitutional, at least insofar as it affected a private litigant who might otherwise have had his case heard under the 1801 Act.

The Jeffersonian leaders, however, were still firmly convinced that judicial power was a major threat, a conviction which Justice Samuel Chase reinforced in May, 1803, by a long political harangue before a grand jury in Baltimore. Chase assailed the philosophy of Jefferson as likely to destroy peace, order, and progress. The judge proclaimed that the 1802 repeal undermined the United States Constitution and also criticized the newly adopted and rather liberal Maryland state constitution as conducive to the destruction of property rights and personal security.[19]

A week before *Marbury* v. *Madison,* Representative Caesar Rodney of Delaware had thrown down a challenge to the Federalist judges: "Judicial supremacy may be made to bow before the strong arm of Legislative authority. We shall discover who is master of the ship."[20] With the challenge apparently accepted by *Marbury,* the next step was to impeach and remove the recalcitrant judges and replace them with reliable Republicans. Just before the *Marbury* decision Jefferson had initiated impeachment proceedings against John Pickering, a district judge in Massachusetts who apparently had become both insane and an alcoholic and was clearly unable to perform his duties in a rational manner.

Despite the President's impatient urging, the House did not impeach Pickering until October, 1803; and the Senate did not convict and remove the judge until March, 1804. "The Constitution ought to be altered," Jefferson had complained, "so that the President should be authorized to remove a Judge from office, on the address of the two Houses."[21]

In January, 1804, at Jefferson's request, the House set up a committee to investigate the conduct of Justice Chase. A month later, speaking through the Chief Justice, the Supreme Court in *Little* v. *Barreme* held void an executive order issued by President Adams because the judges thought it in conflict with an act of Congress. In *Ware* v. *Hylton* (1797) the Court had acted as arbiter between state and nation, a role which Congress had clearly authorized in section 25 of the Judiciary Act of 1789. In *Marbury* v. *Madison,* Marshall had gone beyond the explicit terms of statutory and constitutional authorization and had claimed the right of the judiciary to decide for itself the scope of its power under the Constitution. Now in the Barreme case he had asserted authority to sit in judgment on the distribution of power as between the other branches of the federal government.

THE TRIAL OF JUSTICE CHASE

Anger over the speech-making of Chase and resentment against the moral lecture which Marshall had given Jefferson in the mandamus case apparently blurred precise understanding among Republicans as to exactly how judicial power was growing. Nevertheless, they recognized that this power was increasing in spite of their recent efforts at neutralization. The Chase trial was viewed by many people as the showdown between the Court and the Republicans. If Chase were convicted, it was expected that John Marshall would be the next judge to be removed.[22] To justify their tactics, some Jeffersonians argued that far from being the equivalent of a criminal trial, impeachment was, as Senator Giles said, "nothing more than an enquiry, by the two Houses of Congress, whether the office of any public man might not be better filled by another."[23]

In March, 1804, the House impeached Chase on eight charges of misconduct, and in January, 1805, the dramatic trial began. The Senate chamber was decorated with crimson trappings and the galleries were crowded with curious spectators. Presiding over the trial was Aaron Burr, just returned from his flight after his duel with Alexander Hamilton and still under indictment for murder in New Jersey.

Opposing counsel were some of the most partisan members of either party. The House managers were led by John Randolph of Roanoke, a thin, shrill-voiced orator, characterized by a hostile critic as "that haughty, passionate, eccentric genius" who "personified the aggressive and ruthless Republicanism of the hour."[24] The chief defense attorney was Luther Martin of Maryland, whom Jefferson was to call an "unprincipled and impudent federal bull-dog."[25] Despite his reputation for hard and frequent drinking, Martin was widely considered to be one of the very best lawyers in the country and was far superior in legal skill to Randolph or any of his colleagues. As ardent a Federalist as Randolph was a Republican, Martin's favorite curse was "as great a scoundrel as Thomas Jefferson."[26]

At the trial, Marshall was called as a witness, and according to contemporary accounts the Chief Justice made an unfavorable impression. He gave the appearance of being overly cautious and timid, too anxious to please the House managers. Moreover, his testimony was not very helpful to Chase. Marshall was, in fact, extremely worried by the attacks on the Court. He had written despondently to Chase in 1804 that he thought "the modern doctrine of impeachment should yield to an appellate jurisdiction in the legislature. A reversal of those legal opinions deemed unsound by the legislature would certainly better comport with the mildness of our character than [would] removal of the Judge who has rendered them unknowing of his fault."[27]

Marshall's willingness to capitulate, however, was unnecessary.

Despite its drama, the Chase trial ended in anticlimax. Even though twenty-five of the thirty-four senators were Republicans, the Jeffersonians could muster a simple majority on only three of the charges against Chase and were unable to get the two-thirds majority required on any of the eight counts. The nine Federalist senators had stood firm in defense of Chase, and they had been joined by at least six Republicans on every vote.

The reasons behind the collapse of the attack were complex.[28] Some of them reached beyond any question of Chase's guilt, though without a doubt Luther Martin and his associates had had the better of the legal argument against the House managers. For one thing, Randolph had been inept in personal relations with members of the Senate. Even some Republican senators found his self-righteous, almost arrogant attitude offensive. In addition, like every other national American party, that of Jefferson was an alliance among regional and economic interests;[29] and at the time of the trial internal differences among elements within the coalition were becoming more serious. Squabbles and accusations over the Yazoo land frauds and distrust between the northern and southern wings of the party played a divisive role. There was also a feeling among the more nationally oriented Republicans that Randolph's extreme states' rightism was dangerous and that it would be abetted by a purge of the federal judiciary. It was not unlikely that a basic attitude of respect for the bench played a part, as did sympathy for Chase, who for all his rough and tumble political ways was still an old man who had signed the Declaration of Independence and given his life to public service.

Not all senators were influenced by the same considerations, of course; but in any event the acquittal of Chase meant the end of immediate threats to the Court.[30] Randolph quickly introduced a constitutional amendment to permit Congress to remove judges by a majority vote of both houses, but the proposal was shelved in 1805 just as it was when it was re-introduced in 1806, 1811, and 1816.

MARSHALL, JEFFERSON, AND BURR

The alleged conspiracy of Aaron Burr provided another occasion for conflict between the Court and the other branches of the national government. When, in February, 1807, the Justices[31] ordered the release of two of the accused co-conspirators because of a lack of evidence of treason on their part, Senator Giles of Virginia threatened to revoke the Supreme Court's appellate jurisdiction in all criminal cases, and there was some talk of renewed efforts at impeachment. Later, the Senate considered a bill to remove the Court's authority to issue writs of habeas corpus, but no positive action was taken.[32]

Because of circuit-riding duties, Marshall presided over Burr's treason trial at Richmond during the summer of 1807. Burr and his counsel, as Henry Adams was to interpret it, tried to turn the trial into an attack on Jefferson, and "over this tournament the chief-justice presided as arbiter."[33] At one point in the proceedings, Marshall was so brash as to issue a subpoena to the President. In one of the historic assertions of presidential authority, Jefferson refused to obey the order and sent instructions to the federal marshal in Richmond that no effort at enforcement should be made.[34] Marshall wisely let the matter drop. For his part, Jefferson hoped that Burr's acquittal and Marshall's conduct at the trial would act as a catalyst for adoption of a constitutional amendment to provide a more effective means of removing judges.[35]

TOWARD NATIONAL SUPREMACY

During the thirty years after Chase's acquittal, Court-congressional conflicts were, paradoxically, almost always a result of Supreme Court decisions affirming broad federal—and often congressional—power at the expense of state authority. During this period, however, the state cases were to present the Justices with public policy questions which touched on the most important and controversial political and economic interests of the times.

In 1810, in *Fletcher* v. *Peck,* the Court for the first time held a state law unconstitutional. This litigation was a part of the political maneuvering over the Yazoo land frauds in Georgia, and in all probability the case had been feigned for the purpose of getting a judicial decision on some of the more troublesome policy questions. The Justices were willing to suppress any doubts as to the existence of adverse interests between the parties to the dispute. For the Court, John Marshall ruled that a grant of land by a legislature was a contract, and that the action of a later legislature in revoking the grant because the previous lawmakers had been bribed was forbidden by natural law as well as by the constitutional clause which prohibited states from impairing the obligation of contracts. In *Fairfax's Devisee* v. *Hunter's Lessee* (1813), a dispute dating back to 1777 and involving rich land tracts along the Potomac, the Court held that a Virginia property law was in conflict with the Jay Treaty and that the treaty took precedence.

In 1819, a trio of decisions brought the Court even more deeply into current economic and political conflicts. The Dartmouth College case held for the first time that a state grant of a corporate charter was a contract protected by the Constitution against state abrogation or modification. In *Sturges* v. *Crowninshield,* Marshall, in an opinion which his biographer has termed one of "unyielding conservatism,"[36] ruled that New York's bankruptcy law was unconstitutional impairment of contracts, at least insofar as it applied to debts incurred before passage of the act.

The third decision, *McCulloch* v. *Maryland,* involved the most volatile issue of the time, the Bank of the United States. In this case the Court declared invalid a state tax on the nationally chartered bank on the thesis that "the power to tax is the power to destroy." To justify this conclusion, Marshall first examined and affirmed the authority of Congress to charter such an institution. In so doing he not only declared the bank, hated beyond measure by the agrarian democracy, to be a legitimate instrument of government, but the Chief Justice also ran roughshod over the basic Jeffersonian principles of strict constitutional construction. Broadly interpreting the scope of congressional authority under the "necessary and proper" clause, Marshall wrote:

> Let the end be legitimate, let it be within the scope of the constitution, and all means which are appropriate, which are plainly adapted to that end, which are not prohibited, but consistent with the letter and spirit of the constitution, are constitutional.

Two years later, in *Cohens* v. *Virginia,* the Marshall Court got into one of several struggles with Virginia. The state had convicted two men for selling lottery tickets which had been issued by the federal government, and they appealed their conviction to the Supreme Court. Virginia officials refused to acknowledge any federal jurisdiction over the decisions of state courts, and counsel for the state walked out of the courtroom after arguing the jurisdictional point.

As in *Marbury* v. *Madison,* Marshall managed to speak for a unanimous Court in a bold interpretation of the Constitution and still leave no order which could be defied. On the jurisdictional point, the Chief Justice held most emphatically that the Supreme Court could review a conviction in a state court where a federal question was presented. Such a review, Marshall said, had been authorized by section[25] of the Judiciary Act of 1789 and had not been affected by the adoption of the Eleventh Amendment. Nevertheless, on the merits the Chief Justice affirmed the conviction on the grounds that the statute had authorized sale of the tickets only within the District of Columbia.

At the same term as the Cohens case, the Court in *Green* v. *Biddle* also declared invalid the land laws which Kentucky had enacted to cope with the confused situation in the state over property titles. Justice Story's opinion was less than clear, but the grounds for the decision were apparently that the land laws violated the compact between Kentucky and Virginia, approved by Congress, by which Kentucky had become a state. At the request of Henry Clay, the case was re-argued; but in 1823 the Court once more held the land laws unconstitutional, this time as an impairment of the obligation of contracts.

JEFFERSON PRESCRIBES A REMEDY

It was inevitable that decisions touching such explosive issues, especially when most of them went against the grain of both the political philosophy and economic interests of the dominant political alliance, would have serious repercussions. From retirement at Monticello, Thomas Jefferson wrote letter after letter to political leaders encouraging—and at times urging—them to take some action against John Marshall's Court. *Fletcher* v. *Peck* convinced the former President that the law as interpreted by the Chief Justice was "nothing more than an ambiguous text, to be explained by his sophistry into any meaning which may subserve his personal malice."[37] Writing to John Taylor just after the decision in *Cohens* v. *Virginia,* Jefferson stated contemptuously, "this last act of venality (for it cannot be of judgment) makes me ashamed that I was ever a lawyer."[38]

Jefferson believed that the individual decisions, as objectionable as they were, fitted into an even more dangerous general pattern of centralization of power in the national government at the expense of the states, and an even further concentration in the judiciary of the authority of the national government. When he was President, the latter threat apparently bothered Jefferson more, but in his later years he saw the danger to states' rights as more serious. It was in this period that he called Federal judges a "subtle corps of sappers and miners constantly working under ground to undermine the foundations of our confederated fabric,"[39] and referred to the judiciary as "that body, like gravity, ever acting, with noiseless foot, and unalarming advance, gaining ground step by step, and holding what it gains . . . ingulfing insidiously the special governments into the jaws of that which feeds them."[40] Writing to Charles Hammond in 1821, he expressed his worst fears:

> It has long . . . been my opinion . . . that the germ of dissolution of our federal government is in the constitution of the federal judiciary; an irresponsible body, (for impeachment is scarcely a scarecrow,) working like gravity by night and by day, gaining a little today and a little to-morrow, and advancing its noiseless step like a thief, over the field of jurisdiction, until all shall be usurped from the States, and the government of all be consolidated into one.[41]

The error, as Jefferson saw it, was one of constitutional structure. It was wise to have made judges independent of the executive, but it had been unwise to have made them independent of the nation. "In truth," he wrote, "man is not made to be trusted for life, if secured against all liability to account."[42] Having diagnosed the disease, Jefferson was also prepared to prescribe a cure. Three reforms were necessary. First, the method of impeachment would have to be changed to allow removal by a majority vote of both houses of Congress.[43] Second, the term of judicial offices would have to be limited to four or six years, with the President having authority—with the consent of the Senate—to reappoint judges for a similar term.[44] Third, judges would have to be required to express their views in the pre-Marshall fashion, that is, seriatim. Jefferson believed that "a regard for reputation, and the judgment of the world, may sometimes be felt where conscience is dormant, or indolence inexcitable."[45] Furthermore, with the abolition of judicial "conclaves" and with each judge explaining his personal views in every case, the first two reforms would become far more meaningful.[46]

STATE COUNTERACTION

State officials needed little urging to try to thwart Supreme Court rulings. Pennsylvania used force in 1809. After this tactic was defeated by a federal marshal and his posse, the state legislature drafted resolutions in 1809 and 1810 calling on the other states to request a constitutional amendment for the establishment of an "impartial tribunal to determine disputes between the General and State governments." While these efforts ended in abject failure—indeed, the Virginia legislature went on record at the time as believing the Supreme Court "more eminently qualified . . . to decide the disputes aforesaid in an enlightened and impartial manner, than any other tribunal which could be erected"[47]—other states, including Virginia, were soon to try to curb the Court. During the next fifteen years, the legislatures of six states—Georgia, Kentucky, Maryland, Ohio, South Carolina, and Virginia—were to pass resolutions attacking federal court review of state action.[48]

State judges were to show a similar truculence. The pattern of state judicial resistance was laid down by Virginia following the decision in *Fairfax's Devisee* v. *Hunter's Lessee.* As Charles Warren has noted,[49] this case, reversing as it did a decision of the highest court of the state and awarding a rich tract of land to a British claimant, involved far more than abstract questions of public law. First, the Supreme Court had upheld the claim of an alien enemy against American citizens while the War of 1812 was still in progress. Second, the land in dispute had been the subject of considerable speculation among investors. Third, the chief justice of Virginia was Spencer Roane, one of Marshall's archenemies. Had Marshall's chair been vacated during Jefferson's administration, Roane would probably have become Chief Justice of the United States.

After the Supreme Court decision, the Virginia Court of Appeals denied that the Constitution gave the Supreme Court authority to review decisions of state tribunals, and therefore section 25 of the Judiciary Act of 1789 was unconstitutional. The case, now under the title of *Martin* v. *Hunter's Lessee,* went back to the Supreme Court. The Justices unanimously reaffirmed their power to sit in judgment on decisions of state judges, but they prudently bypassed the Virginia Court of Appeals and sent their order directly to the trial court.

Not unexpectedly, the bank decision was the cause of great consternation.[50] The day after *McCulloch* v. *Maryland, Niles' Register* mournfully commented: "a deadly blow has been struck at the sovereignty of the States."[51] The Richmond *Enquirer* added, "If such a spirit as breathes in this opinion is forever to preside over the Judiciary, then indeed it is high time for the State to tremble."[52] Spencer Roane launched a propaganda counterattack by publishing a series of caustic articles under the pseudonyms "Hampden" and "Amphictyon." These criticisms delighted Jefferson,[53] but they angered Marshall so deeply that he replied in a Federalist newspaper under the pen name "A Friend of the Union."[54]

In Ohio the state legislature adopted resolutions denying the authority of *McCulloch* v. *Maryland.* Ignoring an order from a federal circuit court, state officials enforced an Ohio bank tax by seizing over $120,000[55] from the Chillicothe branch of the Bank of the United States. This action brought the bank question back to the Supreme Court in 1824 in the case of *Osborn* v. *Bank of the United States.* Once again the Justices affirmed congressional power to charter the bank as well as their own authority to invalidate state laws and, despite the Eleventh Amendment, to enjoin state officials from enforcing such laws. In an effort to insulate the Court against charges of partisan politics, Marshall invoked the myth of judicial impotence and neutrality which Hamilton had articulated in *Federalist No. 78:*

> Judicial power, as contradistinguished from the power of the laws, has no existence. Courts are the mere instruments of the law, and can will nothing. . . . Judicial power is never exercised for the purpose of giving effect to the will of the Judge; always for the purpose of giving effect to the will of the Legislature; or, in other words, to the will of the law.

THE CONGRESSIONAL THREAT

The reactions of many congressmen to these decisions were equally as vehement as those of state officials and in the long run perhaps more dangerous to judicial power. Although the governor of Georgia suggested negotiation rather than adjudication as the proper method of settling federal-state problems,[56] and Thomas Jefferson favored something like a popular referendum, three different kinds of countermeasures were seriously discussed on Capitol Hill. These were: (1) giving the Senate appellate jurisdiction over Supreme Court decisions; (2) requiring an extraordinary majority of the Court for a decision to declare a statute unconstitutional; and (3) repealing or modifying section 25 of the Judiciary Act.

In 1821, after the decision in *Green* v. *Biddle* against the Kentucky land laws, Senator Richard M. Johnson of Kentucky—who campaigned as "the man who killed Tecumseh," and who was later to be Vice-President under Van Buren—proposed a constitutional amendment to confer appellate jurisdiction on the Senate in cases where a state desired to become a party because of the constitutional questions presented in the litigation. In defense of his plan, Johnson asked:

> If a judge can repeal a law of Congress, by declaring it unconstitutional, is not this the exercise of political power? If he can declare the laws of a State unconstitutional and void, and, in one moment, subvert the deliberate policy of that State . . . is not this the exercise of political power? . . . If this is not the exercise of political power, I would be gratified to learn the definition of the term, as contradistinguished from judicial power.[57]

The Kentucky senator pointed out that no clause in the Constitution specifically conferred power on judges to invalidate laws. If, as Marshall had claimed in *Marbury,* judges were bound to do so because of their oath, then congressmen—who also took an oath to support and defend the Constitution—were under an obligation to nullify judicial decisions which they felt were in violation of the Constitution. The essence of the matter, as Johnson saw it, was that "Judges, like other men, have their political views. . . . Why then should they be considered any more infallible, or their decisions any less subject to investigation and reversion?"[58]

Senator Johnson's proposal met with little support. Jefferson expressed doubt that the plan was wise, since the smaller states, which had a majority of the votes in the Senate, were likely to support strengthening the national government. Jefferson reiterated that he thought limiting judicial tenure was a better solution.[59]

Even though Marshall had endorsed a similar plan for appellate review in 1804, Justice Story was upset by Johnson's proposal. Writing to Jeremiah Mason in January, 1822, he observed: "The truth is . . . that the Judiciary in our country is essentially feeble and must always be open to attack from all quarters. It will perpetually thwart the wishes and views of demagogues, and it can have no places to give and no patronage to draw around its close defenders." The Justice added self-righteously that the Court's "only support is the wise and the good and the elevated in society; and these, as we all know, must ever remain in a discouraging minority in all Governments."[60] In another few months, however, Story had become more cheerful, as he noted that Senator Johnson's proposal was gathering little support. Indeed, the amendment never came up for a vote in the Senate, though it continued to be discussed for several years.

The second form of threatened congressional counteraction, that of requiring an extraordinary majority of the Justices to invalidate a law, could have been accomplished by a statute rather than a constitutional amendment. The Justices themselves had helped to make a case for such a plan by rendering decisions where, because of absences and dissents, the actual majority consisted of only three out of seven members. The belief was widespread, for example, that both *Fairfax's Devisee* v. *Hunter's Lessee* and *Green* v. *Biddle* had been decided by less than a majority of the Court.[61]

After *Green* v. *Biddle,* the Kentucky legislature requested the state's congressional delegation to secure a law requiring a two-thirds majority of the Justices to invalidate a state statute, or, failing in this, to increase the size of the Court. Senator Johnson responded by proposing, in December, 1823, that the Judiciary Committee inquire into the expediency of increasing the size of the Court to ten and requiring the concurrence of seven of the ten judges, each writing his own opinion, in decisions involving the constitutionality of state or federal laws.[62] The Judiciary Committee, on March 11, 1824, reported a bill requiring a majority of five out of seven Justices to invalidate a state law as well as seriatim opinions in such cases.[63] Notwithstanding this committee victory, the measure failed. On the motion of Van Buren, who had announced the report in the first place, the bill was ordered recommitted.

Similar measures were proposed in the House and Senate in 1825 and 1826, and in the House in 1824, 1827, and 1829. Each of these failed. In 1826 Congress did pass a bill to increase the number of Justices to ten, but the measure never became law because the two houses could not agree on the composition of the new circuits. The desired effect was still achieved since the Justices changed their procedures. In 1834 Marshall explained why the Court was postponing a decision in *New York* v. *Miln:* "The practice of this Court is not (except in cases of absolute necessity) to deliver any judgment in cases where constitutional questions are involved unless four [of the seven] judges concur in opinion, thus making the decision that of a majority of the whole Court."

The most vulnerable link in the judicial armor is that of jurisdiction. Under Article III of the Constitution, the Supreme Court's appellate jurisdiction is exercised "with such Exceptions, and under such Regulations as the Congress shall make." It was thus inevitable that a natural object of attack[64] would be section 25 of the Judiciary Act of 1789, which conferred jurisdiction on the Court to review state decisions where the constitutionality of a state statute had been upheld or a federal act had been declared unconstitutional. Representative Stevenson of Virginia proposed the repeal of this section in 1822, and in 1824[65] Wickliffe of Kentucky suggested either repeal or modification to allow appeal regardless of the decision in the state tribunal.

At the time, neither of these proposals met with any success, nor did several related efforts to amend section 25. And in 1830 *Craig* v. *Missouri* brought up the question of repeal once more. In *Craig,* a 4–3 decision, the Court had held that the issue of state "loan certificates" designed to circulate as local currency violated the constitutional prohibition against a state's issuing "bills of Credit" or making "any Thing but gold and silver Coin a Tender in payment of Debts."

This case again entangled the Court in highly controversial questions of cheap against hard money and decentralized state banking against the centralized control of the Bank of the United States. And, at the next session of Congress, another bill to repeal section 25 was introduced. In January, 1831, the House Judiciary Committee favorably reported the measure. The report stated that the committee's investigation "has resulted in a solemn conviction that the twenty-fifth section . . . is unconstitutional and ought to be repealed." After citing with approval the states' rights theories of the Virginia and

Kentucky Resolutions of 1798–99, the majority of the committee declared that it was "no more necessary to the harmonious action of the Federal and State Governments, that the federal courts should have power to control the decisions of State courts by appeal, than that the Federal Legislature should have power to control the legislation of the States, or the Federal Executive a State Executive, by a negative."[66] A minority report, signed by James Buchanan of Pennsylvania, William D. Ellsworth of Connecticut, and Edward D. White of Louisiana, answered the committee majority point by point and concluded: "It was the imperious duty of Congress to make such a law, and it is equally its duty to continue it. . . ."[67]

"The crisis of our Constitution is now upon us," Marshall wrote Story.[68] Story in turn told a confidant that "if the Twenty-Fifth Section is repealed, the Constitution is practically gone. . . . [O]ur wisest friends look with great gloom to the future."[69] Justice William Johnson suggested privately to John Taylor that the ideal solution to the problems of the Court—and the nation—might be a revival of the plan for a constitutional amendment to allow Senate review of decisions invalidating state laws.[70]

Once again the judges had been overly pessimistic. The pro-Court forces in Congress first postponed a debate on the repeal bill by a parliamentary maneuver.[71] Then, in late January, when the bill came up for discussion once more, they quickly cut off debate by moving the previous question. When the roll call was completed, repeal had been defeated 138–51, with 45 of the 51 votes coming from the South.[72]

JACKSON AND MARSHALL

There is no doubt that the reforms which Jefferson suggested in the 1820's would have hobbled judicial power, but, when President, Jefferson's attitude had been somewhat different. Although he had had little affection for or trust in Marshall and had wanted a more efficient method of removing judges, Jefferson had professed opposition to judicial supremacy rather than to judicial authority to declare unconstitutional acts of Congress or the executive.

This distinction can be both logical and useful. Judicial review of federal action may be thought of in three different ways. First, and most narrowly, it can be seen as the authority of courts to assume primary responsibility for those parts of the Constitution which are clearly directed to judges. Under such a view, for example, if Congress were to permit convictions for treason on the basis of the testimony of only one witness rather than the two witnesses required by the Constitution, judges would be bound to refuse to enforce the statute. Second, and less narrowly, judicial review can encompass the authority of judges to declare unconstitutional any act of the legislature or executive when those departments try to use a law court to carry out policies which judges think invalid.

Neither the first nor the second view denies that Congress and the President are free to follow their own interpretations of the Constitution in performing their duties. But, third, and most broadly, the authority of judges to declare invalid acts which come before them can be viewed as imposing on executive and legislative officials an obligation to follow such judicial interpretations in performing their own functions.

Jefferson asserted that he was opposed only to this third concept. In 1789 he told Madison that independent judges, "kept strictly to their own department," would be an important bulwark of constitutional government.[73] Shortly after *Marbury* v. *Madison* he explained to Abigail Adams why he had pardoned defendants convicted under the Alien and Sedition Acts:

> You seem to think it devolved on the judges to decide on the validity of the sedition law. But nothing in the Constitution has given them a right to decide for the Executive, more than the Executive to decide for them. Both magistrates are equally independent in the sphere of action assigned to them. The judges, believing the law constitutional, had a right to pass a sentence of fine and imprisonment; because the power was placed in their hands by the Constitution. But the executive, believing the law to be unconstitutional, were bound to remit the execution of it; because that power has been confided to them by the Constitution. That instrument meant that its co-ordinate branches should be checks on each other. But the opinion which gives to the judges the right to decide what laws are constitutional, and what not, not only for themselves in their own sphere of action, but for the legislature and executive also, in their spheres, would make the judiciary a despotic branch.[74]

Jackson was to take a somewhat similar position. In 1832 he made no effort to execute one Supreme Court decision, *Worcester* v. *Georgia,* and explicitly refused to recognize any authority of another,

McCulloch v. *Maryland,* over executive action. The first situation arose as one aspect of Georgia's defiance of the Supreme Court. After two preliminary skirmishes between the Court and Georgia officials regarding state encroachments on federally protected lands of the Cherokee Nation,[75] the matter came to a head in 1832 in the Worcester case. There the Court reversed the conviction of two missionaries who had been imprisoned for violating a Georgia law requiring state authorization for whites to live on Indian land. The state legislature instructed the governor to disregard the federal mandate and also directed him "to resist and repel, any and every invasion, from whatever quarter, upon the administration of the criminal laws of this State."[76]

It was at this juncture that Jackson was alleged to have commented, "Well, John Marshall has made his decision, now let him enforce it." Although the remark is probably apocryphal, it is true that the President made no overt effort to see that the Court decision was carried out and that the missionaries stayed in jail until pardoned by the governor. While Jackson's motives have been debated by historians, four factors, as Richard Longaker has shown,[77] certainly played a part in the President's inaction. First, Jackson and his followers had inherited the Jeffersonian distrust of the federal judiciary, and there was also some personal antagonism between the President and the Chief Justice. Second, Georgia's basic Indian policy did not conflict with Jackson's own notions that the tribes should be pushed beyond the Mississippi. Third, the President did not wish to drive Georgia political leaders into an alliance with the nullification forces in South Carolina. The fourth factor was even more practical: The President did not have—or claimed not to have[78]—sufficient forces at his disposal to execute the decision against state resistance.

In the other incident, Jackson clearly refused to follow *McCulloch* v. *Maryland.* In the summer of 1832, as one phase of his war against Nicholas Biddle and the Bank of the United States, the President vetoed a bill extending the life of the bank, giving as one of his reasons that he thought that Congress had no authority to create such an institution. In a statement drafted by Roger Brooke Taney, Jackson disposed of the argument that the Supreme Court had settled the issue of constitutionality:

> Each public officer who takes an oath to support the Constitution swears that he will support it as he understands it, and not as it is understood by others. . . . The opinion of the judges has no more authority over Congress than the opinion of Congress has over the judges, and on that point the President is independent of both.[79]

RETREAT TO PEACE

One of the reasons for the apparent failure of congressional attacks against the Court during the late 1820's and early 1830's was that the judges themselves helped to ease the pressure against their decisions by executing a withdrawal. Both friendly and hostile students of the Marshall Court agree that the Chief Justice's influence declined after 1825. Though still forceful despite his advanced age, Marshall in his last nine years was frequently unable either to keep his older colleagues in line or to win over the newer Jacksonian appointees.[80]

In 1827, *Ogden* v. *Saunders* retreated from much of what had been said in *Sturges* v. *Crowninshield* about bankruptcy laws and the sanctity of contracts; and Marshall for the first time in his career had to write a dissenting opinion on a constitutional question. In the same term the Court reversed a circuit decision of Marshall,[81] and the Chief Justice wrote a lone dissent. *Willson* v. *Blackbird Creek Marsh Co.* (1829) was scarcely compatible with the broad view of federal control of commerce which *Gibbons* v. *Ogden* had taken, but this time Marshall wrote the opinion of the Court, perhaps hoping to soften the effect. *Craig* v. *Missouri* brought out deep cleavages within the Court; and after reading the dissents of Johnson, Thompson, and McLean, Marshall told Story he thought it likely that the Justices themselves would soon effect a repeal of section 25 of the Judiciary Act.[82] In Marshall's last term, the Court was so badly divided that no decision could be handed down in three important constitutional cases, *New York* v. *Miln, Charles River Bridge* v. *Warren River Bridge,* and *Briscoe* v. *Commonwealth Bank of Kentucky*. All three cases were eventually to be decided contrary to the Chief Justice's views.

With the death of Marshall and the appointment of Roger Brooke Taney as Chief Justice, the Court entered a period of comparatively peaceful relations with the other branches of government. But, while the trend of decisions during Taney's chief justiceship was perhaps closer to the constitutional jurisprudence which prevailed during Marshall's last years than during the period 1816–1824, the new Court did not reverse the fundamental policies which Marshall had laid down.[83] As Robert J. Harris has put it, Taney "made significant innovations in constitutional law without destroying its continuity. . . ."[84] Wider scope was given to state police power, but there was little immediate diminution of national power, especially that of the courts, and vested economic interests retained a considerable measure of judicial protection.

SLAVERY

This judicial honeymoon was to be cut short by the slavery question. By 1841 the Supreme Court was being presented with cases which threatened to entangle the bench in the acrimonious debate over the South's "peculiar institution." For a time the Justices skilfully used legal technicalities to sidestep such an involvement.[85] Several of these technical rulings favored slaveholders, but one important decision freed a boatload of Negroes who had successfully mutinied against a slavetrader.[86] Still, the Court was not able to avoid direct decisions sustaining the constitutionality of the fugitive slave act,[87] affirming a civil judgment against a member of the underground railroad,[88] and upholding the validity of an Illinois law making it an offense to assist a fugitive slave.[89]

By the end of the 1840's, the more radical abolitionists had counted the Court, along with the Constitution,[90] as among the enemies of freedom, and had begun an intense propaganda attack against the High Bench's authority and integrity. Equally as dangerous, proposals were being made in Congress that the final settlement of the whole slavery question should be put up to the Court. The Senate actually passed such a bill in 1848, but with both sides fearful that the Court's decision might go against them, the proposal was defeated in the House.[91]

The Court was again drawn into debate when the Compromise of 1850 was being discussed. Senator John P. Hale of New Hampshire charged that "the judicial power has always been in the hands of the South."[92] Salmon P. Chase of Ohio praised the integrity of the judges but warned that they were, "not more than other men, exempt from the bias of education, sympathy, and interest," and that a majority of the Justices had been placed on the bench through slaveholding influence. Chase went on to argue that a Supreme Court decision could not be binding on a co-ordinate branch of the national government.[93]

DRED SCOTT

At a time when these attacks were continuing, the Justices in *Dred Scott* v. *Sandford* (1857) stumblingly fulfilled the most dire predictions of the abolitionists. The legal issue was whether Scott had ceased to be a slave when his master had taken him into a state which the Missouri Compromise had declared to be free. A similar question had been presented in *Strader* v. *Graham* in 1850, and there the Court had ruled that this was purely a matter of state law. Originally, the Justices had agreed to dispose of the Dred Scott case in this same fashion; and an opinion of the Court was being prepared when the majority discovered that Justices McLean and Curtis were writing dissents discussing broader aspects of congressional control over slavery in the territories.

At this point several of the majority Justices agreed to expand their own approach, and Taney took the case away from Justice Nelson and relegated to himself the task of writing the Court's opinion. Justice John Catron, who had already been in touch with James Buchanan, wrote the President-elect and suggested that he put pressure on Justice Grier to join in an opinion settling the issue of congressional control over slavery. Buchanan obliged by writing to Grier, who in turn showed the letter to Taney and Justice Wayne. The three agreed that the Court should try to put the slavery question to rest and also that Buchanan should be advised of the full history of the case.[94]

At his inauguration, Buchanan, utilizing a statement which Catron had drafted, said that there was some doubt as to Congress' power over slavery in the territories. But, the President added, this was a "judicial question," one currently before the Justices of the Supreme Court. "To their decision, in common with all good citizens, I shall cheerfully submit, whatever this may be. . . ."[95] The antislavery groups, however, were not impressed. Greeley commented: "You may 'cheerfully submit'—of course you will to whatever the five slave-holders and two or three doughfaces on the bench . . . may be ready to utter on this subject; but not one man who really desires the triumph of freedom over slavery in the territories will do so."[96]

The day after the inauguration, Taney read his long and disjointed opinion in the case. The Chief Justice tried to make three points: (1) when the Constitution was adopted, Negroes were thought of as inferior persons, having "no rights which the white man was bound to respect," and were not included under the term "citizen" in the constitutional clause giving a citizen of one state an opportunity to use federal courts to sue a citizen of another state; (2) more specifically, no slave could be a citizen, and Scott could not rely on the Missouri Compromise to change his status because that act had unconstitutionally deprived white citizens of their property, i.e., slave, rights; (3) the question of Scott's status was thus a matter of state not federal law, and the Missouri courts had ruled that he was still a slave.

Wayne, Catron, Daniel, Grier, and Campbell filed separate concurring opinions. They differed with Taney on some points, but they all agreed with the Chief Justice that the Missouri Compromise was unconstitutional. Nelson held that the case did present a federal question, but expressed no opinion on the issue of congressional authority. Curtis and McLean, however, fully sustained congressional control over slavery in the territories.

The immediate legal effects of the decision were minor. The Missouri Compromise had been repealed three years earlier, and the Court's decision merely dismissed what was in all probability a trumped up case. On the other hand, the decision's practical effects were as momentous as any ever given by the Court. It was obvious that if the Justices thought the Missouri Compromise unconstitutional they would also invalidate any congressional attempt to control the spread of slavery.

While proslavery groups praised the Dred Scott case, substantial portions of the northern press vilified the Court. Taney's opinion was widely referred to as "a stump speech," and his sentence about the Negro having no rights a white man was bound to respect was torn out of context and represented as the Chief Justice's personal views. Horace Greeley commented editorially that the decision "is entitled to just so much moral weight as would be the judgment of a majority of those congregated in any Washington bar-room." The New York *Independent* solemnly stated that "if the people obey this decision they disobey God." The *New York Evening Post* added that "the moral authority and consequent usefulness" of the Supreme Court had been "seriously impaired, if not destroyed."[97]

The Dred Scott case was debated in the pulpit as well as in the press and condemned as immoral by northern clergy sympathetic to abolition. In Congress the decision was the subject of almost endless discussion, just as it was in political campaigns. Not only were radical abolitionists openly challenging the Court's authority, but even a moderate like Lincoln felt obliged to deny that other branches of government should regard *Dred Scott* as settling the slavery question.[98] During the next year, when *Ableman* v. *Booth,* involving Wisconsin's efforts to nullify the fugitive slave law, was before the Court, another unsuccessful effort was made to repeal section 25 of the Judiciary Act.[99]

Even more significant than the disastrous effect of *Dred Scott* on the Court's prestige was its effect on the nation as a whole. Although intended to end agitation over the slavery issue, the decision, as Carl Swisher has said, "played an important part, not in postponing the conflict between the North and the South, but in bringing on the crisis."[100]

LINCOLN AND TANEY

After Lincoln's election, it was widely expected that the Court would be punished for *Dred Scott*. The *Chicago Tribune* supported plans to curb the Court's power by a constitutional amendment or by "dropping off" a few Justices to make room for men of sounder views. The *New York Tribune* favored increasing the number of Justices to thirteen.[101] This, in light of the three vacancies on the Court, would have given Lincoln an immediate opportunity to make seven appointments. Senator Hale of New Hampshire put forth the most radical plan. In December, 1861, he proposed that the Judiciary Committee be instructed to investigate "abolishing the present Supreme Court and establishing another Supreme Court."[102] Even among the Radical Republicans there were few senators who were willing to go this far, and the resolution was watered down to require the committee to consider the rather vague suggestions the President had made in his first annual message.[103] Undaunted, Hale introduced a second proposal, this one calling for the Judiciary Committee to inquire into "the expediency and propriety of abolishing the present judicial system of the United States, and establishing instead thereof another judicial system. . . ."[104] This resolution was adopted; but ten days later Senator Trumbull of the Judiciary Committee asked that the committee "be discharged from the further consideration of the subject," and the Senate agreed.[105]

Lincoln had no part in these attacks. In his inaugural address he had taken much the same position regarding the Court which he had assumed in the later stages of his debates with Douglas. A decision of the Supreme Court was binding on the parties to the case and was to be treated with respect by other departments of government when similar situations arose. But, Lincoln continued, "the candid citizen must confess that if the policy of the government . . . is to be irrevocably fixed by decisions of the Supreme Court . . . the people will have ceased, to be their own rulers, having, to that extent, practically resigned their government, into the hands of that eminent tribunal." The President added that his remarks were not intended to be an "assault upon the court, or the judges. It is a duty, from which they may not shrink, to decide cases properly brought before them; and it is no fault of theirs, if others seek to turn their decisions to political purposes."[106] With three vacancies on the bench, with three of the remaining six judges believed to be staunch unionists, and with the Chief Justice eighty-five years old, Lincoln could afford to temporize.

The President's first skirmish with the judiciary was to come quickly, however; within six weeks of the outbreak of the Civil War, Lincoln and Taney were to clash over basic constitutional issues.[107] Beset with difficulties in raising troops and harassed by the activities of southern sympathizers in the border states, Lincoln had on his own authority suspended the writ of habeas corpus in a number of states, including Maryland. John Merryman, a prominent Baltimore secessionist, was arrested for his anti-Union activities and imprisoned in Fort McHenry pending trial before a military tribunal.

Merryman's counsel sought a writ of habeas corpus from the U.S. circuit court at Baltimore, over which Taney presided as part of his circuit-riding duties. Taney issued the writ, but the commanding general of the fort refused to obey it. Infuriated, Taney wanted to punish the general for contempt; but with no physical means of doing so, the Chief Justice had to content himself with ruling Merryman's imprisonment illegal. As a civilian, he had a constitutional right to indictment by grand jury and trial by jury before a civil court. Congress could suspend the writ of habeas corpus under certain conditions, Taney noted, but it had not done so. "He certainly does not faithfully execute the laws," the Chief Justice wrote of Lincoln's action, "if he takes upon himself legislative power, by suspending the writ of habeas corpus, and the judicial power also, by arresting and imprisoning a person without due process of law."[108]

For the time, the President was silent; but the press was not. Horace Greeley accused the Chief Justice of having taken "sides with traitors, throwing around them the sheltering protection of the ermine."[109] The *New York Times* called Taney "the Judge who dragged his official robes in the pollution of treason."[110] It was not until more than a month later that Lincoln made his famous reply: "are all the laws, *but one,* to go unexecuted, and the government itself to go to pieces, lest that one be violated? Even in such a case, would not the official oath be broken, if the government should be overthrown, when it was believed that disregarding the single law, would tend to preserve it?"*[111]

THE NEW COURT

In 1862, the national circuit court system was reorganized, and Lincoln made his first three appointments, Noah Swayne of Ohio, David Davis of Illinois (the President's former campaign manager), and Samuel Miller of Iowa. The Union hold on the Court was now stronger, but it was still not guaranteed; and to give the adminis-

* Although Taney's order had been ignored, Merryman was released in a few months and was never brought to trial. The Chief Justice had half expected to be arrested for his decision. This was not an idle fear of an old man, for Lincoln was to prevent the circuit court for the District of Columbia from issuing a writ of habeas corpus in a similar case by subjecting one of the circuit judges to "protective custody," which in fact was nothing more than house arrest. Later Congress completed the fiasco by abolishing the District of Columbia tribunal. See Gerald I. Jordan, "The Impact of Crises upon Judicial Behavior," paper delivered at the 1960 Annual Meeting of the American Political Science Association.

tration a greater margin of safety, as well as to take care of the demands and problems of the Pacific Coast, Congress in 1863 created a tenth circuit for the Far West. To fill this vacancy Lincoln appointed Stephen Field, former Chief Justice of California. The wisdom of having an additional Union-man on the Court was shown when, less than a week before the new act went into effect, the Court in the Prize Cases upheld by a slim 5–4 vote the legality of the blockade measures which Lincoln had undertaken, largely without congressional authorization.

A frustrated and sick man, Taney spent his last bitter days preparing drafts of opinions which he hoped someday to deliver, declaring unconstitutional conscription, paper money, and the Emancipation Proclamation. He died in the fall of 1864 at the age of eighty-eight, and Lincoln named as his fifth appointment Salmon Portland Chase, who had been one of the President's chief rivals within the Republican party.

Although Taney had his defenders, his death was the occasion for the unleashing of abolitionist hatred against the old Court. "The name of Taney," Charles Sumner declared, "is to be hooted down the page of history. . . . He administered justice, at last, wickedly, and degraded the Judiciary of the country and degraded the age."[112] The New York *Independent* claimed that "History will expose him to eternal scorn in the pillory she has set up for infamous judges."[113] Andrew Johnson, who was soon to share the wrath of the Radicals with Taney's memory, wrote gleefully: "Taney is dead! and let freedom and justice rejoice. He has gone into his tomb, remembered only to be despised."[114]

3. THE STRUGGLE FOR POLITICAL SUPREMACY, 1866–1937

Even though Salmon P. Chase had been counted as one of the Radical Republicans, and even though four of his associates on the bench were also Lincoln appointees, his succession to the chief justiceship did not bring about an era of peace like that which had followed Taney's appointment. On the contrary, the Court was quickly drawn into the intrigues, jealousies, and hatreds of the Reconstruction period. Because of Radical distrust of President Johnson, Congress in 1866 passed an act providing that the next three vacancies on the High Bench would not be filled. Many of the Radicals were also apprehensive about the attitude the Justices would take toward the harsher plans for Reconstruction, and events of the next few years were to prove these fears well founded.

MARTIAL RULE AND TEST OATHS

The first Court-congressional conflict was precipitated by civil liberties decisions in the year 1866–67. The most important case was

Ex parte Milligan, which once again involved problems of military trials of civilian defendants. Lincoln had suspended the writ of habeas corpus in Indiana, and during the period of suspension Lambdin P. Milligan, an officer in a secessionist organization, had been tried, convicted, and sentenced to death by a military commission. The Justices were unanimous in affirming Taney's position in the Merryman case that Lincoln's action had been unconstitutional. Furthermore, five members of the Court went beyond the actual facts of the case and offered an opinion that, in situations where civil courts were able to function, even Congress could not validly prescribe trial by military tribunals. "Martial law," Justice Davis wrote for the majority, "cannot arise from a *threatened* invasion. The necessity must be actual and present; the invasion real, such as effectively closes the courts and deposes the civil administration. . . . As necessity creates the rule, so it limits its duration; for if this [military] government is continued *after* the courts are reinstated, it is a gross usurpation of power."

Most immediately, *Milligan* meant that the hasty military trial of several of the alleged conspirators in Lincoln's assassination had been illegal. But of far greater consequence was the fact that the *Milligan* decision implicitly questioned the constitutionality of one of the cardinal principles of Radical Reconstruction, that is, military government of the southern states.

As would be expected, the Radical press was outraged at the Court's action. The *Cleveland Herald* called *Milligan* "judicial tyranny." The *Indianapolis Journal* took solace in the fact that "the Court cannot enforce its reactionary dogma upon the people," and asserted that "the decision carries no moral force, and cannot bind co-ordinate departments." The *New York Herald* called Justice Davis' opinion for the Court "constitutional twaddle." *Harper's Weekly* stated that "like the Dred Scott decision, it is not a judicial opinion; it is a political act."[1]

In a much calmer tone, the *American Law Review* criticized both the craftsmanship and the statesmanship of the Justices:

> Had this unanimous opinion been given simply and directly, it would have established for ever a solid principle of law. . . . It would have been a strong defence against all assaults upon the liberties of the people. . . . But the court did not deliver a unanimous opinion. They divided on a point which was not before them for

> adjudication. . . . They have seemed to forget how all-important it is for the preservation of their influence that they should confine themselves to their duties as judges between the parties in a particular case; how certainly the jealousy of the co-ordinate departments of the government and of the people would be excited by any attempt on their part to exceed their constitutional functions; and how, the more a case before the Supreme Court assumes a political aspect, the more cautious should the judges be to confine themselves within their proper limits.[2]

Congressmen angrily discussed repeal of the habeas corpus laws, reorganization of the judiciary, removal of the Court's appellate jurisdiction, and even impeachment. Thaddeus Stevens spoke of the "murderers that are being turned loose under the Milligan decision." "That decision," Stevens went on, "although in terms perhaps not as infamous as the Dred Scott decision, is yet far more dangerous in its operation upon the lives and liberties of the loyal men of this country. . . . That decision has unsheathed the dagger of the assassin. . . ."[3] After suggesting that Congress could allay its fears of judicial power by "sweep[ing] away at once their appellate jurisdiction in all cases," John A. Bingham of Ohio warned that if the Court began to decide political questions, Congress would "defy judicial usurpation" and propose a constitutional amendment leading to "the abolition of the tribunal itself."[4]

In the middle of this uproar, the Court further antagonized the Radicals by handing down two decisions declaring unconstitutional state and federal Reconstruction acts, requiring from every candidate for certain public professions an oath that he had never aided the Confederacy. The Justices divided 5–4 in holding both statutes to be ex post facto laws and bills of attainder.[5]

While the *Milligan* and two test oath decisions seemed to challenge Radical plans, there were limits as to how far the Justices were ready to go. Following the passage in March, 1867, of the Radical plan for Reconstruction under military rule, attorneys for Mississippi, citing Marshall's subpoena to Jefferson during the Burr trial, asked the Court for permission to file a suit to enjoin President Johnson from executing these laws. If granted, this request would have involved the Court deeper in policy-making than even Taney or Marshall had ever dared go; but, as the New York *Independent* commented, the Court, "already suspecting that, as now constituted, it is regarded as a diseased member of the body politic, will not run the risk of amputation. . . ."[6] For a unanimous bench, the Chief Justice denied Mississippi's request, ruling that the President's duty to take care that the laws be faithfully executed was not ministerial in character, but was "purely executive and political." Since this duty involved considerable discretion, it was beyond the reach of a restraining order.[7] A second effort, this one by Georgia officials seeking to enjoin the Secretary of War, met with a similar judicial rebuff.[8]

THE COURT IS CURBED

The Mississippi and Georgia decisions did not erase congressional distrust of the judiciary; and within a few months the Court was to be presented with another case touching the nerve of the Reconstruction program. William H. McCardle, a Mississippi newspaper editor, had been arrested and held for trial before a military commission. After unsuccessfully petitioning the nearest circuit court for habeas corpus, McCardle's counsel brought his case before the Supreme Court by utilizing the Habeas Corpus Act of 1867, which had been passed to protect officials enforcing the Reconstruction program. In January, 1868, the Court took the case and scheduled it for argument the following March.[9]

Fearing the Justices would invalidate the whole of Reconstruction, the House Judiciary Committee reported and the House quickly passed a bill requiring a two-thirds majority of the Court to hold an act of Congress unconstitutional.[10] The Senate, however, moved more deliberately and avoided a vote on the bill, partly out of fear that more than two-thirds of the Justices would hold the Reconstruction program unconstitutional.[11] The Senate also took no action on a proposal similar to that which Thaddeus Stevens had introduced in the House to prohibit Supreme Court decisions on the validity of the Reconstruction acts.[12]

In March, 1868, as the impeachment trial of Andrew Johnson was beginning, the Radicals struck at the Court by amending a noncontroversial bill in order to remove the Court's appellate jurisdiction under the Habeas Corpus Act of 1867. Clever legislative tactics on the part of the Radicals prevented debate on the repeal, but

Johnson vetoed the bill.[13] This veto provided the opportunity for discussion of the proposal. Since the Radicals wished to avoid a full-scale argument at that time on their plans to dominate the federal government and maintain military rule in the South, the opponents of the bill easily won the debate. Senator Hendricks of Indiana taunted the Radicals: "[Y]ou say you are right, but you will not let [military rule] be tested. That is brave, to say the least of it!"[14] In the House, Woodward of Pennsylvania stated:

> Sir, if this legislation means anything it means just this: that the President shall not exercise the constitutional functions of his office, the judges shall not exercise the constitutional powers vested in them, but the legislative will shall be supreme; which I say is a repeal of the Constitution . . . and a consolidation of all the political power of this Government into the hands of a legislative oligarchy. . . .[15]

The Radicals may have lost the debate, but they lost few votes. The Senate overrode the veto 33–9[16] on March 26, 1868, and the House did so the next day, 114–34.[17]

The Court had had eighteen days between the close of argument in *McCardle* and the enactment into law of the jurisdictional repeal. The Justices used this time with discretion rather than valor, and made no effort to dispose of the case until after the Radicals in Congress had made their move. After the repeal bill was passed, the Court, with Justices Grier and Field dissenting, ordered the case re-argued the next term so that counsel might discuss the effects of the repeal on the litigation. Justice Grier's dissent was biting:

> By the postponement of this case, we shall subject ourselves, whether justly or unjustly, to the imputation that we have evaded the performance of a duty imposed on us by the Constitution, and waited for Legislative interposition to supersede our action, and relieve us from responsibility. I am not willing to be a partaker of the eulogy or opprobrium that may follow. I can only say . . . I am ashamed that such opprobrium should be cast upon the Court, and that it cannot be refuted.[18]

Twelve months later the Justices meekly and unanimously decided that passage of the repeal act had deprived the Court of jurisdiction, and that the McCardle case would have to be dismissed. In a last face-saving gesture, the Court's opinion pointed out that review of habeas corpus denials could still be obtained under the provisions of the Judiciary Act of 1789, which were not affected by the repeal.[19]

On the same day as *McCardle,* the Court made another politic decision in *Texas* v. *White.* Texas had invoked the Supreme Court's original jurisdiction in an effort to recover some federal bonds which the state had owned before the war. The immediate question was one of jurisdiction: whether Texas was a state in the constitutional sense and so entitled to sue in the Supreme Court. This in turn raised questions as to the validity of the Reconstruction program.

While carefully avoiding any discussion of specific Reconstruction acts, the Justices did manage to set forth their general views on the situation. "The Constitution," Chief Justice Chase wrote for the majority, "in all its provisions, looks to an indestructible Union, composed of indestructible States." On this theory, Texas' act of secession was invalid; the state had always legally been a part of the nation and was therefore entitled to sue. This opinion, of course, supported the nationalist principles on which the Civil War had been fought but ran counter to the current Radical concept of the southern states as mere conquered territories. The Chief Justice, however, went on to say that, illegal though it was, secession had not been without effect in Texas, and that it was the constitutional duty of the national government—primarily of Congress rather than of the President—to restore a republican form of government to the rebellious states. The minority judges were of the opinion that, as a matter of political fact rather than of legal fiction, Texas was not a state and therefore not entitled to sue.

HABEAS CORPUS AND POLITICAL QUESTIONS

The Court's refusal to contest the *McCardle* repeal and its conciliatory attitude in *Texas* v. *White* held out hope of less stormy relations with Congress, but peace was to come only after two more crises. The first involved another habeas corpus action, this one under the provisions unaffected by the repeal of 1868. Edward M. Yerger of Mississippi had been charged with murder and was scheduled for a trial before a military commission. After the circuit court had denied his petition for habeas corpus, Yerger appealed to the Supreme Court.

In a brief opinion delivered in October, 1869, the Court unanimously held that it had jurisdiction, thus opening the way for argument and decision on the merits.[20] When Congress reconvened in December, Sumner introduced a bill, favorably reported by the Judiciary Committee, removing all of the Supreme Court's appellate jurisdiction in habeas corpus cases. The Judiciary Committee added an amendment declaring that the status of civil government in the South was a "political question," and "it is hereby declared that all courts of the United States . . . shall be bound by the decisions of the political departments of the Government on political questions."[21] Senator Drake of Missouri,[22] and later Sumner[23] also, wanted to go even further and suggested legislation to forbid any court from holding an act of Congress unconstitutional.

In contrast to the *McCardle* situation, this new attack reverted to the more usual pattern of fierce oratory rather than positive action. Heavy opposition to the Sumner and Drake plans developed both in Congress and in the Republican press. Moreover, the *Yerger* litigation was compromised before the Court could decide the case on its merits.

LEGAL TENDER AND COURT-PACKING

The last crisis of the Reconstruction period centered on the old issue of paper money. The Lincoln administration had partly financed the war through Legal Tender Acts which permitted the printing of greenbacks. In an economy beset with wartime inflation, the value of these paper dollars constantly fluctuated, and they became a cause of financial instability and speculation. Creditors wanted payment in hard money; debtors, among whom were many railroads, wanted to pay off their obligations in depreciated paper. Once again, the Court was drawn into the conflict when, in *Hepburn* v. *Griswold,* it was asked to pass on the constitutionality of the Legal Tender Act of 1862.[24]

By November, 1869, when the Hepburn case was argued, Court membership had been reduced to eight. (Within a month after Grant had succeeded Johnson in the White House, Congress had again raised the number of Justices to nine, but Grant had not yet made an appointment.) In conference, the Court rejected a suggestion that any decision be postponed until the bench was at full strength; and when a vote was taken on the merits, the Justices were divided four to four. Miller, Swayne, Davis, and Grier thought the act constitutional; Chase, who as Secretary of the Treasury had administered the statute, Field, Nelson, and Clifford thought it unconstitutional. This equal division meant that the lower court decision against the validity of the statute would stand, but no opinion would be given and the decision would not have weight as a precedent of the Supreme Court.

The Justices then moved on to the consideration of other litigation. Later, it became apparent that Grier, who at seventy-six was mentally as well as physically infirm, had been confused and was taking a position directly opposite to his vote in *Hepburn.* The matter was brought up again, and this time the Justices were 5–3 against the constitutionality of the act. (By February, 1870, when the decision was announced, Grier had been persuaded by his colleagues to resign, so that the decision was officially 4–3.) The Chief Justice's opinion for the Court settled only the invalidity of the act insofar as it applied to debts incurred before 1862, but the principles of Chase's opinion would also have logically applied to debts contracted after enactment of the statute.

On the day the decision was announced, Grant sent to the Senate the names of two nominees for the Court vacancies, Joseph P. Bradley of New Jersey and William Strong of Pennsylvania. Two weeks before the decision, Chase had warned Secretary of the Treasury Boutwell that the Court was going to void the paper money law; and this information was apparently passed on to President Grant, who chose two new Justices who were thought to believe greenbacks were constitutional. Grant's faith was rewarded when, within fifteen months, Bradley and Strong joined with the old minority of Miller, Swayne, and Davis to reverse *Hepburn* v. *Griswold.*[25]

CIVIL RIGHTS

The quarter century after the Legal Tender Cases constituted another period of relative calm in the Court's relations with the other branches of government. One apparent cause for war passed quietly by. The Thirteenth, Fourteenth, and Fifteenth Amendments had been designed to eradicate the gloss of *Dred Scott* from the Constitution and to establish the Negro as a full-fledged voting citizen who, hopefully, would remember to which party he owed his rise. To protect the Negro's new status, Radical Congresses also passed several sets of civil rights acts. By 1877, however, the Radical movement had spent its energy, and in the great compromise of that year the Hayes-Tilden election was settled with the Republicans retaining the White House but ending Reconstruction in the South and, in effect, leaving the Negro problem to the states.[26]

In a series of decisions beginning in 1876 and culminating in the Civil Rights Cases of 1883,[27] the Court invalidated a large part of the federal civil rights legislation. The Court held that, at least insofar as the Fourteenth Amendment was concerned, the federal government could protect Negroes only against state and not against private action. Justice Harlan protested in vain that this conclusion was based on a "subtle and ingenious" semantic argument which did violence to the plain intent of the framers of the Fourteenth Amendment. During Johnson's administration congressional reaction would have swiftly and decisively supported Harlan; but in the context of their own time, these decisions simply ratified existing political arrangements.[28]

ECONOMIC LIBERTY

If federal protection of Negro rights was a dead issue, questions of public control over the burgeoning corporations were very much alive, and the Court was quickly drawn into this controversy. Initially, a majority of the Justices were sympathetic to state control of business. In the Granger cases (1877), for example, the Court ruled that the fairness of regulation of grain elevator and railroad charges was primarily a legislative rather than a judicial matter. "For protection against abuses by legislatures," Chief Justice Waite wrote, "the people must resort to the polls, not to the courts."[29] In other decisions during Waite's chief justiceship, the Court also qualified the rigid protection of corporate charters which the Dartmouth College case had afforded.[30]

The influence of the American Bar Association—one of whose chief causes for existence was to counter the doctrine of the Granger cases[31]—the writings of Thomas Cooley and Christopher Tiedeman,[32] the appointment of railroad and other corporation lawyers to the bench, and the persistent arguments of counsel against public regulation of business practices turned what had been a minority of the Court into a majority. Gradually, corporations were brought under the protection of the Fourteenth Amendment, and the laissez faire theories of substantive due process began to dominate judicial thinking. Herbert Spencer, Cooley, and Tiedeman replaced Hamilton, Madison, and Marshall as the leading constitutional authorities.

Under this newest of dispensations, the Court tenaciously defended railroad interests in public lands and creditors' interests in municipal bonds, even where fraudulently issued as one of many railroad-building scandals.[33] By 1890, fairness of rates was held to be ultimately a judicial rather than a legislative matter,[34] and within a few years the Court for the first time began to strike down economic and social legislation as denials of "liberty of contract"—a concept discovered to have been implicit in the Fourteenth Amendment.[35] At the same time, congressional regulation of interstate commerce was so narrowly interpreted that the Interstate Commerce Commission was temporarily reduced to "little more than an agency for public information."[36]

This new judicial trend came into full swing in 1895 in three great decisions. *United States* v. *E. C. Knight* held that the Sherman Act could not reach a corporation which refined over 95 per cent of the nation's sugar because production did not "directly affect" interstate commerce. *In re Debs,* on the other hand, sustained both the authority of the executive department to secure an injunction to end a railroad strike and of a district judge to punish summarily for contempt a labor leader whose union had violated the injunction.

The third decision was *Pollock* v. *Farmer's Loan & Trust Co.* After years of agitation by such groups as the Grange, the National Alliance, the Knights of Labor, and the Populists, Congress in 1894 imposed a tax of 2 per cent on all incomes over $4,000.[37] This legislation had been opposed as socialistic, and as soon as the statute was on the books a stockholder's suit was instituted and the federal courts asked "to stop the Communist march." The Supreme Court at first divided 4–4 on the question of the constitutionality of the income tax. Then on rehearing, one judge changed his mind and by a 5–4 vote (Justice Jackson, who had been absent at the first decision, took part in the second and voted to sustain the act) the Court declared the income tax unconstitutional. In spite of precedents as old as 1796[38] and as recent as 1881,[39] the majority ruled that this was a "direct" tax and as such had to be apportioned among the states according to population.

The earlier trend of decision had alienated many Populist leaders —Weaver had warned in 1892 of the "Imperial Supreme Court"[40]— but these three cases were devastating blows to the plans of the Populist party and the Free Silver wing of the Democratic party. Bills were introduced in Congress to curtail the contempt power and to amend the Constitution to permit an income tax. A Senate investigation of the Debs case was also authorized. Senator Tillman spoke of the "one corrupt vote"[41] that had swung the tax decision. Commenting on the Sugar case, an *American Law Review* note stated that the Sherman Act had been "vetoed by the third House of Congress . . . except for the purpose of enabling Federal courts to enjoin railroad strikes,"[42] and Governor Altgeld of Illinois alleged that the *Debs* decision had "established a new form of government . . . government by injunction."[43] Governor Pennoyer of Oregon suggested Congress "impeach the nullifying judges . . . and instruct the President to enforce the collection of the income tax. . . ."[44]

At the 1896 Democratic Convention, William Jennings Bryan denied that the income tax was really invalid. "It was not unconstitutional when it went before the Supreme Court for the first time," he told the delegates. "It did not become unconstitutional until one judge changed his mind, and we cannot be expected to know when a judge will change his mind again."[45] After much wrangling, the Democrats adopted a platform condemning "government by injunction," advocating extension of the right to jury trials in contempt cases, and asserting that it was the duty of Congress to use what constitutional authority remained, or might come from a Court reversal, to enact a new income tax.[46]

The Populists endorsed Bryan and adopted similar planks. Although Free Silver dominated the 1896 campaign, the Court was a subsidiary issue—due in part, perhaps, to a fear that judges who were committed to the economic theories that had condemned the income tax would also invalidate a radical silver act.[47] The Republican victory, however, ended any immediate hope for a reversal of recent judicial action. Over the next dozen years bills were frequently introduced in Congress calling either for enforcement of the 1894 tax or proposing a constitutional amendment to validate the income levy, and Republican leaders, especially Theodore Roosevelt, gave sporadic support to plans to revise the tax in some way acceptable to the Court. But it was not until 1909 that the issue could again be pressed to a showdown, and then it developed out of a fight for a new tariff. To head off a Democratic move to amend the tariff bill with a tax of 3 per cent on incomes over $5,000, Senate conservatives proposed instead a constitutional amendment explicitly authorizing such an excise. While liberals and Progressives recognized the amendment suggestion as designed to bury the income tax in supposedly hostile state legislatures, they felt they had no choice but to support the plan.[48]

These general expectations about the state legislatures were wrong, and within four years the amendment had been properly ratified. In the interim, the Court paved the way for graceful acceptance of defeat (this was made much easier by the fact that none of the *Pollock* majority was still on the bench) by validating a 1909 tax on corporation incomes.[49]

THE COURT IN THE PROGRESSIVE ERA

The trend of decisions after 1890 won for the Court the undying resentment of the Populist and Progressive coalitions. In 1905, *Lochner* v. *New York* declared a sixty-hour work week law for bakers to be an officious interference with freedom of contract. Three years later, the Danbury Hatters case[50] applied the treble damages provisions of the Sherman Act to members of a Connecticut labor union. Federal and state statutes outlawing "yellow-dog" contracts were also voided,[51] and the continued use of restraining orders by judges against labor activities made "government by injunction" a union battle cry. Then, in 1911, the Court increased its supervision of government regulation of business by ruling that the Sherman Act had been meant to prohibit only "unreasonable" restraints of trade rather than, as the statute said, "all" such restraints.[52] This interpretation was made not only in the face of previous Supreme Court decisions to the contrary,[53] but also of congressional refusals to amend the law with a "reasonable" clause.[54]

Despite these decisions, the Court did not by any means invalidate all social and economic legislation challenged during the first eighteen years of the twentieth century.[55] Laws from four states setting maximum hours of labor for women were sustained,[56] though without a direct overruling of *Lochner*. In 1904, the Northern Securities Company case[57] recovered much of the ground given up in the *Knight* decision nine years earlier, and federal regulatory power in other areas was often similarly vindicated. The Court, for instance, held constitutional the Pure Food and Drug Act,[58] a regulatory tax on oleomargarine,[59] an antilottery statute,[60] the narcotics law of 1914,[61] and the Mann Act,[62] as well as the Adamson law which regulated the wages and hours of railroad workers.[63]

Paradoxically, during the period of the 1890's and early 1900's, the cult of the robe became a firmly established part of the lore of American government. In spite of obvious economic partisanship in many decisions—partisanship which Populist groups and, later, Oliver Wendell Holmes mercilessly exposed—judges were widely revered as high priests. They were looked on as men who made neither law nor policy, but acted, in Frankfurter's phrase, as "impersonal vehicles of revealed truth," dispensing divinely ordained justice.

Yet for all its strength this myth of the judicial function was never universally accepted. Theodore Roosevelt's 1912 campaign for the recall of state judicial decisions was an integral part of Populist and Progressive enmity toward the courts.[64] Dissident groups were sometimes even able to get Congress to act to reverse judicial policies. The Webb-Kenyon Act (1913) permitted states to forbid importation of liquor, contrary to the decision in *Leisy* v. *Hardin*. The Elkins (1903), Hepburn (1906), and Mann-Elkins (1910) statutes attempted to restore to the ICC much of the authority which early decisions had denied. Legislation in 1911 tried to slow down federal injunctions against state laws by requiring the convening of special three-judge tribunals to hear suits to enjoin state officials.

The Clayton Act (1914) was a multiple blow against judicial action. Because of fear of the hostile attitude of judges toward government action, Congress established the Federal Trade Commission to enforce the statute. In an effort to negate the effects of the Danbury Hatters case, the Clayton Act declared the "legitimate" activities of labor unions exempt from antitrust laws and forbade injunctions against peaceful persuasion to strike, primary boycotts, or their use in any labor dispute "unless necessary to prevent irreparable injury to property or to a property right." In addition, by adopting somewhat more liberal provisions for jury trials in contempt cases, the act made a weak attempt to counter frequent judicial use of the contempt of court power to punish strikers.

The Progressive influence was also expressed in two of Woodrow Wilson's appointments to the Court. Louis D. Brandeis and John Clarke were both sympathetic to social and economic legislation. On the other hand, Wilson's other appointee, James C. McReynolds, became so conservative in his views that even Taft was to voice concern.[65]

TAFT, LA FOLLETTE, AND LAISSEZ FAIRE

In *Hammer* v. *Dagenhart* (1918) a five-judge majority held unconstitutional as an invasion of state authority protected by the Tenth Amendment congressional efforts to bar from interstate commerce goods made by child labor. Holmes, joined by Brandeis, Clarke, and McKenna, protested in a terse, bitterly eloquent opinion, but *Hammer* marked the beginning of a hardening of judicial attitudes, a change which would be confirmed after 1921 by the four Harding appointees, Taft, Sutherland, Butler, and Sanford.

Probably no Chief Justice had ever come to the bench with as full comprehension of the power and limitations of his office as did Taft.[66] "I am the head of a co-ordinate branch of the federal government," he said, and he immediately proceeded to contact every lower federal judge, as well as every state chief justice, to try to harmonize relations within the judiciary. Taft also maintained cordial relations with Harding and his Attorney General, Harry Daugherty, and attempted, often successfully, to influence the appointment of federal judges at every level. In addition, the new Chief Justice worked with conservative members of Congress to get needed reforms in the judicial system. Perhaps most important, Taft thoroughly understood the magic which the cult of robe bestowed on judges,* and he had a

* Before his appointment to the Court, Taft had written: "It is well that judges should be clothed in robes, not only, that those who witness the administration of justice should be properly advised that the function performed is one different from, and higher, than that which a man discharges as a citizen in the ordinary walks of life; but also, in order to impress the judge himself with the constant consciousness that he is a high-priest in the temple of justice and is surrounded with obligations of a sacred character that he cannot escape. . . ." *Present Day Problems* (New York: Dodd, Mead & Co., Inc., 1908), pp. 63–64.

definite concept of the role of the Supreme Court as the ultimate guardian of property interests—a concept shared by more than a majority of his colleagues.

In 1922–23, the Court struck two major blows at government regulation of business and at the same time extended government regulation of labor. After *Hammer* v. *Dagenhart,* Congress had again tried to control child labor by means of taxation. The Court had sustained similar regulation of oleomargarine and narcotics; but in the Child Labor Tax Cases,* the Justices, with only Clarke dissenting,[67] invalidated this new effort as a mere subterfuge. Taft, who wrote the opinion of the Court, confided to his brother that the tax law was "a mere effort of good people, who wish children protected throughout the country, to compel certain States to conduct their police power in accord with the views of the good people, as well as an effort by the manufacturers of Connecticut and Massachusetts to increase the cost of production of commodities in which they compete with the Southern States, by depriving them of child labor."[68]

In *United Mine Workers* v. *Coronado,* which grew out of a bloody union–mine company war in Arkansas, the Court for the first time ruled that a labor union could be sued for damages in a federal court. (The Danbury Hatters litigation had been directed at individual members of the union.) Even though Taft's opinion held—with "regret"—that in this particular case a suit under the Sherman Act could not be maintained because of lack of evidence of any effect on interstate commerce, the Chief Justice condemned "the outrages, felonies, and murders" which the union had allegedly committed.[69]

A third decision, *Adkins* v. *Children's Hospital,* moved even Taft to dissent. Dividing 5–3 (Brandeis did not participate), the Court invalidated a District of Columbia minimum wage law for women. Speaking through Justice Sutherland, the majority stated that "free-

* The day after the decision was announced, Solicitor General James M. Beck wrote to Taft: "You may be surprised to know that, although I presented the Government's contention in the Child Labor Cases as strongly as I was able, yet none who heard you deliver the opinion may have welcomed the decision more than I. Had the Court adhered tenaciously to the views of the late Chief Justice White in *McCray* v. *United States* [the oleo tax case], our form of Government would have sustained a serious injury." Taft replied cordially: "I had the impression that your soul was not wrapped up in the Child Labor cases, although you certainly made as strong a case as could be made out of the previous authorities." Several months later, when the Chief Justice heard that Beck was a candidate for the Court, he commented cryptically to Van Devanter: "The President could not make a weaker appointment." Beck to Taft, May 16, 1922; Taft to Beck, May 17, 1922; Taft to Van Devanter, August 31, 1922; Taft Papers.

dom of contract is . . . the general rule and restraint the exception; and the exercise of legislative authority to abridge it can be justified only by the existence of exceptional circumstances." Resting his decision squarely on *Lochner* v. *New York,* Sutherland brushed aside the sociological evidence supporting such laws for women as "only mildly persuasive."

The reaction was typical of that which, during the previous 130 years, had greeted other Court decisions on important policy issues. Samuel Gompers asked for a constitutional amendment permitting Congress to revise Supreme Court rulings,[70] and the Brotherhood of Railroad Trainmen adopted a resolution calling for a constitutional amendment providing for popular election of federal judges.[71] Senator Owen of Oklahoma introduced a bill declaring that judges had no authority to hold acts of Congress unconstitutional.[72] Representative John McSwain of South Carolina and Senator William Borah of Idaho proposed legislation to require a minimum vote of seven Justices to invalidate a statute.[73]

It was Senator Robert M. La Follette who made the most blistering attack on the judicial system. In a speech before the American Federation of Labor, La Follette named several district judges who had handed down antilabor decisions as "petty tyrants and arrogant despots." Noting that Chief Justice Taft had been repudiated by the voters in 1912, La Follette charged:

> By a process of gradual encroachments . . . sovereignty has been wrested from the people and usurped by the courts. To-day the actual ruler of the American people is the Supreme Court of the United States. The law is what they say it is, and not what the people, through Congress, enacts. Aye, even the Constitution of the United States is not what its plain terms declare but what these nine men construe it to be. In fact, five of these nine men are actually the supreme rulers, for by a bare majority the court has repeatedly overridden the will of the people as declared by their Representatives in Congress, and has construed the Constitution to mean whatever suited their peculiar economic and political views.[74]

"The time has come," La Follette continued, "when we must put the ax to the root of this monstrous growth upon the body of our Government." He then proposed a two-point program: (1) No inferior judge should be allowed to declare an act of Congress unconstitutional; (2) if the Supreme Court found such a law void, Congress might repass the statute and so nullify the Court's decision.

Representative Frear of Wisconsin followed up La Follette's speech with a fundamental attack of his own on judicial power,[75] and formally introduced a constitutional amendment authorizing Congress to set the minimum number of Justices who could invalidate a law and providing for congressional reversal of Supreme Court decisions by a two-thirds vote of both houses.[76]

These proposals were widely debated in Congress, in the popular press, in law reviews, and in academic journals. While the bar as a whole defended the Court,[77] several state judges, most notably Walter Clark, Chief Justice of North Carolina, joined the Progressive attack.[78] John Clarke, who had resigned from the Court because of dislike for judicial work, publicly suggested that the Justices would be well advised to adopt voluntarily a rule requiring at least a 7–2 vote to invalidate an act of Congress.[79] Despite this publicity, all the anti-Court bills died in committee, though Congress did propose a constitutional amendment allowing national regulation of child labor.

Undeterred, the Progressives tried to make judicial reform a campaign issue in 1924. Their platform called for constitutional amendments to make all federal judgeships elective for ten-year terms and to authorize Congress to override Supreme Court decisions. In addition, the Progressives supported the ratification of the child labor amendment and abolition of the injunction in labor disputes.[80]

As an old political enemy of the Progressives, Taft was piqued at their attacks on the Court. He characterized Senator George Norris as "an ugly kind of individual, at odds with the world generally,"[81] and linked him with men "of communistic and socialistic tendencies."[82] Borah he dismissed contemptuously as a "demagogue,"[83] "unstable as water,"[84] and as "a poser . . . utterly without any constancy of conviction or thought."[85] The Chief Justice held La Follette in equally low esteem.[86]

Taft, however, did not let his personal dislikes cloud his political judgment. For one thing, he knew that even if any of these measures became law, he would have an opportunity to sit in judgment on them.[87] More basically, he did not think that the Court foes could win in the legislative process. While warning Justice Sutherland that the Court faced a decade of conflict similar to that which had confronted Marshall[88] (Taft had just read Charles Warren's history of the Court), the Chief Justice put his finger on the Progressives' great weakness:

> I may of course be mistaken, but my impression is that the sooner the fight comes, the better. . . . One of the safeguards of the existing status is the personal ambition of the various would-be leaders of radicalism. La Follette must be first or he will not play at all. [Senator Hiram W.] Johnson has the same feeling, and he hates La Follette with a perfect hatred; and Borah is disgusted with both. The farmers really have no use for the labor unions and the labor unions no use for the farmers when it comes to the last analysis of their real problems.[89]

The Progressives were at the additional disadvantage of preaching reform in a period of what was, except for farmers, a time of relative plenty. As John D. Hicks has observed, "Whatever index of prosperity one cares to choose, the evidence is overwhelming that during the Coolidge era the country was experiencing a business boom of unprecedented proportions."[90] Disillusioned by the war, and mesmerized by material progress, the American people had no time for a political crusade.

Taft caught this let-alone attitude toward politics in advising Calvin Coolidge just after Harding's death, when the usually taciturn Coolidge had confessed to being awed by his new responsibilities. "I told him," the Chief Justice recounted a short time later, "to do nothing. I told him that the public were glad to have him in the White House doing nothing. . . ."[91] And, of course, the cult of the robe was still flourishing. It was Charles Evans Hughes rather than La Follette who reflected the more popular mood during the 1924 campaign when he said, "It is only from the Supreme Court that we can obtain a sane, well-ordered interpretation of the Constitution."[92]

The Progressives received only one-sixth of the popular vote in 1924,[93] and with their defeat the Court issue was for all practical purposes shelved. Neither Congress nor the lethargic administrations of Coolidge or Hoover endangered judicial leadership. Within the Court, Taft's care in selecting judges during his own Presidency (Van Devanter was to remain on the bench for ever seven years after Taft's resignation), as well as his influence on Harding's appointments, paid dividends. Only Holmes and Brandeis and, later, Harlan

Stone were fundamentally opposed to his views on the judicial function.

Brandeis warned Taft in private that it was "not good statesmanship to clamp down safety valves," and he publicly castigated the Court's policies as those of a "super-legislature."[94] But Brandeis' strictures were generally no more effective than those from outside the Court. A majority of the Justices joined Taft in putting aside hostile criticism as "the yawping of Gompers and La Follette,"[95] and with only occasional exceptions they relentlessly struck down state regulations of business. During Taft's chief justiceship, the Court invalidated state legislation in 141 cases, two-thirds of which were decided under the due process clause of the Fourteenth Amendment.[96] At the same time, the Justices ignored the congressional rebuff in the Clayton Act and continued to apply the antitrust laws to union activity.[97] The Taft Court did sustain several federal regulations of interstate commerce,[98] but the FTC suffered much the same fate during the 1920's as had the ICC thirty years earlier.[99]

Liberals might have agreed with Borah that the Supreme Court had become "the economic dictator" of the country, but for the time there was little that they could do. They could criticize the Justices' economic biases. They could harass Court nominees seeking Senate confirmation, as they did with Charles Evans Hughes in 1930. But the Court foes won only three victories: the passage by Congress in 1924 of a proposed constitutional amendment giving Congress full control over child labor, the defeat of John J. Parker's nomination for the High Bench, and the adoption in 1932 of the Norris–La Guardia Act, denying jurisdiction to federal courts to issue injunctions in labor disputes. Furthermore, the first two turned out to be hollow triumphs. The child labor amendment died in the state legislatures, and Parker was not only eminently qualified to be a Justice but was probably more sympathetic to the social and economic aims of the liberals than was Owen J. Roberts, whom Hoover nominated after Parker was rejected.

THE NEW DEAL

In the 1932 presidential campaign, the liberal groups which Taft had seen as mutually antagonistic finally found a bold leader who could unite them into a winning coalition. Roosevelt brought to the White House not only vigor and imagination but also a grand concept of his office. As a practical politician, FDR was willing to work with the Justices, and he had shocked judicial sensibilities by intimating that he would welcome an opportunity to discuss some sort of mutual accommodation with members of the Court.[100] Compromise was one thing, surrender quite another; under no circumstances was Roosevelt about to permit judges to govern the United States.

Each of the Justices found some aspects of early New Deal policies offensive,[101] but their opposition varied in scope, intensity, and in thoughts of counteraction. On the right the four conservatives, Sutherland, Van Devanter, McReynolds, and Butler, were ready to use judicial power to wreck the New Deal. Brandeis, Cardozo, and Stone were not only less opposed to the ultimate aims of the administration, but also less willing that the Court should be used as the principal force to change current federal policies. Hughes and Owen J. Roberts were uncommitted to either wing of the Court and they held the balance of power.

At first it seemed that the Chief Justice would swing the Court along the path of compromise. In 1934, Hughes and Roberts sided with the "less conservative" trio to uphold a Minnesota mortgage moratorium.[102] By the same vote, *Nebbia* v. *New York* sustained New York's attempt to combat the depression by stabilizing milk prices. Splitting along identical lines, the Court the next year refused to invalidate the federal government's repudiation of the gold clause in its bonds.[103] When the decision was announced, McReynolds said from the bench, "The constitution as many of us have understood it, the constitution that has meant so much is gone."*

If Roberts and Hughes continued to vote in this fashion, some sort of compromise was possible. But if either Hughes or Roberts

* This quotation differs from that usually ascribed to McReynolds. I have used the version published in the *Wall Street Journal,* February 23, 1935, p. 1, which McReynolds corrected in his own handwriting. The McReynolds Papers, The Alderman Library, the University of Virginia. The full quotation (as corrected by McReynolds) in which this sentence appears is as follows:

"It is impossible to overestimate the result of what has been done this day. The constitution as many of us have understood it, the constitution that has meant so much is gone. The guarantees which men and women heretofore have supposed protected them against arbitrary action, have been swept away. The powers of Congress have been enlarged to such an extent that no man can foresee their limitations. We stand today stripped of the fundamental guarantees we heretofore supposed stood between us and arbitrary action."

switched into a permanent alliance with the four conservatives, conflict would become inevitable. And the opportunities for conflict were crowding the Supreme Court docket. The business groups which had been trammeled in Congress had not accepted defeat of their old ideals; instead, aided and abetted by the Liberty League, they had utilized another avenue of access to political power by taking their lost cause to the judges.

On May 6, 1935, Roberts supplied the fifth vote to invalidate the Railroad Retirement Act.[104] Then, on May 27, 1935, full-scale war broke out. On one Monday afternoon the Court struck down the National Industrial Recovery Act as both an unconstitutional delegation of power and a regulation of local rather than interstate commerce.[105] Next, the Frazier-Lemke Act for relief of farm debtors was held unconstitutional.[106] Pouring salt in the President's wounds, the Court also ruled that Roosevelt had exceeded his authority in removing a member of the Federal Trade Commission;[107] the Justices refused to admit that dicta from a Taft opinion on presidential power to hire and fire directly supported FDR's action.[108] Worst of all, the three decisions were unanimous. Cardozo had filed a concurring opinion in the NIRA case, saying "this is delegation run riot," and Brandeis had written the opinion laying the ax to the Frazier-Lemke Act. After the opinions had been read, Brandeis called Thomas Corcoran into the robing room and told him:

> This is the end of this business of centralization, and I want you to go back and tell the President that we're not going to let this government centralize everything. It's come to an end. As for your young men, you call them together and tell them to get out of Washington—tell them to go home, back to the states. That is where they must do their work.[109]

At his press conference four days later, Roosevelt delivered what was in effect a scorching dissent against what he termed the "horse and buggy" ideas of the Justices.[110] Yet the President made no immediate move to curb the Court. Instead, he intensified his legislative program. He pushed, pulled, and whipped Congress into passing fresh reforms, and the New Deal went into its second Hundred Days.

The judiciary was also pushing its program. Within the next two years some 1,600 injunctions against enforcement of acts of Congress were signed by district judges,[111] and in Washington the Supreme Court's guillotine was kept busy. On January 6, 1936, *United States* v. *Butler* ruled unconstitutional the tax on which the Agricultural Adjustment Act depended. Roberts' opinion for the Court was long, perplexing, and contradictory. Stone, with Brandeis and Cardozo concurring, wrote such a scathing dissent that Roberts asked the Chief Justice to persuade Stone to soften his criticism.[112] Labeling the reasoning of the majority "a tortured construction of the Constitution," Stone charged his brethren with invalidating the tax because of personal distaste rather than conflict with the Constitution. It was here that Stone wrote his famous warning to the Court that while the other branches of government were subject to judicial review, "the only check upon our own exercise of power is our own sense of self-restraint."

A week later the Court struck down the 1935 amendments to the AAA program.[113] In February, the administration won a limited victory in being allowed to sell electric power generated by TVA.[114] On the same day, however, Roberts joined the four extreme conservatives to void the Guffey Act, which was intended to bring order out of the chaos of the coal industry.[115] On the following decision Monday, the Court again divided 5–4 in holding the Municipal Bankruptcy Act to be an invasion of rights guaranteed the states by the Tenth Amendment,[116] even though the statute specifically stipulated that no city could utilize its provisions unless permitted to do so by state law.

The Tenth Amendment had been used to cut a wide swath in federal legislation, and the Court's opinions during the New Deal fight had conveyed the impression that the Justices had been protecting state authority.[117] But the more conservative Justices were opposed to all social and economic regulation, federal or state. In June, 1936, *Morehead* v. *New York* brought out this opposition with a clarity that blinded even many of the Court defenders. Dividing 5–4 once again, the ultraconservatives and Roberts ruled that New York's regulation of minimum wages was a violation of due process.

With the Morehead case judicial supremacy reached its apogee. According to one commentator, "Probably more than any other action this New York minimum wage decision revealed the grim and fantastic determination of the narrow Court majority to preclude legislative intervention in economic and social affairs."[118] Justice Stone was equally emphatic. He wrote to his sister: "Our latest exploit was a holding by a divided vote that there was no power in a state to regulate minimum wages for women. Since the court last week said this could not be done by the national government, as the matter was local, and now it is said that it cannot be done by local governments even though it is local, we seem to have tied Uncle Sam up in a hard knot."[119]

Roosevelt took the new Court decisions with outward calm, but other Democrats were less patient. Senator Guffey of Pennsylvania asked his colleagues: "How much longer will we let the Supreme Court sanctify the sweatshop and pervert democratic processes?" Representative Cross of Texas stated dramatically that "this country's Nemesis is the Supreme Court," and predicted that Congress would soon "dethrone this judicial oligarchy and issue another proclamation of emancipation that will wipe out this 'no man's land' of sweatshop slavery."[120]

While Raoul Desvernine would boast for the dwindling proponents of laissez faire that the Court had stood as a "bulwark of defense" against the New Deal,[121] other conservatives were disappointed and shocked at the tragedy of the Morehead case. Even the Republican party platform of 1936 repudiated this decision. Meeting at Cleveland, the Republican convention pledged to:

> Support the adoption of State laws and interstate compacts to abolish sweatshops and child labor, and to protect women and children with respect to maximum hours, minimum wages and working conditions. *We believe that this can be done within the Constitution as it now stands.*[122]

ROOSEVELT STRIKES BACK

The story of the 1937 Court fight is a twice-told tale.[123] In brief, FDR made three great tactical decisions. First, he decided to curb the Court with legislation rather than a constitutional amendment and chose to try to increase the number of Justices—"Court-packing" it would be called. His plan asked for authority to make an additional appointment whenever a Justice reached seventy and did not retire, with the maximum size of the Court to be set at fifteen. Second, Roosevelt decided to present his plan not as a frank means of overcoming judicial efforts to block needed legislation, but as a general reform to promote "efficiency" in the administration of justice. The third decision was Roosevelt's determination to keep his plan secret until the last moment. Indeed, the public announcement of his plan caught by surprise many high executive officials as well as congressmen. Attorney General Cummings was the only cabinet member to know of the proposal in advance, and no congressional leader was told of the plan until a few minutes before it was released to the press.

The first decision may or may not have been politically wise, but the other two spelled disaster for Roosevelt. By keeping his plan secret, FDR had offended many legislators and interest groups whose help he would need if his bill were to get through Congress. His tactic of calling congressional leaders in on the morning his plan was to be sent to Congress, telling them of his ideas without asking advice, and then immediately leaving to talk with reporters smacked of domination that was insulting to independent and sensitive legislators. Almost immediately Hatton Summers, chairman of the House Judiciary Committee, defected. The old-line Progressive Burton K. Wheeler pulled out to head the anti-Court-packing coalition, and stolid liberals like Joseph O'Mahoney of Wyoming were not far behind. When the presidential message was being read in the Senate, Vice-President Garner expressed his opinion by holding his nose and pointing thumbs down.

With top administration leaders alienated and no groundwork laid either with Congress or friendly interest groups, or even within the executive department itself, the Court bill was obviously going to have a rough time. And the deviousness of the presentation was too transparent to deceive anyone. In fact, it allowed the opponents of the plan to heap ridicule and moral indignation on the scheme. Conservative Democrats like Carter Glass, Harry Byrd, and Edward R. Burke of Nebraska pumped this line for all it was worth. The Republicans, under the guidance of Senate Minority leader Charles L. McNary of Oregon, shrewdly avoided public protests and let the Court issue tear the Democratic party to shreds. Public opinion, fired by conservative newspapers and fanned by bar association pronouncements, was more incensed at the deviousness and crassness of Roosevelt's scheme than at the Court decisions. For once FDR's assertion that "the people are with me" was wrong.

Because of Summers' defection, the bill was pushed first in the

Senate, and it seemed initially that administration pressure would force the measure through the upper chamber. But, as the fight developed and as the liberal-conservative coalition turned the hearings into a semifilibuster, it became apparent that no more than thirty senators were ready to support the President's plan.

The unexpected strength of the opposition forced Roosevelt to drop his deceptive "reform" pose. Quoting at length from Justice Stone's dissents, FDR explained to the people in one of his "fireside chats" the necessity of curbing judicial power. The administration was also compelled to depend more and more on Senate Majority leader Joseph T. Robinson, a conservative Southern Democrat from Arkansas. Robinson and his friends were spurred on by a promise that he would get the first new seat on the bench. All this was still not enough. The President had managed to sway some segments of public opinion and Robinson drove himself frantically, but few votes were corralled. FDR's usually astute sense of politics had failed him. The New Deal faithful were at best lukewarm, at worst frigid. And the opposition, led by Wheeler and, behind the scenes, Borah, was exploiting every advantage.

In one of the master strokes of the campaign, Wheeler arranged for the Chief Justice to send him a letter exploding every point of Roosevelt's "reform for efficiency." Not content with pointing out that the Court was completely abreast of its docket and predicting that an increase in membership would slow rather than speed work, Hughes went on to offer the advisory opinion that it would be unconstitutional for the Supreme Court to sit in several divisions to hear cases. Although he had consulted only Brandeis and Van Devanter, the Chief Justice's letter gave the impression that it represented the views of the other Justices.[124]

The letter had the desired effect of attracting widespread newspaper headlines which gravely hurt the President's cause; but Hughes had more bombs to drop on Roosevelt's scheme. Three weeks before the 1936 election, the Court had denied a rehearing in the New York minimum-wage case; but a little more than a month after the election, a similar case from the state of Washington was argued, and Roberts* told the Chief Justice that he would vote to sustain the

* Roberts' switch was the butt of many jibes as well as the source of much theorizing about the Supreme Court, election returns, and threats of congressional retaliation. Since Roberts had voted in *Parrish* well prior to any announcement of FDR's Court-packing plan, there could have been no direct relationship there, although an anti-

law. The opinion in this case, *West Coast Hotel* v. *Parrish,* came down on March 29, 1937, a week after Hughes's letter was made public. Sutherland and his three associates protested bitterly against the reversal but to no avail. States could now regulate wages as well as hours without offending "freedom of contract."

On the same day, a revised Frazier-Lemke Act for farm relief was sustained by a unanimous bench.[125] Again 9–0, the Court upheld the mandatory collective bargaining provisions of the Railway Labor Act, even as applied to "back shop" employees who repaired train equipment.[126] The Court also refused to invalidate the National Firearms Act, a tax so heavy as to end legitimate sale of sawed-off shotguns.[127] Stone delivered the unanimous opinion in this case and vindicated his position on the AAA twenty-seven months earlier: "Inquiry into the hidden motives which may move Congress to exercise a power constitutionally conferred upon it is beyond the competency of the Courts."

Then, on April 12, the Court decided in a set of 5–4 decisions[128] that the Wagner Act was constitutional. Speaking for the majority, the Chief Justice found in the first case that the operations of the Jones and Laughlin steel company "directly affected" interstate commerce and therefore labor relations within an individual company plant were subject to congressional regulation. In his opinion, Hughes emphasized the widespread operations of the massive corporation, activities which included ownership of iron mines in Minnesota and Michigan, ore ships on the Great Lakes, coal mines in Pennsylvania, warehouses in New York, and barge and railroad lines which connected with national transportation systems. Although the other two cases involved the Fruehauf truck company and a small clothing manufacturer in Richmond, Virginia—both very different in style and scope from the giant steel company—Hughes disposed of the burden of argument by citing the *Jones & Laughlin* decision and

---

Court plan of some sort was generally expected. Roberts left with Felix Frankfurter a memorandum explaining his position on *Morehead* and *Parrish.* He voted as he did in *Morehead,* he said, simply because New York had not asked the Court to overrule the basic doctrine of *Adkins* v. *Children's Hospital* (1923). He should, Roberts admitted, have filed a separate opinion to this effect. In *Parrish,* the *Adkins* doctrine, he claimed, was directly challenged, and he voted to overrule that earlier decision (Felix Frankfurter, "Mr. Justice Roberts," 104 *U. Pa. L. Rev.* 311 [1955]). Yet Roberts was not oblivious to the temper of the times, and in 1954 he told a Senate subcommittee about the "tremendous strain" to which the Justices had been subjected (Senate Committee on the Judiciary, *Hearings on S. J. Res. 44,* 83/2 [January 29, 1954], p. 9).

stating: "We hold that the principles there stated are applicable here."

These decisions, as Edward S. Corwin observed,[129] represented nothing less than a constitutional revolution. Yet the Chief Justice's opinions gave little hint that the Court was repudiating its former dogma. In *Parrish* Hughes had directly reversed *Morehead* as well as the Adkins case on which *Morehead* had been based. But in the interstate commerce opinions he distinguished rather than overruled the holdings of the earlier New Deal decisions. With a touch of his magic pen, the Chief Justice transformed into mere problems of semantics the constitutional barriers which Sutherland and his colleagues had so painstakingly constructed. In the Wagner Act opinions, Hughes managed to convey the impression that Roosevelt in his Court-packing scheme had been playing Othello to the Court's Desdemona. Six weeks later, as if to drive home the Chief Justice's point, a majority of the Justices sustained the Social Security and Unemployment Insurance legislation.[130]

On May 18, Justice Van Devanter struck another blow from the High Bench. He announced that he would retire at the end of the current term. The old Justice had carefully co-ordinated his timing with Wheeler and Borah; and on the same morning as the retirement plans were published, the Judiciary Committee recommended, 10–8, that the bill "do not pass."[131] Coming as a one-two punch, the report and the creation of a vacancy further demoralized FDR's supporters on the Hill.*

* Although perhaps not an altogether precise measure of American public opinion, the findings of the Gallup polls provide an interesting commentary on the popularity of the Court-packing plan. In August, 1935, 59 per cent of those interviewed answered "no" to the question whether the Supreme Court should be curbed. In November, 1935, 63 per cent said they opposed "as a general principle" limiting judicial review of acts of Congress. In December, 1936, 54 per cent gave a negative reply to this second question. (American Institute of Public Opinion, press release, February 28, 1937.) The table below provides a running account of AIPO's findings during the battle in the Senate over the Court bill. (The dates are those of the press releases and not of the actual pollings.)

Date	Per Cent Favoring FDR's Plan	Per Cent Opposing FDR's Plan
February 28, 1937	47	53
March 28, 1937†	48	52
April 23, 1937	49	51
May 2, 1937‡	47	53
May 23, 1937	46	54
June 6, 1937	42	58
June 20, 1937	41	59

† Poll taken after two nationwide radio speeches by FDR.
‡ Poll taken after the Court's decision in the Jones & Laughlin case.

For a time, Roosevelt was unable to accept defeat. His position had been complicated by Van Devanter's retirement and his promise to Robinson, since it was doubtful that, once safely on the bench, Robinson would be any less conservative than Van Devanter. Not until June, after the Senate had been further angered by the President's apparent renege on a promise, did FDR seek a compromise. By then it was much too late. The Majority leader fought on loyally, but the struggle was too much for one man. On July 14, 1937, Robinson died of a heart attack, and the Court bill was buried with him at Little Rock. Roosevelt got a compromise measure modifying some lower court procedures, but the final statute made no reference at all to the number or power of Supreme Court Justices.

Two years after the Senate fight, the President claimed that he had lost the battle but won the war.[132] Without the appointment of a single new member the Court had radically changed its course. On the contrary, a biographer of Roosevelt concluded in 1956 that the President had lost the battle, won the campaign, but lost the war.[133] The mighty New Deal coalition that had triumphantly swept forty-six states in November, 1936, had splattered like Humpty Dumpty the next spring.* After the Court fight FDR got through Congress only one more major piece of domestic New Deal legislation; and the failure of the congressional purge of 1938 created an impasse between the executive and the legislature.

The Court had also suffered. Once again the speciousness of the myth that judges only discover the law was exposed to public view. But old myths, like old soldiers, fade away rather than die. While the Court's sudden defection to the New Deal was perhaps the sharpest blow to the official myth since the McCardle case, belief in the distinction in judicial decision-making between will and judgment persisted, though now it became an ideal image of how judges had behaved in a lost and golden past.

As a sidelight on the May 2, 1937, release, AIPO reported that in answer to the question whether they thought the President would get congressional approval for his Court bill, 61 per cent said "yes."

* According to the American Institute of Public Opinion, the Court fight had also damaged Roosevelt's personal popularity. In February, 1937, before the announcement of the Court plan, 65.5 per cent of respondents told Gallup they approved of FDR's general policies as President. In March this "popularity rating" fell to 65.2 per cent; in April to 62.8 per cent; and in June to 60.2 per cent (AIPO release, June 20, 1937).

STRUGGLE FOR POLITICAL SUPREMACY

THE PERSPECTIVE OF HISTORY

By the close of Marshall's chief justiceship, almost all of the basic measures to curb the Court had been seriously suggested or actually tried: impeachment, reduction of jurisdiction, congressional review of decisions, limited tenure, requirement for an extraordinary majority to invalidate a statute, Court-packing, presidential refusal to enforce a decision, and (at the state level) nullification and even resort to force. But despite all the threats, no anti-Court legislation passed Congress between the judiciary acts of 1802 and the Civil War. Furthermore, the Court's prestige grew and flourished in the environment of conflict, and that prestige remained at a high level until 1857.

Perhaps the most disappointing feature of historical literature on the Court before the Dred Scott case is the absence of convincing and systematic explanations for the failure of the early congressional attacks; and this criticism holds only slightly less for the literature on the Court up to 1937. Most commentators have been content to record the collapse of the attacks and to add only a smattering of theorizing about the causes of these failures or their implications for understanding the Court's relations with Congress. Reserving more general explanations for the final chapter of this book, it would seem that certain facts stand out in the pre–Dred Scott attacks.

First—and this most obvious point holds true for later periods as well—the issues of conflict were questions of the distribution of political and economic power. Moreover, on these issues constitutional language was ambiguous, and there was little in the way of generally accepted agreements as to how these problems should have been solved. The absence of explicit language in the Constitution or consensus in society increased the controversial nature of Court decisions and made efforts at reversal or retaliation more likely. On the other hand, this absence also made it more difficult to mount and maintain a sustained attack at the national level.

Second, until 1857 the Justices usually took a broad view of congressional authority. Even the claim of judicial review in *Marbury* v. *Madison* involved a statute regulating Court procedure and jurisdiction; and, at any rate, it was the moral lecture to the Jefferson administration which caught public attention. There was much friction over how the country should be governed, but the Court made no overt effort to bar Congress or the President from sharing that power. Senators and congressmen attacked the Court because of pressure from their constituents and/or because they disagreed with the policies the Court was supporting. They did not attack the judges because the Court was preventing members of Congress from exercising what they thought were legitimate powers.

Third, in curbing state authority, the Court never faced a unified enemy. By definition, states' righters are localists. Furthermore, not all Virginians or Kentuckians or Georgians were states' righters. The moneyed classes in these states could hardly have objected to the Court's striking down bankruptcy laws, strictly interpreting the contract clause, or sustaining the Bank of the United States. Nor were Jeffersonian politicians always ready to support states' rights as a principle when expediency dictated otherwise. For instance, although the invalidation of Kentucky's land laws in *Green* v. *Biddle* was greeted with outrage in that state, there was little inclination on the part of Virginia leaders to join the attack on that particular issue because the decision had favored the claims of Virginia citizens. In addition, occasional decisions, like that in *Gibbons* v. *Ogden,* combining, however accidentally, political nationalism with antimonopoly economics, were almost universally popular. In violation of the military and political maxim of massing forces, the states' righters and the economic interests they represented fought piecemeal against the Court and the interests it was protecting, and they were defeated piecemeal.

Fourth, and this point also applies to later periods, the Justices were acutely aware of the attacks against their decisions, and they were willing to make concessions when they felt that danger had become too threatening. The inclination to round off the edges of some of the decisions against state power after 1825 was influenced, of course, by the appointing process.

In the era of the Civil War and Reconstruction, the judges found themselves faced with different kinds of conflict. The Court in the *Dred Scott, Milligan,* and test oath decisions, and the Chief Justice in the Merryman case, had interposed judicial authority against that of Congress and the President on issues of great and far-reaching moment. The addition of a tenth Justice, threats of wholesale packing, demands for abolishing the Court, and the actual removal of jurisdiction in the McCardle case were direct fruits of this immediate challenge.

After the end of Reconstruction and the shelving of the Negro question as a federal problem, Court conflicts took on another aspect. Whereas pre–Civil War clashes had been largely over problems of federalism heavily mixed with economic controversy, the new battles were fundamentally over economic policy, with federalism receding to the status of an instrumental concept. Until 1937 the Court was able to use either states' rights or national supremacy as a means of striking down government regulation which the Justices thought unwise.

The attacks of the Populists and Progressives failed for many reasons, but the root cause was similar to the localist difficulty which had beset the states' righters during the Marshall era. Neither the Populists nor the Progressives were able to unite and focus, on a national basis, the political power of dissident farm and labor groups. Laissez faire in its purest form may not have been widely accepted in America; on the other hand, the mass of voters were never persuaded that they should buy a full program of government regulation of the economy, at least not in one neat package.

In the New Deal period, some of the Justices, perhaps thinking that the triumph of judicial supremacy was permanent, tried to insist that public officials had no authority to tamper with the inexorable laws of the business cycle. These efforts to hold back the clock were doomed from the start, and the attack against the Court collapsed once again. In part this failure was due to the tactical blunders of an overconfident President; in part it was due to the Court's own strategic retreat. But there were also important institutional considerations involved. Congressional resentment against the Court was tempered by fear of executive dominance. Although it was inevitable that the Court's laissez faire dogmas would be reversed either by legislative or judicial action, it was not inevitable—nor was it even probable—that jealous congressmen and senators would assist an ambitious Chief Executive to enhance substantially presidential influence over members of the Supreme Court.

II THE WARREN COURT

4. JUDICIAL RESTRAINT FROM STONE TO WARREN

Justice Van Devanter's retirement and Senator Robinson's death opened the way for Roosevelt to make his first Court appointment. He chose Hugo Lafayette Black, a shrewd and tough New Deal senator from Alabama, a man anathema to most conservatives but whose confirmation was protected by the senatorial rule of courtesy which discouraged strenuous objections to the appointment of a colleague. In 1938 Sutherland decided to step down, and Roosevelt appointed in his place Solicitor General Stanley Reed, a moderate Kentucky Democrat who had first come to Washington to work for the Hoover administration. Cardozo died in July, 1938, and the chair that he had taken over from Holmes went to Felix Frankfurter, professor of law at Harvard. Frankfurter had been close to the President both as an intimate personal adviser and as a one-man employment agency sending bright young Harvard men like Thomas Corcoran to Washington jobs.

In February, 1939, Brandeis retired at the age of eighty-two, and

William O. Douglas, former Yale Law School professor and chairman of the Securities and Exchange Commission, was appointed. Pierce Butler died in November, 1939, and to replace him Roosevelt selected Attorney General Frank Murphy, former governor of Michigan. In 1941, McReynolds, the last of the old guard, gave up the fight and presented FDR with his sixth opportunity to name a Supreme Court Justice. This time Senator James F. Byrnes of South Carolina was nominated. Then, at the end of the term, Hughes retired and Roosevelt passed over the most obvious candidate, his gifted and ambitious Attorney General, Robert H. Jackson. Instead, FDR promoted Harlan Fiske Stone to the center chair and appointed Jackson to take Stone's place as an Associate Justice.

By July, 1941, only Stone and Roberts were left from the Hughes Court. The next year, Roosevelt asked Byrnes to become an assistant to the President to aid the war effort, and the former senator resigned from the High Bench. Wiley Rutledge, then a judge on the Court of Appeals and formerly dean of Iowa Law School, became the seventh New Deal appointee.

THE ROOSEVELT COURT SEEKS A NEW ROLE

The revolution that the Hughes Court had begun was continued by the new Justices. Congressional control over interstate commerce was found to be ample authority for a slightly revised AAA program,[1] a prohibition against shipments of "filled milk,"[2] and extension of jurisdiction over navigable waters to include streams potentially navigable or even tributaries whose flow might affect navigability.[3] The *Jones & Laughlin* trend was accelerated to embrace congressional regulation of wages and hours as well as child labor in huge or small industries which might somehow touch on interstate commerce.[4] The Court even went so far as to rule that Congress could control the agricultural production of a farmer who was growing a few acres of wheat solely for his own consumption and not for sale.[5]

In these decisions the Justices repeatedly held that state authority was no bar to the exercise of congressional power, and in 1941 the Court relegated the Tenth Amendment to the status of a "truism" which had been meant to explain the relation between the states and national government and not to limit federal authority.[6] The

Roosevelt Court also ended the doctrine of Substantive Due Process as a limitation on state economic power. As Justice Douglas said in 1955, summing up the decisions of the previous eighteen years, "The day is gone when this Court uses the Due Process Clause of the Fourteenth Amendment to strike down state laws, regulatory of business and industrial conditions, because they may be unwise, improvident, or out of harmony with a particular school of thought."[7]

The High Bench, now largely restaffed, had made peace with the other branches of government, and it seemed as if the New Deal Justices would enjoy another era of good feeling. But no such honeymoon took place. Lacking a major enemy in the White House or on Capitol Hill, the brilliant, ebullient Roosevelt appointees lashed out at one another. Unable to agree on what their new role should be, the Justices splintered into angry factions, each using official opinions to hurl charges and countercharges in language matched only by the most brash critics of the 1930's.[8]

Harlan Stone tried to formulate a new theory for the judiciary.[9] In matters of general economic and social regulation, the courts were to defer to legislative judgment. The primary check on government was to be the political check of the ballot box. Judges were to intervene only to protect the integrity of the political process—especially where questions of freedom of speech or press were concerned—or to guard rights of minorities which could not hope to achieve political power.

It was over Stone's theory that the Justices divided so bitterly. Black, Douglas, Murphy, and Rutledge were the superlibertarians; they adopted Stone's belief in the "preferred position" of First Amendment freedoms and extended it to presume unconstitutional legislation affecting freedom of press, speech, or religion. Frankfurter denied the Stone thesis, though on occasion he put it into practice. He insisted that since the Constitution established neither firsts nor seconds in rights and duties, self-restraint was the proper judicial theme in all cases. Jackson's attitude was ambivalent, but he tended to reach the same result as Frankfurter more often than he agreed with the four libertarians. Although in 1956, shortly before his retirement, Reed apparently accepted the preferred freedoms doctrine,[10] during the 1940's he frequently protested against its application. Roberts went his own way; he had little sympathy for any of the new factions.

The disagreement between the Black-Douglas-Murphy-Rutledge coalition and that of Frankfurter and Jackson consisted less in belief in the value of civil liberties than in emphasis on the proper function of the Court. The four libertarians would not sit idly by and countenance injustice in the name of self-restraint. For different reasons and in an entirely different context, they were as determined to use judicial power to achieve policy aims as had been Sutherland, Van Devanter, Butler, and McReynolds. And the four new appointees, at least during their early years on the Bench, made little effort to deny that they were freely choosing among policy alternatives. On the other hand, Frankfurter and Jackson were continually fearful of a return to judicial oligarchy. Furthermore, Frankfurter and, to a lesser extent, Jackson often screened from both the public and themselves their inevitable reliance on personal value judgments—again, just as had Sutherland and his confreres.

Clashing personalities and ambitions sharpened doctrinal divisions. Several new Justices were, both publicly and privately, severely critical of each other, and the Black-Jackson feud simmered for years before it blew up in 1946. Nor was there love lost between the older Justices. Roberts still bore the scars from Stone's lashing dissent in the AAA case, and now there was even deeper enmity between Roberts and Black. Stone's lack of ability as a presiding officer aggravated existing ill-feeling. Under his direction, the Saturday conferences turned into angry wrangles in which emotion and insult often substituted for reason and intelllectual discussion.

Despite internal discord, the Roosevelt Court was peculiarly sensitive to the claims of three different groups—labor unions, Jehovah's Witnesses, and Negroes. During the decade after 1937, as labor's access in Congress sharply declined, unions could count on the Court to protect their interests in almost all situations. By 1947, however, the political demise of labor began to be paralleled in the judicial process.

Once the compulsory flag salute was declared unconstitutional in 1943,[11] the claims of Jehovah's Witnesses to freedom of speech, assembly, and religion found a staunch champion in the Supreme Court. The third special group was the Negro. The National Association for the Advancement of Colored People had assumed direction of the Negro's fight for full citizenship, and its astute legal staff had exploited the advantages of the judicial process. The Hughes Court had been attentive to many constitutional rights of Negroes, and the Roosevelt Justices were even more willing to use their power to stop legalized racial discrimination. Sophisticated voting barriers and methods of exclusion from jury service were struck down; unions utilizing federal bargaining machinery were forbidden to discriminate, and the erosion, begun in 1938, of the "separate but equal" doctrine was continued.[12]

THE VINSON COURT: RESTRAINT VEERS TOWARD ABNEGATION

Roberts' retirement in 1945 gave President Truman his first chance to appoint a Justice; the nomination went to Harold H. Burton, Republican senator from Ohio. Then in April, 1946, Stone suffered a fatal stroke while delivering an opinion. As thirteenth Chief Justice of the United States, Truman appointed his Secretary of the Treasury, Fred M. Vinson, former congressman from Kentucky and judge on the Court of Appeals. These two appointments shifted but did not radically change the balance of power on the High Bench. Although Vinson was notably less inclined to protect civil liberties than Stone, Burton took a position quite similar to that of Roberts.

In 1949, there was a fundamental change in the structure of Court power. That summer Frank Murphy and Wiley Rutledge died, and in their places Truman named Sherman Minton and Attorney General Tom C. Clark, a long-time protégé of fellow Texan Tom Connolly. Minton had been an avid New Deal senator in the late 1930's, and Roosevelt had seriously considered him for Van Devanter's chair. But the Indiana senator had supported his friend Hugo Black. In 1941 Roosevelt had appointed Minton to the Court of Appeals for the Seventh Circuit, and eight years on the bench had drained most of his liberalism.

When Stone was Chief Justice, the four activist libertarians had usually been able to pick up a fifth vote from Stone, Frankfurter, or Jackson, and the Roosevelt Court had established a solid record of support for individual rights. Vinson was less libertarian than Stone, but the chances of the four becoming a majority were still good. Clark and Minton, however, joined Burton, Vinson, and Reed to form a cohesive five-judge bloc that was markedly less sensitive to claims of civil liberties than Black and Douglas or Frankfurter and Jackson.

After the 1936 deluge, the Court under Hughes, Stone, and Vinson had declared only three acts of Congress unconstitutional.[13] All of these were relatively minor statutes, and only one caused major stirrings on Capitol Hill. That decision was *United States* v. *Lovett*, where a majority of the Justices voided as a bill of attainder a prohibition against the payment of salaries to three named federal employees who had run afoul of the House Un-American Activities Committee.

Even though there was no war with Congress, there was more or less intermittent guerrilla fighting. In 1946 Senators Styles Bridges of New Hampshire and James O. Eastland of Mississippi introduced a constitutional amendment to "unpack" the Court by forcing all but the first three of Roosevelt's appointees to retire.[14] This proposal did not even clear the Judiciary Committee, but its failure did not deter sniping by congressmen who disapproved of the New Deal figures on the High Bench or who opposed specific decisions.

The Negro cases were a frequent source of irritated attacks by southern politicians. Eastland charged in 1948 that the decision ordering Oklahoma to admit a Negro to the state university[15] was "not judicially honest."[16] When the Justices held racially restrictive real estate covenants to be unenforcible in either state or federal courts,[17] Representative Rankin of Mississippi commented angrily:

> Mr. Speaker, there must have been a celebration in Moscow last night; for the Communists won their greatest victory in the Supreme Court of the United States . . . yesterday, when that once august body proceeded to destroy the value of property owned by tens of thousands of loyal Americans in every state of the Union. . . .[18]

During this period an old technique was often used to avert the policy implications of Court rulings based on statutory interpretation.[19] Business groups in particular were effective in getting statutory amendments to reverse the future effects of Supreme Court decisions touching on their interests.* Some of this legislation, like

* According to Charles Warren, this tactic was first used in 1852 to overcome the decision in *Pennsylvania* v. *The Wheeling and Belmont Bridge Co.* (1852). The statute was sustained four years later in another case under the same title. For details, consult Warren, *The Supreme Court in U.S. History,* II, 234–36. For early twentieth-century instances, see above, chap. 3.

that involving "tidelands oil" or the application of the Sherman Act to insurance companies, attracted national attention. But, on the whole, these groups worked without much publicity and were sometimes able to present their cases to Congress without arousing opposition groups. In this fashion a number of specific Court decisions were quietly reversed.

While the public was generally unaware of what was going on, this legislative action had two important, long-run implications for Court-congressional relations. First, it provided an opportunity for business groups to perfect legislative tactics to reverse Court decisions, a set of tactics which could conceivably be quite useful in the future. Second, and conversely, it built up among many influential members of congressional committees and their staffs a readiness to examine Court rulings supercritically—a "Well, what have they done wrong this time?" attitude which damaged judicial prestige at a point where it would be most needed in a period of crisis.

For the time being, however, there was only friction, not open conflict. Despite an occasional outcry charging usurpation of power, none of the Court decisions complained of involved a denial of congressional authority. There was, in substance, only a relatively minor series of clashes over group interests. The only occasion on which the Justices directly challenged legislative authority was in the Lovett case, and there Congress had reluctantly acceded to the judgment of the Court.

The Court's deference to Congress was due in some part to the fact that the New Deal statutes either explicitly carried out or could easily be interpreted to carry out the policy preferences of the Roosevelt and Truman appointees. But liberalism on economic matters and liberalism on civil liberties issues are entirely separate political attitudes, and it was on questions of civil rights rather than on economic regulation that the Justices were most likely to disagree with Congress. Yet even this conflict failed to materialize. During World War II a majority of the Court twice refused to invalidate the army's policy—authorized by Congress—of herding Japanese-Americans into concentration camps.[20] This retreat in the face of national security pressures served as a guide for the Vinson Court when cold war internal security measures posed the next great challenge to civil liberties. Although striking down one state loyalty-oath statute and interpreting another to insure constitutionality,[21] the Vinson Court, usually with Black and Douglas and sometimes Frankfurter and Jackson dissenting, managed to sidestep or to sustain almost every question of federal power.[22]

A majority of the Justices upheld the Taft-Hartley requirement that labor leaders swear they were not members of the Communist party; and by a 4–4 division the High Bench affirmed a Court of Appeals decision that Congress could also exact an oath denying *belief* in the violent overthrow of the government.[23] *Bailey* v. *Richardson* caused another 4–4 division. Here Vinson, Burton, Minton, and Reed (Clark did not participate) voted to affirm a lower court decision that a government worker could be dismissed from her job as a security risk on the basis of unsworn, secret evidence submitted by unnamed persons. The only instance in which a federal loyalty-security measure was invalidated was a decision ordering the Attorney General to remove the names of three groups from his list of subversive organizations.[24] But the five majority Justices (Burton joined Black, Douglas, Frankfurter, and Jackson) could not agree as to why the Attorney General's act was illegal, and they filed five separate opinions in the case.

Although the Vinson Court managed to avoid most of the substantive questions posed by congressional investigations, it did meet the basic issue of the constitutionality of the Smith Act of 1940, which made it a crime to advocate or conspire to advocate the violent overthrow of the government. In 1949, Eugene Dennis and ten associates had been convicted in their famous trial before Judge Medina, and the Court of Appeals had upheld the convictions. The Supreme Court sustained the constitutionality of the Smith Act and affirmed the convictions by a 6–2 vote.[25] There was no institutional opinion of the Court, however, since Frankfurter and Jackson refused to join in Vinson's opinion. The two Roosevelt appointees, in separate opinions, expressed little faith in the wisdom or efficacy of the Smith Act, but they could not deny that its enactment was within the power of Congress. Only Black and Douglas attacked the authority of Congress to frame such a statute.

All in all, the record of the Vinson Court in loyalty cases showed a consistent support of security measures. Liberals, who believed that the years after 1948 constituted an era of hysteria, criticized the Court just as sharply for its self-restraint as they had attacked the Hughes Court for its activism in the 1930's. One authority, though admitting great achievements in race cases, charged that the Vinson Court had committed the same errors as had the French generals in World War II: a majority of the Justices had used tactics which would have been exceedingly wise in 1935–36, but which were disastrous in the context of their own times.[26] Other critics were less restrained. A law school professor summed up the Court's loyalty decisions:

> The tragedy . . . is that the Supreme Court's majority, with the most magnificent opportunity ever granted so small a group to show the world the profound difference between the humanity of a democracy and the brutality of a dictatorship, so miserably failed; that the Court—except in the Negro cases—while purporting to fight a foreign tyranny, actually aped it.[27]

This sort of criticism may have stung the Justices and aroused civil liberties groups, but it did nothing to bring down the anger of the executive or Congress upon the Court. The Vinson Justices, after all, were simply performing one of the highest functions of the Bench, that of imparting the benediction of constitutional orthodoxy upon political decisions.

Congress, far more than the President, had reasons to be grateful to the Court. In 1952, after long and fruitless government-labor-management negotiations, a steel strike had broken out which threatened to cut off ammunition production for the Korean War. After failing to bring the contestants to an agreement, Truman boldly seized the mills and ordered them operated under federal control. The steel companies immediately took to the courts, and the case quickly reached the High Bench. By a 6–3 vote the Vinson Court ordered the mills returned to their owners.[28] The Justices were again divided in their reasoning. Each member of the majority wrote his own opinion. All six acknowledged the paramount power of Congress to provide for such a seizure, subject to restitution for damages, but they could not agree whether Congress had not authorized the President to take such action or whether Congress had instructed him to proceed in a different manner from that followed by Truman.

Congressmen and senators were jubilant over the denial of presidential power. When the news came over the ticker tape, Senator Tobey stood up and shouted, "Hurrah. Thank God for the Supreme Court."[29] Senator McCarran spoke warmly of "our former colleague" Hugo Black, who had delivered the official opinion of the Court;

and other senators joined in lavish praise of the majority decision. Truman was disappointed and chagrined, but facing a hostile Congress, and realizing that public opinion was against him, ordered his Secretary of Commerce to return the mills.

Perhaps as an indication of pleasure at the Court's preference of congressional over presidential authority, the Senate on May 11, 1954, expressed a willingness to surrender two of the great political checks on the judiciary. It approved by an overwhelming vote a constitutional amendment, drafted by the American Bar Association and introduced by Senator John Marshall Butler of Maryland, which provided that the number of Justices would be frozen at nine and retirement at seventy-five would be mandatory. In addition, Congress was to give up its control over the Court's appellate jurisdiction insofar as cases involving questions of constitutional law were concerned.[30]

For once, the House of Representatives was more jealous of congressional prerogatives than the Senate was, and Butler's proposal died in committee. Ironically, in light of the conflict the Court would soon engender, it was largely the liberals who opposed the amendment and conservatives who favored its adoption.

THE APPOINTMENT OF EARL WARREN

Fred Vinson died suddenly in September, 1953, and as his successor Eisenhower chose Earl Warren, the affable, hard-working, perennial governor of California, who, under the state's weird cross-filing system, had charmed his way into becoming the gubernatorial nominee of both parties. Warren had long been recognized as a leader of the liberal wing of the Republican party; and although unsuccessful as Thomas E. Dewey's vice-presidential running mate in 1948, he had retained sufficient influence within the party organization to be a major candidate for the 1952 presidential nomination.

The appointment was eminently political. For the President it not only paid off a campaign debt to liberal Republicans but also bolstered the "New Republicanism" which Eisenhower was advocating during his first years in the White House. For the Republican party it rewarded a party stalwart who would be more than acceptable to the Democrats. For the Court, Warren's appointment brought an energetic chief, a man short on judicial experience but long in the administrative expertise so vital to the office of the Chief Justice. His background as both a state official and a politician with national ambitions promised understanding of the policy-making problems which constantly face the Court. In addition, the Justices could hope that Warren's reputation for smooth and persuasive leadership might ease some of the personal friction within the Court.

The most loaded legacy Fred Vinson had willed his successor was a collection of cases which went under the innocent titles of *Brown* v. *Topeka* and *Bolling* v. *Sharpe*. These were suits from Delaware, Kansas, South Carolina, Virginia, and the District of Columbia directly challenging the constitutionality of segregation in public schools. One or more of these pieces of litigation had been rattling around the federal court system since 1950; but through a series of delays, including an order for reargument, the Supreme Court had managed to avoid settling the issue.

Decision Monday after Monday went by in the 1953 Term until there were less than four weeks left before the time scheduled for adjournment. Then on May 17, 1954, the first opinion read was that in the Brown case. In the tradition of the great Chief Justices, Warren took upon himself the responsibility of explaining the reasoning behind the momentous decision to end the legal life of Jim Crow and to shake the very foundations of southern life and culture. After delivering the judgment of the Court that "separate facilities are inherently unequal," the Chief Justice announced that reargument would be heard during the next term on the question of how soon and by what means school segregation practices should be ended.

The immediate reaction of the South, except for that of a few professional race-baiters, was one more of stunned silence than of violent resentment. Within a year, however, apathy had turned to action, and the Supreme Court was reviled as it had not been since *Dred Scott*. The typical comment of the southern politician referred to the Justices as "9 men lacking in judicial capacity," "indoctrinated and brainwashed by left-wing pressure groups." May 17, 1954, became "Black Monday," the day of "shameful and cheap capitulation," and of "the most fraudulent and hypocritical surrender of principle in the history of this republic."[31]

Southern reaction did not stop with verbal assaults. State legislatures began to pass reams of new segregation statutes as well as resolutions of interposition "nullifying" the *Brown* decision. Almost every segregation state government vowed to abolish public education rather than submit to "intermingling" and "race mongrelization." In Congress, nineteen southern senators and seventy-seven representatives signed a "Manifesto" pledging "to use all lawful means to bring about a reversal of this decision which is contrary to the Constitution and to prevent the use of force in its implementation."[32]

Thus, after little more than a year under Warren's leadership, the Court was moving toward another of its historic conflicts. This struggle was initially only with a group of states rather than with one of the co-ordinate branches of the federal government; but, as John Marshall had learned, no serious state-Court fight could pass unnoticed in Congress. And, due to longevity, seniority, and nominal loyalty to the Democratic party, southern influence in both House and Senate far exceeded mere numerical representation.

THE 1953 AND 1954 TERMS

Warren's opinion in the School Segregation cases gave an impression that his first term had been one of radical revolution, but this impression could hardly have been more false. Even the *Brown* decision had not been revolutionary. In case after case since 1938, the Court, first under Hughes, then Stone, and then under Vinson, had been eroding the legal bases of segregation. After 1950 every careful student of constitutional law knew that, given the climate of judicial—as well as national—opinion, the "separate but equal" formula was doomed.

Nor did the other decisions during Warren's first term indicate a turn to radical libertarianism, either by the Chief Justice or by the Court as a whole.[33] *Barsky* v. *Board* allowed New York to suspend a physician's license to practice medicine because he had refused to co-operate with a congressional investigation. *Galvan* v. *Press* permitted the Attorney General to deport a resident alien because of past membership in the Communist party, even though this association had been terminated in 1946, four years before the statute involved had become law. The majority also went on to hold that under the Internal Security Act of 1950 an alien's merely joining the Communist party was sufficient to justify deportation; innocent membership was no defense.

In *Irvine* v. *California* a five-judge majority affirmed a state conviction based on evidence obtained through illegal searches and seizures. Even though four of the majority admitted that in gathering the evidence California police had committed acts of "trespass and probably a burglary" and the fifth Justice described the official conduct as "incredible," they refused to judge state administration of justice by the same standards demanded of federal courts.* *United States* v. *Harriss* sustained, against a First Amendment challenge, the vaguely worded federal lobbying legislation. In each of these decisions the Chief Justice was not only with the majority, but Black and Douglas dissented in every instance. Indeed, in not one civil liberties case disposed of by full opinion did Warren join Black and Douglas in dissent.

The 1954 Term, like that of 1953, was dominated by the segregation issue, and Warren aligned his eight colleagues behind the nebulous "with all deliberate speed" formula to guide integration. But hardly more than in the previous year was there anything like a significant shift in Court policy. *Peters* v. *Hobby* was the only other important civil liberties decision of the term. There, Dr. John P. Peters of Yale directly attacked the constitutionality of the secret witness procedure in the Federal Loyalty-Security Program. The Court majority, however, artfully dodged this issue by ruling that the Loyalty Review Board, which had ordered Peters' dismissal after two clearances by agency loyalty boards, did not have jurisdiction to review such a case unless the employee so requested.

The 1954 Term did provide a change in personnel. Robert H. Jackson died in October, and Eisenhower nominated John Marshall Harlan to take his place. Grandson of the eccentric and forthright Justice Harlan, whom Holmes had called "the last of the tobacco-chewing judges," the younger Harlan had served for less than a year on the Court of Appeals for the Second Circuit. Like most freshman Justices,[34] Harlan took a center position on the Court, along with Frankfurter and Warren.

* In *Mapp* v. *Ohio* (1961), the Court reversed *Wolf* v. *Colorado* (1949), the precedent on which *Irvine* was based.

LEFT TURN

When the 1955 Term opened, there had been eighteen years of relative peace between the Court and the other two branches of the federal government. Some observers felt that disuse had atrophied the Court's ability to oppose either Congress or the Presidency.[35] But before the term was over the outlines of a new legislative-judicial struggle for political power had begun to take shape.

The Court got off to a ringing start in its first full opinion of the year by declaring unconstitutional that section of the Uniform Code of Military Justice which allowed trial by court-martial of discharged GI's for offenses allegedly committed while on active duty.[36] The case was relatively minor in itself, but it was significant in that it was only the fourth instance since the conflict between the Hughes Court and the New Deal that the Justices had invalidated an act of Congress.

Griffin v. *Illinois* established another constitutional bench mark. Illinois required defendants who wished to appeal a conviction to furnish a bill of exceptions. This frequently necessitated a transcript of the trial. Indigent defendants under a death sentence were given a free transcript, but all others had to buy a copy of the trial record. In the Griffin case, two men convicted of armed robbery had been denied appellate review because they could not pay to have a record prepared. Warren, Black, Douglas, Clark, and Frankfurter found the Illinois law to be a denial of equal protection and a violation of due process. "In criminal trials," Justice Black wrote, "a State can no more discriminate on account of poverty than on account of religion, race, or color. Plainly the ability to pay costs in advance bears no rational relationship to a defendant's guilt or innocence. . . ."

A number of state officials were offended by the Griffin case because of its "interference" with local judicial procedures; but even more pertinent to the brooding clash between Congress and the Court were six cold war decisions. In two of these, demands of security were held to override claims of individual freedom, but in the other four the judges tipped the scales against the government.

Over a moving dissent from Douglas and Black that the "right of silence created by the Fifth Amendment is beyond the reach of Congress," seven Justices, in *Ullmann* v. *United States,* sustained federal power to compel a witness, in cases involving treason, espionage, or national defense, to testify concerning past and possibly criminal acts in exchange for a blanket promise of immunity from prosecution.

Black v. *Cutter Laboratories* contested the firing by a pharmaceutical company of an employee accused of being a Communist. The union had taken the worker's case before an arbitration board, and the board decided that the Communist charge had been only a pretext and the real basis for firing had been union activity, and therefore ordered reinstatement of the employee. The California Supreme Court reversed the arbitration board, and a majority of the U.S. Supreme Court held that the case did not present a substantial federal question.

Justice Douglas, joined by Black and Warren, dissented, asserting emphatically that there was a very substantial federal question in the case. State action in the form of a decision by the California Supreme Court had brought the First and Fourteenth Amendments into play. Douglas read the California decision as sustaining the employee's discharge on the basis of her membership in the Communist party, and this, he thought, amounted to punishment for beliefs. "I do not think we can hold consistently with our Bill of Rights that citizens can be proscribed from making a living on the assumption that wherever they work the incidence of sabotage rises or that the danger from Communist employees is too great for critical industry to bear."

In the other four cold war cases, Black and Douglas were joined not only by Warren and Frankfurter, but three times by Harlan, twice by Clark, and once by Burton. *Slochower* v. *Board* held that a city college could not dismiss a college professor solely because he had invoked the Fifth Amendment before a congressional committee. Justice Clark deserted the right wing to write the opinion for himself, Black, Douglas, Warren, and Frankfurter. "At the outset," Clark stated, "we must condemn the practice of imputing a sinister meaning to the exercise of a person's constitutional right under the Fifth Amendment. . . . [A] witness may have reasonable fear of prosecution and yet be innocent of any wrongdoing. The privilege serves to protect the innocent who otherwise might be ensnared by ambiguous circumstances." While New York officials might well have found as a result of a proper inquiry that Slochower's continued employment was not in the public interest, no such inquiry had even been attempted. The employee had been fired under a statute which provided for automatic discharge where the constitutional right to silence had been invoked. "We hold," Clark concluded, "that the summary dismissal of appellant violates due process of law."

In *Communist Party* v. *Subversive Activities Control Board,* a six-judge majority speaking through Frankfurter sent back for further proceedings the Subversive Board's finding that the Communist party of the United States was a Communist action organization in terms of the Internal Security Act of 1950. The basis of the decision was the party's claim—unchallenged by the Justice Department—that three government witnesses, including Harvey Matusow, had committed perjury in their testimony before the board.

> The untainted administration of justice is certainly one of the most cherished aspects of our institutions. Its observance is one of our proudest boasts. This Court is charged with supervisory functions in relation to proceedings in the federal courts. Therefore, fastidious regard for the honor of the administration of justice requires the Court to make certain that the doing of justice be made so manifest that only irrational or perverse claims of its disregard can be asserted.

Clark, dissenting with Reed and Minton, thought the majority was not only wrong in holding the tainted evidence to have influenced the board's decision—he noted that the Communist party had pressed the perjury point before the board—but that the Court was also coyly seeking a procedural flaw to avoid the duty of passing on the constitutionality of the Internal Security Act.

In *Cole* v. *Young,* just as in *Peters* v. *Hobby,* the Court resorted to statutory interpretation as a means of avoiding constitutional issues raised by the Federal Loyalty-Security Program. In a narrow, exacting legal essay written by Harlan, six Justices held that Congress in the Summary Suspension Act of 1950 had not authorized summary dismissal of civil service employees in "non-sensitive" positions. Such workers could be fired for loyalty-security reasons, but only through normal civil service procedures.

Clark, speaking for himself, Reed, and Minton, dissented, stating that the majority opinion "flies directly in the face of the language of the Act and of the legislative history. The plain words of § 1 make the Act applicable to 'any civilian officer or employee,' not as the majority would have it, 'any civilian officer or employee *in a sensitive position.*'" As a postscript, Clark added:

> We believe the Court's order has stricken down the most effective weapon against subversive activity available to the Government. It is not realistic to say that the Government can be protected by applying the Act to sensitive jobs. One never knows just which job is sensitive. The janitor might prove to be in as important a spot security-wise as the top employee in the building.

The most significant decision of the 1955 Term was *Pennsylvania v. Nelson.* Steve Nelson had been convicted in a county court on a charge of sedition against the United States, but the Pennsylvania Supreme Court had reversed the conviction on the ground that by the Smith Act Congress had superseded state legislation punishing sedition against the United States. Warren, speaking for himself, Black, Douglas, Frankfurter, Clark, and Harlan, affirmed the ruling of the Pennsylvania Supreme Court and, in effect, by so doing invalidated in part sedition statutes in forty-two states, Alaska, and Hawaii.

The Chief Justice distinguished state authority to protect itself against subversion from state authority to guard the United States against similar action. The first the states retained in full; the second the states retained only insofar as its exercise was compatible with the action and intent of Congress. Warren concluded that: (1) the scheme of federal subversive regulation—including the Smith Act, the Internal Security Act of 1950, and the Communist Control Act of 1954—was so pervasive as to imply that Congress had left no room for supplementary state action; (2) the federal interest in protecting national security was so dominant that the congressional action had to be presumed to preclude parallel state laws; and (3) enforcement of state legislation might present a "serious danger of conflict with the administration of the federal program."

In a dissent in which Minton and Burton concurred, Justice Reed quietly but effectively attacked the majority opinion. He could find no congressional intent to pre-empt the states from the sedition field, nor could he see any "clear and direct" conflict between state and federal legislation in the area. Indeed, in § 3231 of Title 18 of the *U.S. Code*—the title under which the Smith Act and other federal criminal laws were collected—Congress had specified that: "Nothing in this title shall be held to take away or impair the jurisdiction of the courts of the several States, under the laws thereof."*

Reed was equally unimpressed with the danger of state interference with federal administration. He quoted from the *amicus curiae* brief of the Justice Department: "The administration of the various state laws has not, in the course of the fifteen years that the federal and state sedition laws have existed side by side, in fact interfered with, embarrassed, or impeded the enforcement of the Smith Act."

CONGRESSIONAL REACTION

One fact of strategic importance clearly emerged from the statistics of the 1955 Term. Warren had shifted from his position at the center of the Court and had solidly established himself in the left wing with Black and Douglas. Not only had the Chief Justice joined the two liberals in six of the seven cold war cases, but Black, Douglas, and Warren had voted together in 83 of the 91 full opinion cases in which all three had participated. Equally revealing was the bare statistic that in 89 of these 91 cases, or 39 of the 41 decisions on which the Court had divided, Warren and Black had reached the same result, an internal agreement markedly higher than that between Black and Douglas. In only 13 of the 83 cases in which the newly formed trio agreed were they in dissent, and on five of these occasions they had picked up a fourth vote to reinforce their protest.

Outside the Court other alliances were also forming. The segregationists were still angrily adamant in their opposition to the Court, and now the cold war cases had given them a second theme for their chant. Representative Andrews of Alabama asked his colleagues in the House: "How much longer will this Congress continue to permit the Supreme Court to usurp the power of Congress, write the laws of the land, destroy States rights and protect the Communist Party?"[37]

Joining with the segregationists were the ultraconservative and security-conscious of both parties, men like Francis Walter of Pennsylvania, Noah Mason of Illinois, and Styles Bridges of New Hampshire. Two weeks after the Nelson case, Mason charged that the

* In a footnote to his opinion, Warren stated that the sentence from Sec. 3231 which Reed had quoted had been designed to qualify the grant of exclusive jurisdiction to federal courts to try offenses against the United States. "There was no intention to resolve particular supersession questions by the Section."

Court had "completely overlooked or deliberately ignored" the intent of the Smith Act. "Mr. Speaker, where is the usurpation of States' rights by the United States Supreme Court going to end? It is only a question of time before the States will be deprived of all power and sovereignty. . . ."[38]

After Mason's speech, a covey of southern representatives rose to compliment him and to echo his dire predictions. Davis of Georgia called the *Nelson* decision "a brazen and irresponsible attack on the sovereignty of all the States," and another example of the Court's efforts to achieve "a complete judicial dictatorship." Rivers of South Carolina pleaded that "something has got to be done to stop that Supreme Court. They are a greater threat to this Union than the entire confines of Soviet Russia. If some way is not found to stop them, God help us." Williams of Mississippi warned that if the states did not resort to interposition and if Congress did not side with the states, "this generation will live to see the day when individual human liberty and freedom will become nothing more than a sacred memory."[39]

In the Senate Karl Mundt of North Dakota drafted legislation to reverse what he termed "the tortured interpretation of the English language" represented by *Cole* v. *Young*. "I am introducing remedial legislation in an effort to plug another hole in the defense bastions of America which has been created by another unrealistic and unhappy decision by six isolated members of our Supreme Court." Accusing the Court of "endeavoring to become a legislative body," Mundt urged the Senate to reject judicial "decisions which stultify the power of the Government of the United States to defend itself."[40]

Senator McCarthy, in spite of the fact that his magic had become faded and tarnished by 1956, jumped into the Court fight with his usual gusto. He called the *Nelson* decision "the most outrageous instance of judicial legislation that has ever come to my attention." Turning to the Slochower case, he claimed that "the Court reached a new low in judicial irresponsibility. And it has handed another solid victory to the Communist Party. . . . It is bad enough that a majority of the justices have fallen hook, line, and sinker for the leftwing view of what taking the fifth amendment implies; but that the Court should have gone further, and said that a contrary interpretation by a competent State body is impermissible is—as a matter of constitutional law—outrageous."[41]

Senator Russell of Georgia interrupted at this point to register his agreement. "The whole trend of the actions of the Supreme Court in recent months, including the two decisions which the Senator has mentioned, indicates that the Court has dedicated itself to abolishing completely the States and federalizing the American people. Such actions can only lead to the destruction of the rights and liberties of the American people."[42]

Segregationists and the ultra-security-conscious had found a common foe in the Court and had found common ground for opposition in the concepts of states' rights and virulent anticommunism. In exchange for much needed aid in the fight for segregation as a way of life, Southern Democrats were willing to swallow their pride and to forget if not forgive the McCarthy wing of the Republican party for 1952 campaign charges of "twenty years of treason." Cobelligerency promised a heavier attack on the Justices, and tarring the Supreme Court with the red brush of "soft-on-communism" would mean a loss of judicial prestige, with a consequent weakening of the desegregation policy.

This alliance between Southern Democrats and northern conservatives was formally ratified by the junior senator from Wisconsin and Senator Eastland of Mississippi:[43]

> EASTLAND: "Is there any more certain road to the destruction of the American system of Government than an irresponsible Supreme Court usurping the power of Congress?"
>
> MCCARTHY: "You are right. And I may say, Mr. Chairman, that I think one of the reasons why we are getting such bad decisions, while I hate to engage in personalities, I think it is because we made the mistake of confirming as Chief Justice of the Supreme Court a man who had no judicial experience, who had practically no legal experience except as a district attorney for a short time and whose entire experience was as a politician."
>
> . . . .
>
> EASTLAND: "We have politicians instead of lawyers on the Court."
>
> MCCARTHY: "Unfortunately so, and they do not understand the function of the Court. They apparently feel that it is the function of the Court to legislate and not to interpret the laws."
>
> EASTLAND: "Senator McCarthy, in the Steve Nelson case the Court has deprived the state of its most fundamental powers."
>
> MCCARTHY: "Right."

EASTLAND: "What greater blow could be struck at the American system of Government?"

A similar set of ratifications was exchanged a month later:[44]

EASTLAND: "Could I ask you a question there?"

MCCARTHY: "Yes, sir."

EASTLAND: "There is just one pro-communist decision after another from this court, is there not?"

MCCARTHY: "You are so right."

EASTLAND: "What other explanation could there be except that a majority of that court is being influenced by some secret, but very powerful Communist or pro-communist influence?"

MCCARTHY: "It is impossible to explain it. Either incompetence beyond words, Mr. Chairman, I would say, or the type of influence which you mentioned."

. . . .

EASTLAND: "You have heard one communist after another come before this committee and take the position that the Communist Party was just another political party; in fact, that is the Communist line, is it not?"

MCCARTHY: "That is strictly the Communist line."

EASTLAND: "Is not that the line that the Chief Justice of the United States takes?"

MCCARTHY: "Unfortunately, yes, Mr. Chairman. And I may say that I follow what is said in communist publications, to follow their line, rather closely. And the Communist Daily Worker applauded this decision, the Nelson decision, and other decisions of the Supreme Court.

"In their book Earl Warren is a hero.

"Now, I do not accuse Earl Warren of being a Communist, not even remotely. But there is something radically wrong with him. And I think it is extremely unfortunate that he was confirmed as Chief Justice. I cannot understand why a man with practically no legal background, almost nothing but a political background, and a left-wing one at that, was ever selected as a Supreme Court Justice."

EASTLAND: "Of course, I am not accusing him of being a party member—of course not. I am not accusing him of being a Communist, but he takes the same position that the Communists take when they attempt to protect themselves."

This ideological alliance was reinforced by another, more economically oriented, conservative group. Several business organizations were very much concerned about Supreme Court decisions affecting labor relations. Since the access of business to state legislatures seemed to be improving, the question of states' rights had become increasingly important to management. And the Court, although it had refused to void state right-to-work laws as violations of the First and Fourteenth Amendments or of the Contract Clause,[45] still posed a threat to state legislation restricting union power.*

The Roosevelt Court, of course, had been known as a labor tribunal, and, indeed, the doctrine of pre-emptive federalism, which had been applied in *Nelson* to annul state subversive regulations, had been used to invalidate state labor legislation on the ground that Congress, in the Wagner and Taft-Hartley laws, had "occupied the field."[46] In the 1955 Term, *Railway Employees* v. *Hanson* over arguments presented by the attorneys general of nine states, the National Right to Work Committee, the Chamber of Commerce, the National Association of Manufacturers, and the American Farm Bureau Federation—struck down Nebraska's right-to-work statute insofar as it applied to railroad workers. Douglas' opinion for the Court held that Congress had specifically permitted a union shop in the Railway Labor Act, and under Article VI of the Constitution, state legislation to the contrary had to give way. There were no dissents in *Hanson,* and to add to the firmness of the decision rumors in Washington had it that the Justices had almost handled the case via a terse *per curiam* opinion in order to emphasize that they thought the issue "too settled" to merit discussion.

The Taft-Hartley legislation had a clause authorizing a union shop, but only if the state in which the agreement was made permitted such an arrangement. This would have seemed like ironclad protection for state right-to-work laws had *Pennsylvania* v. *Nelson* not run roughshod over a similar, though less specifically worded, provision in the Federal Criminal Code. The *Nelson* ruling plus the Court's firmness in *Hanson,* the known sympathy of several of the Justices with the labor movement, as well as another 1955 Term decision which held that states were still precluded from control over a union in interstate commerce even though the union had failed to

* In December, 1957, Ernest G. Swigert, president of the National Association of Manufacturers, keynoted the Sixty-second Congress of American Industry with a plea to work to reverse the trend toward government control, a trend caused in large part, Swigert declared, by the "distortion" of the Supreme Court into "an instrument of social change" (*New York Times,* December 5, 1957, 1:3).

file the non-Communist affidavits required by the Taft-Hartley oath[47] —all of these made right-to-work backers fearful that such state statutes might fall under the pre-emptive rule.[48] And even if that drastic event never came to pass, states were still barred from comprehensive control of labor relations unless Congress took positive action or the Court reversed itself.

HOWARD SMITH'S PROPOSAL

A number of groups had found a common enemy in the Supreme Court, a common battle cry in "states' rights," and a common remedy had been made available as well. Representative Howard Smith of Virginia,* a conservative banker, segregationist, and author of the Smith Act, had played the part of the broker. On January 5, 1955, he had introduced H.R. 3 in an effort to end the doctrine of pre-emptive federalism before the High Bench could decide the Nelson case. H.R. 3 stipulated that

> . . . no Act of Congress shall be construed as indicating an intent on the part of Congress to occupy the field in which such Act operates, to the exclusion of all State laws on the same subject matter, unless such Act contains an express provision to that effect. No Act of Congress shall be construed as invalidating a provision of State law which would be valid in the absence of such Act unless there is a direct and positive conflict between an express provision of such Act and such provision of the State law so that the two cannot be reconciled or consistently stand together.

By backing this bill, the segregationists could curb the Court, psychologically if not physically, since the pre-emptive rule was largely judge-made. The ultra-security-conscious could revitalize state sedition laws. The right-to-work people could get the specter of federal supremacy removed from their legal closets. And conserv-

* Howard Worth Smith (1883—), LL.B., University of Virginia, 1903, was born in Broad Run, Virginia. He served as Commonwealth attorney for Alexandria from 1918 to 1922. From 1922 to 1928 he was a judge of the Alexandria Corporation Court, and in 1928 he was appointed judge of Virginia's Sixteenth Judicial Circuit. He resigned in 1930 to run for the House of Representatives. Elected in 1931 to the Seventy-second Congress from Virginia's Eighth District, Smith has been re-elected to every succeeding Congress. He quickly built up—and stoutly maintained—a reputation as an anti-New Deal, antilabor, ultraconservative Southern Democrat. FDR once called him "the greatest obstructionist in Congress," and tried to purge him in 1938.

ative groups generally would be freer to exploit their access to state legislatures.

COMMITTEE ACTION

Emanuel Celler of New York,* chairman of the House Judiciary Committee, was the antithesis of all that Smith represented. A liberal, anti–big business New Dealer who represented a predominantly Jewish and Italian neighborhood in Brooklyn, Celler was a staunch champion of minority civil rights. His personality as well as his politics continually clashed with those of Howard Smith. And in recent years, each man had been able to frustrate the other, Smith through his control of the powerful Rules Committee and Celler through his chairmanship of the Judiciary Committee. But while Celler would have been delighted to pigeonhole H.R. 3, within the Judiciary Committee there was a coalition of Southern Democrats and conservative Republicans strongly in favor of at least exploring the bill's potential; and they were able to persuade the chairman to allow Representative Francis Walter's subcommittee #1 to hold hearings during the spring and summer of 1955.[49] Walter, as chairman of the House Un-American Activities Committee, had no sympathy with the *Nelson* decision or any of the other security cases which had been decided against the government.

H.R. 3's proponents lined up supporting testimony from the National Association of Manufacturers, the American Farm Bureau Federation, the Southern Regional Council of Attorneys General, as well as the attorneys general of New Hampshire, Missouri, and Illinois. The NAM expressed the "very deep interest and concern of the members of this association over the continuing trend toward centralization of power in the Federal Government resulting from numerous recent decisions pre-empting various areas which Federal legislation has touched, even, in some instances, by implication." The NAM statement also noted that it was in the field of labor rela-

* Emanuel Celler (1888––) was born in Brooklyn and received his A.B. and LL.B. from Columbia University. Like Smith he had considerable experience as a bank executive. Celler was first elected to Congress in 1922, and in the Eighty-first Congress he became chairman of the Judiciary Committee. A member of many Jewish civic organizations, Celler has also been prominently associated with Zionism. He published his autobiography, *You Never Leave Brooklyn* (New York: John Day Co., Inc.), in 1953.

tions that the need for such a bill was most immediately apparent. "Employment, as we all know, is essentially a local relationship between local parties living and working under local conditions with other local people all subject in most respects to local law. Their employment, however, is being increasingly regulated from Washington."

The House Judiciary Committee took no further action after the summer hearings; but in the next session of Congress the committee held more public hearings,[50] while in the Senate hearings were also opened on two similar bills.[51] This time the attorneys general of twenty-four states urged an end to the pre-emptive rule, and they were joined by Governor Shivers of Texas and Associate Justice Musmanno of the Pennsylvania Supreme Court. In addition to the NAM and AFBF from the previous year, the U.S. Chamber of Commerce, the Missouri Chamber of Commerce, the California Manufacturers Association, the Forest Management Committee of the National Lumber Manufacturers Association, and the National Association of State Aviation Officials either sent favorable witnesses or mailed statements strongly backing H.R. 3.

During these second hearings the forces opposing H.R. 3 were also able to get themselves on record. The AFL-CIO and the Railway Labor Executives Committee saw the bill as a threat to the protection that federal labor legislation had been offering unions and warned that "chaos and confusion" would result if both the states and the federal government were to engage in concurrent regulation of labor matters. The two groups suggested that if Congress was displeased with a specific Supreme Court decision (the Court had affirmed the Pennsylvania decision in the Nelson case just three weeks before the 1956 hearings began), remedial legislation might be better directed at re-establishing congressional intent in that limited area rather than using the scattergun approach of H.R. 3.

The Association of American Railroads, frightened by nightmares of double compliance with complex state and federal transportation regulations, joined the two labor groups in opposing H.R. 3 as it then stood. The railway owners were willing to support the bill only if it were amended so as not to apply to them. They requested that the following clause be added to the proposal: "This Act shall not apply to laws of Congress relating to carriers by railroad subject to Part I of the Interstate Commerce Act."

Joseph Rauh testified for the Americans for Democratic Action, opposing H.R. 3 for the same general reasons as the labor groups; but Rauh also objected to more specific proposals to reverse the Nelson case. The ADA, Rauh said, believed that a conspiracy of the scope of the Communist party could only be fought effectively by the national government. "Entrusting such a task to frequently overzealous or misguided State officials not only cannot aid enforcement, but must necessarily hamper the Federal program. Its likely result is the prosecution of racial and political minorities rather than Communists."[52]

Clarence Mitchell of the NAACP appeared before the House committee and stated that the bill "in its legislative setting" constituted a double threat to the civil rights of American Negroes. Mitchell explained that H.R. 3 could destroy the integration gains the Negro had won through the Interstate Commerce Commission order banning segregation in facilities used for interstate transportation. In addition, the Court decisions holding that unions utilizing federal bargaining machinery could not discriminate against Negro workers would be jeopardized since a number of states would allow a dual code of employment rights.[53]

In the summer of 1955, the bill received significant support when it was approved in principle by the American Bar Association's House of Delegates[54] and was specifically indorsed as needed legislation by the National Association of Attorneys General.[55] Balancing these victories were sharp criticisms from the Interstate Commerce Commission and the Department of Justice. Each of these governmental agencies stressed the vagueness of the measure, but the memorandum from Deputy Attorney General William Rogers was especially strong:

> The rule of interpretation proposed in the bill would radically change the rules applied by the courts since the early days of this country. . . . More importantly, by its application to all Federal statutes whenever enacted, this bill would create great confusion in important areas, raising difficult and substantial legal and practical problems. It would require persons who are operating in full conformity to Federal statutes which wholly govern their field of operations suddenly to conform their operations also to the rules of each State in which those operations may be conducted. . . . Besides the question of constitutional authority of the Congress to enact such a

> provision, the breadth of its application raises serious legal and practical problems, not only for those who administer the laws, but more particularly for those who must obey them.[56]

Celler managed to keep H.R. 3 shelved for eighteen months, but in the summer of 1956 the conservative coalition within the committee forced him to put the measure to a vote. In July, 1956, the committee favorably reported the bill, although Celler and his liberal followers had been able to secure a major revision.[57] As reported, H.R. 3 would have lifted the pre-emption ban only as to state sedition laws. In effect it would have reversed the Nelson case and have left the pre-emptive doctrine intact.

The committee version was completely unsatisfactory to Smith, and he intended to try to return the bill to its original form by amendment once it got to the floor. However, at this time neither House Speaker Sam Rayburn nor Majority leader John McCormack favored H.R. 3 as originally written; and they planned to call up the committee version of the bill under a suspension of the rules, a move which would have precluded any amendments. Smith objected to this procedure, and H.R. 3 was shelved for the remainder of the Eighty-fourth Congress.[58]

THE BAR ASSOCIATION AND THE GOVERNORS

Time Magazine reported in June, 1956, that criticism of the Warren Court was "more emotional than cerebral."[59] This thesis received support when, in October, one hundred lawyers from all parts of the country published a manifesto defending the Court against "heedless," "reckless," and "dangerous" attacks.[60] Yet as emotional, even demagogic, as many of the assaults on the Court were, they had a wide and firm base, as shown by the support H.R. 3 had amassed. And the hundred lawyers had issued their pronouncement only after they had been unable to persuade the American Bar Association to adopt it the previous summer.[61]

The ABA's action was negative, a failure to support the Court. The 1956 Governors' Conference took positive action in adopting a resolution critical of the *Nelson* decision and the pre-emptive doctrine. Although not specifically mentioning H.R. 3 by name, the governors approved its purposes and principles:

> Members of this Conference are gravely concerned by decisions of the Supreme Court of the United States which have held that Congressional enactments supersede state laws on the matters involved and thereby pre-empt those fields for the federal government alone. Judicial interpretations of this character seriously handicap the states in the regulation and administration of their internal affairs. . . . [The] Governors' Conference recommends to the Congress that federal laws should be framed that will not be construed to pre-empt any field against state action unless this intent is stated, and that the exercise of national power on any subject should not bar state action on the same subject unless there is positive inconsistency.[62]

PROSPECTS FOR THE FUTURE

The Court foes had suffered failure in their first skirmishes. They had been able to get only an unsatisfactory version of H.R. 3 out of committee and, of course, had not succeeded in getting any legislation adopted. The manifesto of the hundred lawyers was damaging to their prestige, and the northern press was showing little sympathy for their cause. Yet the Court foes had been able to effect a loose alliance among their divergent forces, and this alliance included important interest groups as well as some of the most influential members of Congress. The Court foes had also received encouragement from the American Bar Association and from the Conference of State Governors. Moreover, the same interests were still being threatened, the same states' rights slogan was still available, and H.R. 3 could be reintroduced in the Eighty-fifth Congress to provide another rallying point. The anti-Court factions had only lost a little time; and if the Warren Court continued its indicated trend of decisions, this might turn out to have been no real loss at all.

5. THE RESURGENCE OF JUDICIAL POWER

By *the end* of the 1955 Term, the seeds of a new Court-Congress conflict had been sown and had taken root. No matter how often liberal leaders characterized H.R. 3 as ludicrous and preposterous, the harsh facts remained that Smith's proposal was not only gaining support but that it was only one of more than seventy anti-Court bills which had been introduced in the Eighty-fourth Congress. Writing in the May 18, 1956, issue of *U.S. News and World Report,* former Associate Justice James Byrnes had issued a call to arms. "Power intoxicates men. It is never voluntarily surrendered. The Supreme Court must be curbed."[1] The Georgia legislature rallied around the former governor of South Carolina by demanding that the House of Representatives impeach the Chief Justice and five Associate Justices for giving aid and comfort to the Communist enemy as well as other high crimes and misdemeanors "too numerous to mention."[2]

Yet judges, like other statesmen, may be gauged by the enemies they make. Opposition by segregationists and the former followers of McCarthy might be considered as the inevitable lot of a liberal tribunal. And many ultraconservative businessmen had never forgiven the Court for its 1937 switch on economic legislation. Something more than alienation of the extreme right wings of the two political parties would be needed to translate border skirmishes, however bitter, into a full-scale war. Either the President or the middle-of-the-road majority of Congress would have to shift far to the right, or the Court would have to do something more radical to stir up serious opposition among the moderates.

NEW FACES

Two changes of personnel took place in the 1956 Term. Sherman Minton retired in October, and Eisenhower gave a recess appointment to William Joseph Brennan, Jr., of New Jersey. Brennan was a relatively young man (only fifty), a Roman Catholic—there had been no Catholic on the High Bench since Justice Murphy's death in 1949—a Democrat, and most important for critics of Court appointments, a man of considerable judicial experience. He had served for three years as a state lower court judge and for more than four years on the New Jersey Supreme Court.

In February, 1957, Stanley Reed retired; and the fourth Eisenhower appointment went to Charles Evans Whittaker of Missouri, a fifty-seven-year-old Republican. Like Brennan, Whittaker had prior judicial service, two years as a federal district judge and about ten months on the Court of Appeals for the Eighth Circuit. Whittaker did not take office until late March and so was able to participate in only a few important decisions. On the other hand, Brennan's recess appointment allowed him to sit through all but the first days of the term, and his votes and opinions became critical factors in the decisions which led to the crisis of the Warren Court.

Brennan was a clear exception to the normal rule that a new Justice positions himself in the center of the Court for a few terms before joining one of the opposing wings.[3] Although his first months on the Bench gave little hint as to his underlying judicial philosophy, before his initial term was over he had moved into the camp of Black, Douglas, and Warren, re-establishing a four-judge libertarian bloc similar to that of the old Roosevelt Court. With this reinforcement a judicial counterattack against cold war assaults on traditional civil liberties became a reality.

JENCKS V. UNITED STATES

The first decision of the 1956 Term again involved Steve Nelson. This time the Communist leader had come to the Court seeking review of a federal Smith Act conviction. The Justice Department conceded that one of the prosecuting witnesses had possibly committed perjury, and the Solicitor General requested that the case be remanded to the trial court to allow the judge to decide whether a new trial should be granted. Over dissents from Harlan, Frankfurter, and Burton (Brennan did not participate), the Court reversed the conviction and ordered a new trial.[4] "The dignity of the United States Government," the Chief Justice wrote, "will not permit the conviction of any person on tainted testimony."

This was a dramatic beginning, and it was an accurate omen of what was to come later in the term. In many ways the most startling decision was that in *Jencks* v. *United States,* the appeal of a New Mexico labor leader from a perjury conviction for falsely taking the Taft-Hartley non-Communist oath. At the trial, Jencks's attorney had asked two government witnesses, J. W. Ford and Harvey Matusow, if they could recall what they had told the FBI about Jencks in their reports made during the time period (1948–49) about which they were testifying. Neither witness could recall the contents of these reports, and the defense attorney then asked the court to secure the FBI files in question and to examine them for possible discrepancies. The trial judge refused this request, and after the conviction his refusal was sustained by the Court of Appeals.

Justice Brennan, speaking for himself, Warren, Black, Douglas, and Frankfurter, reversed the conviction. Giving Jencks more than he had asked for, Brennan's opinion held that the defense and not the trial judge should be allowed to inspect relevant reports of the witnesses in the possession of the government, because only the defense attorney could know what was important to his case. "Justice," Brennan concluded, "requires no less." Recognizing that there might be information vital to national security which could not be revealed, the Court gave the Justice Department an option: "The criminal action must be dismissed when the Government, on the ground of privilege, elects not to comply with an order to produce, for the accused's inspection and for admission in evidence, relevant statements or reports in its possession of government witnesses touching the subject matter of their testimony at the trial."

In a separate concurring opinion, Burton and Harlan agreed that the conviction should be reversed, but thought that the trial judge and not the defendant should be given the FBI documents so that admissibility could be determined. Material withheld from the defense could be sealed so that an appellate court could review any possible error. In this way, the two Justices thought, the competing and conflicting demands of national security and procedural guaranties could best be balanced.

Justice Clark dissented. Declaring that the Court had opened a "veritable Pandora's box of troubles," he directed his opinion less at his colleagues on the Bench than at the Court's neighbors in the domed building across Capitol Plaza. "Unless the Congress changes the rule announced by the Court today, those intelligence agencies of our Government engaged in law enforcement may as well close up shop, for the Court has opened their files to the criminal and thus afforded him a Roman holiday for rummaging through confidential information as well as vital national secrets."

LIMITING THE POWER TO INVESTIGATE

Just two weeks after *Jencks,* on June 17—"Red Monday" the Court's foes would call it—the Supreme Court unleashed another set of lightning bolts. *Watkins* v. *United States* twisted the tail of the congressional lion by restricting the jealously guarded power to investigate. John T. Watkins, a United Automobile Workers organizer, had appeared before the House Un-American Activities Committee in 1954. While candidly confessing his own past part in aiding the Communist party, he had refused to give the committee names of reformed party members, claiming that such questions went beyond the scope of the investigators' authority. For this refusal he was convicted of contempt of Congress.

Dividing 6–1, the Supreme Court reversed Watkins' conviction.

For the majority, the Chief Justice wrote a rambling thirty-five-page opinion. Conceding the investigatory power of Congress was "inherent" as well as "broad," Warren still would not hold that it was unlimited. "There is no general authority to expose the private affairs of individuals without justification in terms of the functions of the Congress . . . nor is the Congress a law enforcement or trial agency. These are functions of the executive and judicial departments of government. No inquiry is an end in itself; it must be related to and in furtherance of a legitimate task of Congress." Viewing the Court's task as one of seeking an accommodation between the power of Congress to obtain information and the right of the citizen to privacy, Warren also declined to assume that "every congressional investigation is justified by a public need that overbalances the private rights affected."

So far there was little new doctrine, although the language emphasizing limitations on congressional inquisitorial power was stronger than any since *Kilbourn* v. *Thompson* in 1881. But the Chief Justice proceeded to mount the pulpit and preach to Congress of its recent sins of overindulgence. "In the decade following World War II, there appeared a new kind of congressional inquiry unknown in prior periods of American history. . . . The new phase of legislative inquiry involved a broad-scale intrusion into the lives and affairs of private citizens." Not only did those intrusions probe deeply into the citizen's right to be let alone, but, Warren added, Congress had failed in its duty to frame with particularity the areas to be examined by its subordinate bodies. On this count, the mandate to the House Un-American Activities Committee to investigate those forces and groups which threaten "the principle of the form of government guaranteed by our Constitution," was a flagrant sin of omission. "It would be difficult to imagine a less explicit authorizing resolution. Who can define the meaning of 'Un-American'? What is the single, solitary 'principle of the form of government guaranteed by our Constitution'?" And, despite the fact that this special committee had conceived of its task in "the grand view of its name," the House had repeatedly extended the body's life, and had finally made it a standing committee.

After this sermon, Warren shifted to other, though related faults. The sweeping scope of the legislative authorization turned out not to have been the cardinal error of *l'affaire Watkins.* Now the grave sin was found in the actual questioning of the witness. In spite of Watkins' objection to the relevancy of the questions to a valid legislative purpose, the committee chairman had never made any such relevance clear. Indeed, after a trial and one review, even a majority of the Supreme Court remained "unenlightened as to the subject to which the questions asked [Watkins] were pertinent. Certainly if the point is that obscure . . . it was not adequately revealed to [Watkins] when he had to decide at his peril whether or not to answer. Fundamental fairness demands that no witness be compelled to make such a determination with so little guidance."

Thus the whole inquiry suffered from the "vice of vagueness." Since Watkins had not been "accorded a fair opportunity to determine whether he was within his rights in refusing to answer, his conviction is necessarily invalid under the Due Process Clause of the Fifth Amendment."

Once again Clark filed an acid dissent, denouncing the majority opinion as a "mischievous curbing of the informing function of the Congress." The requirements set by the Court, he claimed, were "both unnecessary and unworkable." In addition, Clark disputed the fact of any vagueness. "I think the committee here was acting entirely within its scope and that the purpose of its inquiry was set out with 'indisputable clarity.' " Singling out Black and Frankfurter for special treatment, Clark cited as authorities for his dissent their work and writing during the 1920's and 1930's when they had urged "Hands off the Investigations."

FREE SPEECH: THE DISTINCTION BETWEEN ADVOCACY AND INCITEMENT

The echoes from the *Watkins* blasts had hardly been absorbed by the velvet draperies when Justice Harlan began reading the majority opinion* in *Yates* v. *United States,* a case which reversed Smith Act convictions of fourteen Communist leaders. The Vinson Court in its 1951 decision in *Dennis* v. *United States* had sustained the constitutionality of the Smith Act, and the Warren Court did not reverse

* So labeled in the official reports; but of the seven participating Justices only Warren and Frankfurter did not dissent from one or more points. In his dissent Justice Clark referred to Harlan's opinion as the "principal opinion" rather than as the majority opinion.

Dennis, although it did "explain" the earlier case to such an extent that a Court of Appeals judge baldly stated that the statute had been reduced to a "shambles."[5]

Taking up first the charge that the defendants had conspired to organize a group to teach the violent overthrow of the government, Harlan's meticulous opinion began with a nine-page discussion of the meaning of the term "organize." Finding that the intent of Congress was unclear, Harlan concluded that the Court should follow the historic judicial rule of interpreting criminal statutes narrowly. "Organize" thus applied only to the actual establishment of the Communist party, not the day-to-day activities necessary to keep it functioning. Since the American Communist party had been refounded in 1945, and since there was a three-year statute of limitations on this section of the Act, that part of the 1951 indictment was fatally defective.

Next Harlan considered the trial judge's instructions to the jury and found that the judge had blurred the distinction between permissible speech, that is, advocacy of an abstract doctrine, and incitement to illegal action. "The essential distinction is that those to whom the advocacy is addressed must be urged to *do* something, now or in the future, rather than merely to *believe* in something." While he conceded that this difference was "subtle and difficult to grasp," Harlan nevertheless felt that it went to the heart of the matter, and that the jury had to be clearly instructed that they could not convict unless incitement to action had been proved.

The third point in Harlan's opinion was that the evidence against five of the defendants had been "entirely too meager to justify putting them to a new trial," and their acquittal was ordered. The evidence against the remaining nine was not found to be too tenuous to prevent a retrial.

Justice Burton concurred in the result and in Harlan's opinion except for the definition of the word "organize." Black and Douglas concurred in part and dissented in part. They agreed with the Court in reversing the convictions, but thought that acquittals should have been directed for all fourteen defendants. Adhering to their dissenting views in the Dennis case, Black and Douglas asserted that the Smith Act was a violation of free speech. "The First Amendment provides the only kind of security system that can preserve a free government—one that leaves the way wide open for people to favor, discuss, advocate or incite causes and doctrines however obnoxious and antagonistic such views may be to the rest of us."

Once again Clark dissented, charging the majority with frustrating the purpose of Congress in its definition of "organize," and of usurping the functions of a jury in ordering an acquittal. As for the trial judge's instructions to the jury, Clark professed that Harlan's "artillery of words" concerning proper distinctions between privileged and punishable speech had left him "confused."

RIGHTS IN GOVERNMENT EMPLOYMENT

In a third decision handed down that day, the Court by an 8–0 vote, Clark not participating, ordered the reinstatement of John Service who had been discharged from the State Department for alleged disloyalty.[6] Subjected to what David Fellman has termed "perpetual jeopardy,"[7] Service had been cleared five times by departmental loyalty boards and twice by the Loyalty Review Board. On the third review of his fifth clearance, however, the review board found reasonable doubt as to Service's loyalty and so advised the Secretary of State. The Secretary, solely on this advice and without any independent examination of the record, invoked the authority of the "McCarran Rider," which gave him "absolute discretion" to fire employees in the national interest, and ordered Service discharged.

Harlan's opinion for the Court declared this action of the Secretary had violated the State Department's own rules and was therefore invalid. The Court, applying a principle of administrative law later described by Frankfurter as "he that takes the procedural sword shall perish with that sword," held that the Secretary of State was obliged to follow his own regulations. "While it is of course true that under the McCarran Rider the Secretary was not obligated to impose upon himself these more rigorous substantive and procedural standards . . . having done so he could not, so long as the Regulations remained unchanged, proceed without regard to them."

STATE POWER TO INVESTIGATE

In *Sweezy* v. *New Hampshire,* Red Monday's fourth cold war case, the Court imposed the same restrictions and much the same sermon on state inquisitorial power as *Watkins* had placed on congressional investigations. Louis Wyman, New Hampshire's attorney general, acting as a one-man legislative committee investigating subversion, had been balked by Paul Sweezy, a classical Marxian professor. Sweezy had refused, on First Amendment grounds, to answer a number of questions concerning his political beliefs, his affiliations with Henry Wallace's Progressive party, or the content of lectures he had delivered at the University of New Hampshire.

This time there was no institutional opinion for the Court. The Chief Justice announced the decision to reverse Sweezy's contempt conviction and wrote another long, discursive essay in which Black, Douglas, and Brennan concurred. The gist of Warren's prolix opinion was that the "sweeping and uncertain" nature of the authorization for the investigation had failed to set proper and ascertainable constitutional limits to the inquiry.

Frankfurter, joined by Harlan, filed a masterful concurring opinion. He was willing to accept the claim that the specific questions Wyman asked Sweezy had been authorized by the legislature, but Frankfurter contended that the investigation itself had infringed on First and Fourteenth Amendment rights to political and academic freedom.

> For a citizen to be made to forego even a part of so basic a liberty as his political autonomy, the subordinating interest of the State must be compelling. . . . Inviolability of privacy belonging to a citizen's political loyalties has so overwhelming an importance to the well-being of our kind of society that it cannot be constitutionally encroached upon on the basis of so meagre a countervailing interest of the State as may be argumentatively found in the remote, shadowy threat to the security of New Hampshire allegedly presented in the origins and contributing elements of the Progressive Party and in [Sweezy's] relations to these.

Answering the New Hampshire Attorney General's assertion that it had been necessary to question Sweezy about his university lectures to determine if violent overthrow of the government was being taught, Frankfurter countered:

> When weighed against the grave harm resulting from governmental intrusion into the intellectual life of a university, such justification for compelling a witness to discuss the contents of his lecture appears grossly inadequate. Particularly is this so where the witness

> has sworn that neither in the lecture nor at any other time did he ever advocate overthrowing the Government by force and violence.

Then, paraphrasing the late Robert H. Jackson's reply in the second Flag Salute case[8] to his own eloquent and moving dissent against that decision, Frankfurter spelled out what he thought to be the proper function of the judiciary in such instances:

> To be sure, this is a conclusion based on a judicial judgment in balancing two contending principles—the right of a citizen to political privacy, as protected by the Fourteenth Amendment, and the right of the State to self-protection. And striking the balance implies the exercise of judgment. This is the inescapable judicial task in giving substantive content, legally enforced, to the Due Process Clause, and it is a task ultimately committed to this Court.

Clark, joined by Burton, wrote a searing, three-and-a-half-page dissent. "The short of it is that the Court blocks New Hampshire's effort to enforce its law. . . . I thought we had left open a wide field for state action, but implicit in the opinions today is a contrary conclusion. They destroy the fact-finding power of the State in this field and I dissent from the wide sweep of their coverage."

RACE, BUSINESS, AND LABOR

Piled up on these cold war cases were a number of other decisions from the 1956 Term which further antagonized the Court opposition. In November, *Gayle* v. *Browder* had extended the ban against segregation to public transportation at the intrastate level. Later in the term, *Guss* v. *Utah* and companion cases from Ohio and California held that even where the National Labor Relations Board refused to exercise its jurisdiction, the states still did not necessarily have authority to handle labor disputes affecting interstate commerce.

Many business executives and corporation lawyers were alarmed when Justice Brennan for a four-judge majority—Clark, Harlan, and Whittaker not participating—ruled that section 7 of the Clayton Act had been aimed at vertical as well as horizontal monopolies.[9] This decision held illegal Du Pont's acquisition of General Motors stock in 1917–19 and, many businessmen feared, opened the doors for widespread and, in effect, ex post facto government action against firms which had purchased stock in customer corporations.

Equally as significant as these cases was the *Girard College* decision,[10] which applied a dentist's drill to the exposed nerve of conservatism—liberty of free disposal of private property. In a unanimous *per curiam* opinion the Court ruled that, notwithstanding a clause in Stephen Girard's will that the school to be established by his trust fund was to be for whites only, the institution would have to admit Negroes. The inclusion of the City of Philadelphia as one of the trustees was declared to have brought into play the Fourteenth Amendment's prohibitions against racial discrimination.

CROSSING THE BAR

Not content with this agitation of its opponents, the Court had gone on to make new enemies in the form of organized bar associations and law enforcement officials. The legal profession was angered by a pair of decisions which put constitutional limitations on the guild's hitherto almost absolute power to regulate admission to its ranks. In *Schware* v. *New Mexico* the Court found a denial of due process in the State Board of Bar Examiners' refusal to admit the petitioner to law practice because of a lack of good moral character. The board based its decision on Schware's admitted membership in the Communist party during the 1930's, his use of aliases, and his record of several arrests.

Black's opinion for the Court rejected the contention that arrest without prosecution, or use of aliases, explained by the petitioner as an effort to avoid anti-Semitism, could sustain a judgment of bad moral character. Nor would Black concede that mere membership in the Communist party, membership terminated fifteen years earlier, could justify such a conclusion. "There is nothing in the record that gives any indication that his association with that party was anything more than a political faith in a political party. . . . Assuming that some members of the Communist Party . . . had illegal aims and engaged in illegal activities, it cannot automatically be inferred that all members shared their evil purposes or participated in their illegal conduct."

Justices Frankfurter, Harlan, and Clark concurred in a separate opinion written by Frankfurter, making the decision, at least, a unanimous one. But in *Konigsberg* v. *California,* the second bar case, the Court divided 5–3 (Whittaker took no part in either decision). The California examining committee had refused to certify Raphael Konigsberg as a man of good moral character who did not advocate the violent overthrow of the government. The evidence against the petitioner included testimony of an ex-Communist that Konigsberg had attended party meetings in 1941, as well as Konigsberg's own published criticisms of American participation in the Korean War. But the chief count against him seems to have been his persistent refusal to tell the committee whether he was or ever had been a Communist. To answer these questions, he stated, would mean yielding his First Amendment rights to freedom of belief and association.

Black, Warren, Douglas, Brennan, and Burton felt that, even if true, 1941 membership in the Communist party, without more, "could not support an inference that [Konigsberg] did not have good moral character." Nor was criticism of American foreign policy evidence of disloyalty or even disaffection. As for the third point, the majority thought it obvious "the State could not draw inferences as to his truthfulness, candor or his moral character in general if his refusal to answer was based on a belief that the United States Constitution prohibited the type of inquiries which the Committee was making."

Frankfurter dissented because he thought it very possible that the state decision might have been based on non-federal grounds. Harlan and Clark shared Frankfurter's jurisdictional doubts but also dissented on the merits. "What the Court has really done," Harlan wrote, "is simply to impose on California its own notions of public policy and judgment. For me, today's decision represents an unacceptable intrusion into a matter of state concern."

POLICE DETENTION

When in *Mallory* v. *United States* the Court moved away from Communist cases to matters of "normal" criminal jurisprudence, the Justices also managed to offend a number of people. Although the *Mallory* decision immediately affected only federal police practices, it worried state and federal law enforcement officers. In this case, the Court ordered a retrial of a brutal rapist on an apparent technicality. District of Columbia police had arrested Andrew Mallory, a dull-witted, nineteen-year-old Negro, at two o'clock in the afternoon. Contrary to the command of Rule 5(a) of the Federal Rules of Criminal Procedure, that an arrested person should be arraigned "without unnecessary delay"—i.e., brought before a magistrate, informed of the charge against him, and told of his constitutional rights—the officers questioned Mallory intermittently for about seven and a half hours. Not until he had submitted to a lie detector test, had confessed, and had repeated his confession did the police make an effort to abide by the arraignment requirement.

Speaking through Justice Frankfurter, the Court unanimously held that a confession obtained in violation of the Rules of Criminal Procedure was inadmissible in a federal court. This exclusionary rule based on delay in arraignment was not new. The basic decision, *McNabb* v. *United States,* had been made fourteen years earlier. But *Mallory* did represent a more rigid application of this rule since in earlier cases defendants had been held from thirty hours to several days. To make the situation more stringent from the point of view of police operations, Frankfurter's opinion stressed that "unnecessary delay" was to be given a literal and exact definition. Rule 5(a) "allows arresting officers little more leeway than the interval between arrest and the ordinary administrative steps required to bring a suspect before the nearest available magistrate."[11]

THE WORK OF THE WARREN COURT

Once again decisions of the Supreme Court had squarely collided with the views espoused by other government officials. The political offender decisions had aroused anger among ultra-security-minded congressmen and administrators and had stirred doubts in the minds of many moderates and even some liberals. Of all previous Court conflicts the strongest parallel—perhaps because it was so recent—seemed to be with the action of the Hughes Court on May 27, 1935, when the Justices had struck down the Frazier-Lemke Act, the NIRA, and had thrown out what FDR had considered gratuitous insults in its opinion denying him authority to fire a member of the Federal Trade Commission.

The parallel was there on the surface, but close analysis would reveal that the analogy was shallow. There were significant differences in approach between the Hughes Bench and the Warren Court. The racial decisions after 1954 had been grounded on the Constitution, as had some of the civil liberties cases which had not involved cold war problems. But, on the other controversial issues of the time, the Warren Court, unlike the majority of the Hughes Court before 1937, had not, or not yet, put a constitutional block in the path of congressional power to govern.

In cases where subversion, threatened or real, was the key issue, the Warren Court uniformly decided the outcome on procedural or statutory grounds. *Pennsylvania* v. *Nelson* and *Cole* v. *Young* had settled only questions of statutory interpretation. *Service* v. *Dulles, Peters* v. *Hobby,* and, in the main, *Slochower* v. *Board* cited procedural rather than constitutional flaws as reasons for reversal. The opinion in *Yates* v. *United States* was based on statutory interpretation, though the directed acquittal for lack of evidence might be called a reversal for a procedural error.

Even where constitutional clauses were invoked, as in *Watkins, Sweezy, Slochower,* and the bar admission cases, it was a specific set of circumstances which tainted the particular governmental action; the action itself was not inherently invalid. The basis of *Jencks,* however, was a mystery. In his sixteen-page opinion, Brennan never found time to explain whether the FBI reports had to be produced because of the general commands of due process of law or because of the more specific commands of the Federal Rules of Criminal Procedure, or whether the Supreme Court, in its capacity of overseer of the administration of justice in federal courts, was establishing this production requirement as a rule of judicial procedure. In any event, read in its entirety, the *Jencks* opinion scarcely lived up to the nightmarish picture which Justice Clark's flamboyant dissent painted; it was not an invitation for a Communist "Roman holiday" of rummaging through secret FBI files.

None of these cases denied congressional authority to punish subversion or to permit removal of security risks from public employment; nor did they deny the states similar authority if Congress would unequivocally allow state intervention to protect the federal government. As one commentator wrote in the summer of 1957: "That the 1956 Term holdings erect no important substantive bars in the subversion field is, in fact, an evaluation too obvious to merit much further elaboration."[12]

What Warren had been able to do was to lead the Court into a reassertion of judicial power, largely by means of the indirect approach of statutory interpretation.[13] The Court declared in bold, almost belligerent terms that if public officials wished to prosecute Communists, the prosecutions would have to be based on defendants' acts or attempts or plans to act, not on their political beliefs, no matter how repugnant; that if congressional and state investigators were to delve into private affairs, they would have to justify their probes by a valid legislative purpose, a specific authorization, and a reasonable demonstration of a government interest overriding individual rights to privacy; that if state and federal governments wished to fire employees as loyalty-security risks, they had to do so with scrupulous regard for procedural niceties; and that if a state wished to deny a person access to a public profession, there had to be sound and convincing evidence of serious prior misconduct or some other clear connection between the individual's record and the government's proscription.

The Justices had refused to admit that Congress, if not the states, had intended to push the hunt for Communists and security risks to the extreme of dispensing with normal procedural regularities of American law. The opinions of the Warren Court admonished the other branches of government to use their authority calmly, wisely, and justly; the Court did not forbid the use of political power to cope with problems of internal subversion.

But fourteen Communist leaders had been freed, two suspected Communists apparently had been allowed to practice law,* a "security risk" had been ordered reinstated, and state and congressional investigations had been frustrated. These results, played up by newspaper headlines which were often as exaggerated as Justice Clark's dissents, provided ready ammunition for the Court's enemies. Nor could the general indirectness of the Warren Court's approach mask from jealous members of Congress the incontrovertible fact that the

* The state bar committee refused to certify Konigsberg a second time, this time on the ground that he had obstructed an investigation into his qualifications to practice law. The Supreme Court upheld this second exclusion, *Konigsberg* v. *California* (1961). Warren, Black, Douglas, and Brennan dissented.

Justices were setting public policy in major areas of national affairs. That they were doing so more adroitly than had previous judges was an added source of irritation. Thus a dangerous mixture of ire at "mistaken" decisions, indignation at the moral lecture delivered in *Watkins,* and fear of an invasion of important fields of legislative jurisdiction was brewing on Capitol Hill.

THE PRESS SPEAKS

Reaction to the 1956 Term cases was even more booming than that of the previous few years.[14] Not unexpectedly, Communists were jubilant. A leader of the party in California claimed that *Yates* "will mark a rejuvenation of the party in America. We have lost some members in the last two years, but now we are on our way."[15] The *People's World* crowed: "We rejoice. Victory is, indeed, sweet." And the *Daily Worker* picked up the theme: "Monday's Supreme Court decisions go a long way towards restoring civil liberties for all Americans. These landmark rulings in one great flash illuminate the recent McCarthyian darkness and light up the promise of a restored Bill of Rights."[16] Eugene Dennis wrote a report to the party's national executive committee stating that it was "essential" for Communists "to popularize the democratic significance and portent of the Court's [*Yates*] decision for all Americans, Communists and non-Communists alike. And it is necessary to emphasize the new grounds which now exist to fight from, plus the heavy responsibilities of labor and the popular forces in this situation."[17]

On the other hand, the old Court foes were enraged. The *Richmond News Leader* charged the Justices with "arrogant incompetence," "gross dereliction of duty," and "flagrant and wilful disregard of the judicial function." David Lawrence demanded loyalty checks for Supreme Court law clerks and suggested popular election of judges as the only sure remedy against continued abuse of power.

Other segments of the conservative press added to the tumult. The *Washington Star* and the *New York Herald Tribune* expressed grave doubts as to the wisdom of the recent decisions. The *Chicago Tribune,* which thirteen years earlier had eulogized the Court for protecting free speech of American Nazis during World War II,[18] blasted the *Yates* decision as a "crippling blow to the efforts of Congress to deter the Communists." "The boys in the Kremlin," the *Tribune* added, "may wonder why they need a 5th column in the United States so long as the Supreme Court is determined to be so helpful." The *Cleveland Plain Dealer* was equally irate: "Well, Comrades, you've finally got what you wanted. The Supreme Court has handed it to you on a platter. From now on you have the right to teach and advocate the forcible overthrow of the Government of the United States, just as long as you speak in general principles and don't plot specific acts of violence. So, Comrades, come and get us."

In New York, the *Daily News* termed the *Yates* decision "a masterpiece of hair-splitting," and the *Daily Mirror* charged that the Court had brought about a "moment of weeping" in "making the Communists superior to every other citizen in the country." Pointing out that Justice Clark had reproached the *Yates* majority for usurping the function of a jury, the *Philadelphia Inquirer* remarked that "many persons are likely to believe that the functions of Congress may have been usurped as well." The American Legion *Firing Line* added that "unless immediate remedial legislation is enacted, irreparable harm will be done the entire security program."

Although somewhat critical of the political offender decisions,[19] the *Wall Street Journal* was more concerned about the Du Pont case. It quoted an NAM official as calling the decision "incredible" and a Chamber of Commerce officer as saying, "it looks like another instance of the continued trend of the Court to disregard precedent." For its part, the *Journal* added:

> It seems to us, then, that what the Supreme Court has done is to throw away all past standards and put no practical ones in their place. . . . The effects of this ruling on du Pont and General Motors . . . seem to us as minor compared to the potential effects on the business community in general of a decision so sweeping that it throws suspicion on any corporation that does business with any other company any of whose stock it may own.[20]

The *New York Herald Tribune* agreed:

> The whole American corporate structure is shaken. . . . Certainly this is not in the public interest; certainly this could not have been the intent of Congress. . . . Obviously it is necessary to revise the [Clayton] Act again. It must be clear to Congress, not only that "bigness" is in itself not illegal nor contrary to the best interests of the country, but that business cannot function with the time bomb

of Section 7 ticking away in its gear box. And Congress must in turn make these points clear to the Courts.[21]

But the 1956 Term had also awakened the friends of the Court both among liberal and conservative sectors of the press. "These are good decisions," the *Baltimore Sun* wrote. Praising the Court as "the most courageous of our three branches of Government," the *New York Times* called June 17 a "day for freedom."[22] The *Washington Post and Times-Herald* claimed the decisions were "especially needed and long overdue." In Philadelphia, the *Bulletin* noted that "the Supreme Court has wisely taken the position that individual rights and freedoms must weigh heavier in the balance where a choice has to be made, than the objective of total exposure and punishment of any connection, however remote, with the Communist conspiracy." The *New York Post* congratulated the Justices for having shaken the pillars of "know-nothingism," and articles in the *Nation* and the *New Republic* as well as editorials in the *Detroit Free Press* and the *St. Louis Post-Dispatch* joined the cheering.

Even religious publications were drawn into the debate. The Jesuit magazine *America* was worried about the creation of legal loopholes for Communists, although generally pleased with the constitutional principles of the June decisions.[23] The other leading Catholic periodical, *Commonweal,* had nothing but praise: "The recent decisions of the Supreme Court of the United States have reaffirmed both the strength and the glory of democracy."[24] Not to be outdone, the *Christian Science Monitor* editorialized: "While liberals will hail the Court's actions, its opinions are basically conservative. For they mark an emphatic return to constitutional guarantees of liberty. The Court has restored a balance which has been upset in recent years by the cold war and popular fears for national security."

The *Jewish Frontier* characterized the 1956 Term decisions as "a signal triumph," leading the nation "back to the Bill of Rights."[25] The *Christian Century,* which had remarked on June 12, 1957, that "the mantle of Calhoun has fallen upon pigmies," printed excerpts from Warren's *Watkins* opinion as the lead editorial in its July 24, 1957, issue. To make its position even more emphatic, the *Century* added its praise for the High Bench for "fostering civil courage." Taking the opposite view, the *Methodist Challenge* printed in September an article entitled "A Subversive Court."

RUMBLINGS ON CAPITOL HILL

Reaction in Congress was divided. A number of liberals hailed the Court's decisions as a justification of their fight against McCarthyism. Senator Wayne Morse of Oregon called *Watkins* "one of the great landmarks in the protection of the rights of the individual citizen."[26] Senator Thomas Hennings of Missouri announced that criticism of the Supreme Court should be turned and directed at "the unconstitutional and unlawful procedures which have been permitted to develop in this country in recent years. Rather than being denounced for its decisions of recent weeks, the court should be praised for fulfilling its function as the ultimate guardian of human rights and freedom in our society."[27]

Other members of Congress were less pleased. In a prepared statement, Senator Styles Bridges of New Hampshire, chairman of the Republican Senate Policy Committee, attacked "this ultra-liberal policy motivated court."[28] And Francis Walter, chairman of the House Un-American Activities Committee, reprimanded the Court for conducting an "invasion of the legislative field." Walter expressed his doubts whether the Justices could have made their decisions of the 1956 Term if they had really understood the nature of communism.[29]

The segregationists were eager to join their allies in battle. Howard Smith of Virginia observed that he could not recall a case which the Communists had lost before the Warren Court. Representative Davis of Georgia claimed that the political offender decisions constituted a "wild orgy of usurpation of power" which had destroyed national security. "I believe that no court and no group of men no matter how constituted could possibly achieve such a record of error by fortuitous chance. . . ."[30]

In the Senate, J. Strom Thurmond of South Carolina added the *Mallory* decision to the list of Court offenses. "Mr. President, the Supreme Court—which has recently handed down decisions to give greater protection to Communists and criminals—has now issued an edict which will give greater protection to such heinous criminals as rapists and murderers. . . . '[T]he choice we face in this country today is judicial limitation or judicial tyranny.' Congress must take action to limit the power of the Court."[31]

There was also a scattering of impeachment demands. On July 7,

Thurmond appeared on the nationally televised program "Open Hearing," and suggested such a move against every Justice who voted with the majority in *Watkins* and *Jencks*. In the House, Claire Hoffman of Michigan urged his colleagues to impeach the Justices "on the theory that the Court is attempting to overthrow the Government through fallacious reasoning, rendering decisions which make constitutional provisions void."[32] A few days later, Noah Mason of Illinois and George Andrews of Alabama announced that they were hiring "one of the best lawyers in America to prepare an impeachment resolution against all members of the High Court."[33]

Bill after bill was added to the Eighty-fifth Congress' burgeoning inventory of Court-curbing proposals.[34] The suggestions included plans to give the Senate appellate jurisdiction over the Supreme Court, to allow Congress to reverse the Court's interpretation of the Constitution, to require a unanimous decision to invalidate a state law, and even one measure which would have ordered lower courts to disregard any Supreme Court decision "which conflicts with the legal principle of adhering to prior decisions and which is clearly based upon considerations other than legal."[35] In addition to these bills there were at least eleven plans to change the method of selecting Justices and a half-dozen devices to take away judicial authority to hear or review school segregation disputes.

Far more ominous than wild-haired radical schemes was the quiet but unmistakable undertone on Capitol Hill, a fear not only among conservatives but among moderates as well as some liberals that the Justices had gone too far in protecting individual rights and in so doing had moved into the legislative domain. This center group of representatives and senators seldom resorted to long speeches in the *Congressional Record,* but what little they said and did was significant. House Minority leader Joe Martin, a respected conservative associated with neither McCarthyism nor segregation, appeared on a national television program and flatly stated that the Watkins case had "crippled the investigating committees." Martin also described the *Jencks* decision as "very inimical to the country."[36]

Kenneth Keating of New York, who had the fence-straddling reputation of being both an extremely security-conscious conservative and a pro-Negro civil rights liberal, introduced a trio of bills to reverse the *Mallory* ruling, to redefine "organize" in the Smith Act to counter *Yates,* and to modify *Jencks* along the lines of Burton's concurring opinion.[37] In the Senate it was not a conservative Republican or a Southern Democrat, but Joseph O'Mahoney, long-time liberal from Wyoming, who introduced the Justice Department's bill to reshape the rule of evidence laid down in *Jencks*.[38]

THE PRESIDENT ABSTAINS

Sixteen blocks northwest on Pennsylvania Avenue, Eisenhower was trying to keep out of the controversy, just as he had attempted to refrain from public comment on the segregation question during the previous three years. At the news conference on June 19, 1957, Dayton Moore of the United Press asked the President if he thought the Supreme Court had gone too far in protecting individual rights. Eisenhower replied:

> Well, I wouldn't want to answer that question in the specific nature that you—the specific way you seem to expect. Like all laymen in the law, I have my fixed convictions about these things, and I suppose they are, on one side or the other, very strong. But the actual decisions are being studied in the Justice Department. If there seems to be any action we should take through asking for legal action of any kind, they will come up with it. But until that is done, I don't want to comment.[39]

The next week reporters returned to the same issue, asking if the President viewed it as part of his duty to defend the Court against attack. Eisenhower answered by denying that the Justices were without means of defending themselves. Then, after expressing his firm faith in the necessity for an independent judiciary and his respect for the Supreme Court, he added: "Possibly in their latest series of decisions there are some that each of us has very great trouble understanding."[40]

DISSENTS FROM THE FLOOR

The fight was being waged outside of the federal government as well, and pressures were building up against the Court. In Sun Valley, Idaho, New Hampshire's Attorney General Louis C. Wyman, the defeated party in the Sweezy case, availed himself of the losing litigant's ancient right "to retire to the nearest tavern or cross-roads and cuss the court." Wyman told the 1957 meeting of the National Association of Attorneys General[41] that the Supreme Court had "tortured [the Constitution] out of all rational historical proportion," "insulted" state sovereignty in language that was "pure sophistry," and had "set the United States back twenty-five years in its attempt to make certain that those loyal to a foreign power cannot create another Trojan Horse here."

Wyman's speech was criticized by some of his colleagues. Pat Brown of California commented that the only suggestion Wyman had not made "was that we adopt the court-packing plan of Franklin Delano Roosevelt." Pennsylvania's assistant attorney general, Joseph Donnelly, was more direct, castigating Wyman's address as an "angry, hysterical, and unwarranted" as well as a "low and underhanded" attack with which his state would not be connected. But in contrast to the heavy applause which Wyman had received, there was only dull, flattening silence when Donnelly sat down.

To make clear the general agreement with Wyman, a resolution was introduced which called for Congress "to re-affirm and reactivate Federal and state internal security controls rendered ineffective or weakened by recent decisions of the Supreme Court." After a short floor fight, the convention agreed to eliminate what Minnesota's attorney general termed a "gratuitous insult" to the Court by deleting the last eleven words of the resolution. Then, by a 31–10 vote, the association appointed a special committee of five (Wyman was one of the members) to study the Supreme Court security decisions and recommend remedial legislation to Congress.

The American Bar Association experienced a similar controversy at its summer meetings in New York and London. First, in New York, the assembly of the ABA voted down a resolution by Judge Palmer Hutcheson of Dallas which would have expressed the bar's support of the High Bench and its repudiation of recent criticism.[42] The association then went on to London for the second half of its proceedings. There, former Maryland State Senator Herbert O'Conor, chairman of the Committee on Communist Strategy and Tactics, delivered a report raking the Court for its new decisions and recommending a six-point legislative program to reverse the security rulings from *Nelson* to *Yates*. Since no action by the House of Delegates had been requested, the committee's report was simply accepted and filed.[43]

In 1955, the ABA had recommended that Congress reverse the Nelson case and adopt H.R. 3, but that action had been taken quietly and with decorum. In London, the critics of the Court were far less restrained in private conversation than in public speeches, and the British were taken aback by the frequency and vehemence of the American lawyers' attack on their own highest tribunal.[44] Both the outgoing president of the ABA, David Maxwell, and the incoming president, Charles S. Rhyne, felt obliged to caution the legal profession against "loose and vituperative" Court criticism; but even Maxwell could not resist charging the Court with acting as a "superstate" in its 1957 bar admission cases.[45]

Back in the United States, the Conference of State Chief Justices, meeting in July, registered "profound concern for the retention and exercise of the constitutional power of state governments." But the conference voted down proposals to censure the U.S. Supreme Court for usurping state power and to urge public pressure on Congress to curb the Court. Instead, the state Chief Justices selected a special committee to study the role of the judiciary as it had affected the distribution of state-federal power.[46]

The 1957 Governors' Conference, meeting at Williamsburg, Virginia, just a week after "Red Monday," heard more than what had come to be regarded as the normal amount of criticism of the High Bench. The Court foes, however, had no hope of obtaining the governors' collective indorsement of segregation, and they were even unable to follow up their 1956 successes by securing a resolution urging reversal of any of the political offender decisions. They had to be content with a mild resolution praising the FBI and expressing "concern that the effectiveness of the Federal Bureau of Investigation will be continued and preserved, and our hope that all possible avenues will be explored to protect the security of our nation, while affording its citizens all possible personal protection consistent with that security."[47]

In Honolulu, the International Association of Chiefs of Police, angry and frightened at the potential implications of the Mallory case for state as well as federal law enforcement agencies, loudly applauded sharp criticism of the High Bench by Chiefs William H. Parker of Los Angeles and Francis J. Ahern of San Francisco. The association's legislative committee then delivered a report charging that recent Supreme Court decisions represented a threat to law and order in the United States.[48]

In September, 1957, the American Legion's national convention—in 1956 the Legion had approved resolutions indorsing "dual sovereignty" as against the pre-emption doctrine and urging a congressional investigation of the NAACP, as well as other recommendations to Congress that the Nelson case be reversed and that all federal employees be required to take a loyalty oath—leaped formally onto the anti-Court bandwagon. The convention went on record:

> That it does condemn and deplore as dangerous to the security of this nation the specific decisions referred to above [*Yates, Jencks, Mallory, Nelson, Schware, Konigsberg, Watkins,* and *Sweezy*] and others of similar nature, which serve not to protect civil liberties, but, to the contrary, to release law violators to prey, unmolested, upon the citizens of our great country; be it further resolved . . . that legislation be enacted by the Congress designed to establish proper qualifications for all federal judges so that henceforth only those who are imbued with the fundamental concepts of our republic and basic tenets of our system of jurisprudence may be appointed to the judiciary.[49]

TENSIONS WITHIN THE COURT

By goring assorted oxen on a wholesale scale, the decisions of the 1956 Term transformed congressional criticism into militant opposition; and, within the Court, the tensions which Warren had managed to charm into hibernation during his first three terms had been reawakened. Dissenting votes were up markedly from the previous term,[50] and Clark's strident calls for Congress to overrule the Court supplied glaring evidence of the severest sort of division. Not only were the old differences among the Justices still very much alive, but new differences were being created. Within a few months Warren and Frankfurter would be bickering with one another in open court.

Moreover, the technical skill of the Court's work left much to be desired. Of the most important cases, probably only against *Nelson* in 1956 and *Du Pont* and *Konigsberg* in 1957 could a strong, objective legal argument be made that the decision had gone the wrong way. But the Warren Court had exhibited a marked deficiency in judicial craftsmanship, a deficiency which troubled even its defenders.[51]

In *Jencks,* Brennan not only engaged in judicial homework in granting the defendant access to FBI files when he had only asked that the trial judge examine the reports, but to support his decision Brennan quoted John Marshall and quoted him out of context. By use of ellipses, Brennan managed to convey the impression that in Aaron Burr's treason trial Marshall had laid the foundation for the *Jencks* decision. At best, the Burr case was irrelevant because the information Burr had sought had been in the personal possession of the President. At worst, the Burr case blatantly contradicted *Jencks* because Marshall had allowed the trial to proceed after Jefferson had refused to give the court the secret letters of General Wilkinson which Burr had claimed were necessary to his defense.[52]

Just as serious was Brennan's failure in his opinion ever to say whether the decision was based on constitutional or statutory grounds, or to spell out in unmistakable terms what portions of the FBI reports should be given to the defense, by whom such a determination would be made, or at what point in the litigation the information could be obtained. Under J. Edgar Hoover's charismatic leadership the FBI had become the most sacrosanct of Washington's many sacred cows. The Justices could have hoped to bring that organization to task only on unimpeachable legal grounds. To have relied on faulty craftsmanship was a grave mistake.

In *Du Pont,* Brennan repeated his mis-citation error and was caught in the act by the dissenters. But perhaps even more damaging than Brennan's obvious flaws was the general style of the Chief Justice's writing. The School Segregation opinion had clearly been no work of art. Its candor had embarrassed many friends of the Court, and it had given the Court's enemies a means of self-justification without the necessity of facing up to the basic moral and legal questions presented by an apartheid policy in a supposedly democratic society. The legislative history of the Smith Act and the Justice Department's denial of administrative conflict weakened the reasoning of the *Nelson* opinion. In *Watkins* and *Sweezy* Warren wrote disjointed, emotional essays rather than crisp legal opinions.

The point was not that Warren's opinions suffered in comparison with those of Vinson, Stone, Hughes, Taft, White, Fuller, Waite, Chase, or even Taney. On the contrary, they did not. The point was rather that the Warren Court was not going to receive the sort of support from the American bar that, for example, the Court under Fuller, White, Taft, or Hughes had received when attacked. The Warren Court's opinions, therefore, had to be markedly superior to those of previous benches to meet the attacks from the press, the bar, and members of Congress; and although probably well above the judicial average, the Chief Justice's opinions did not quite reach the needed levels of law and literature.

Harlan, a meticulous craftsman, would not be guilty of Brennan's mistakes of overanxiousness or Warren's literary vagaries. His opinion in *Yates* was a model of technical correctness—and dulness. The careful student of constitutional law could appreciate the precise legalisms; the general public would see only that more Communists were being freed. And, in spite of his precision, Harlan failed to emphasize that he was following the great free speech tradition of Holmes and Brandeis. In light of the opposition such a decision would inevitably engender, the Court badly needed a vivid phrase, a slogan as ear-catching as Holmes's "clear and present danger" to dramatize its defense of the First Amendment. Instead, Harlan produced a nine-page definition of "organize" and an admittedly subtle set of semantic distinctions. For all their good sense and constitutional correctness, these could never be rallying cries.

Two decades of internal wrangling, conflict sharpened by personal friction, competing ambitions, and clashing dogmas had caught up with the Court at a crucial hour and had deprived the Justices of their vital ability to communicate and popularize their ideals and goals. The Chief Justice, Harlan, and Brennan were each unable to perform these functions, and Clark would not. Whittaker was barred from participating in most of the decisions, and it was doubtful where he stood on basic policy issues. This left Burton, Black, Douglas, and Frankfurter. Burton's opinions were even more tedious than Harlan's, and they lacked Harlan's saving grace of painfully accurate scholarship. Black, Douglas, and Frankfurter each had a superb mastery of the law as well as an eloquent writing style, but the extreme libertarianism of Black and Douglas frequently made their views unacceptable to any of their colleagues except Warren and Brennan.

While Frankfurter's ideological alloy of libertarianism and judicial self-restraint put him in the center of the Bench, this middle-of-the-road position was more the result of doctrinal choice than of an effort to effect a compromise between the other Court factions. Equally important, during the previous eighteen years his differences with other Justices had not always been on an impersonal plane. Moreover, the Frankfurter-Warren break which would come out in the open in the fall of 1957 was probably brewing during the 1956 Term. It is worth noting that although Frankfurter voted with the majority in six of the seven major cold war cases of the term,[53] the Chief Justice did not assign him any of these opinions to write.

The Warren Court had aroused an alliance of powerful enemies, and then, while less than half-armed, had gone into battle against these foes. Although the Court was spared the agony of internal criticism of the caliber of Johnson, Curtis, Grier, Harlan, Holmes, Brandeis, Cardozo, or Stone, it could neither find a single spokesman whose opinions could provide leadership, learning, and literature, nor synthesize its massive individual talents to accomplish these tasks in the political offender cases.

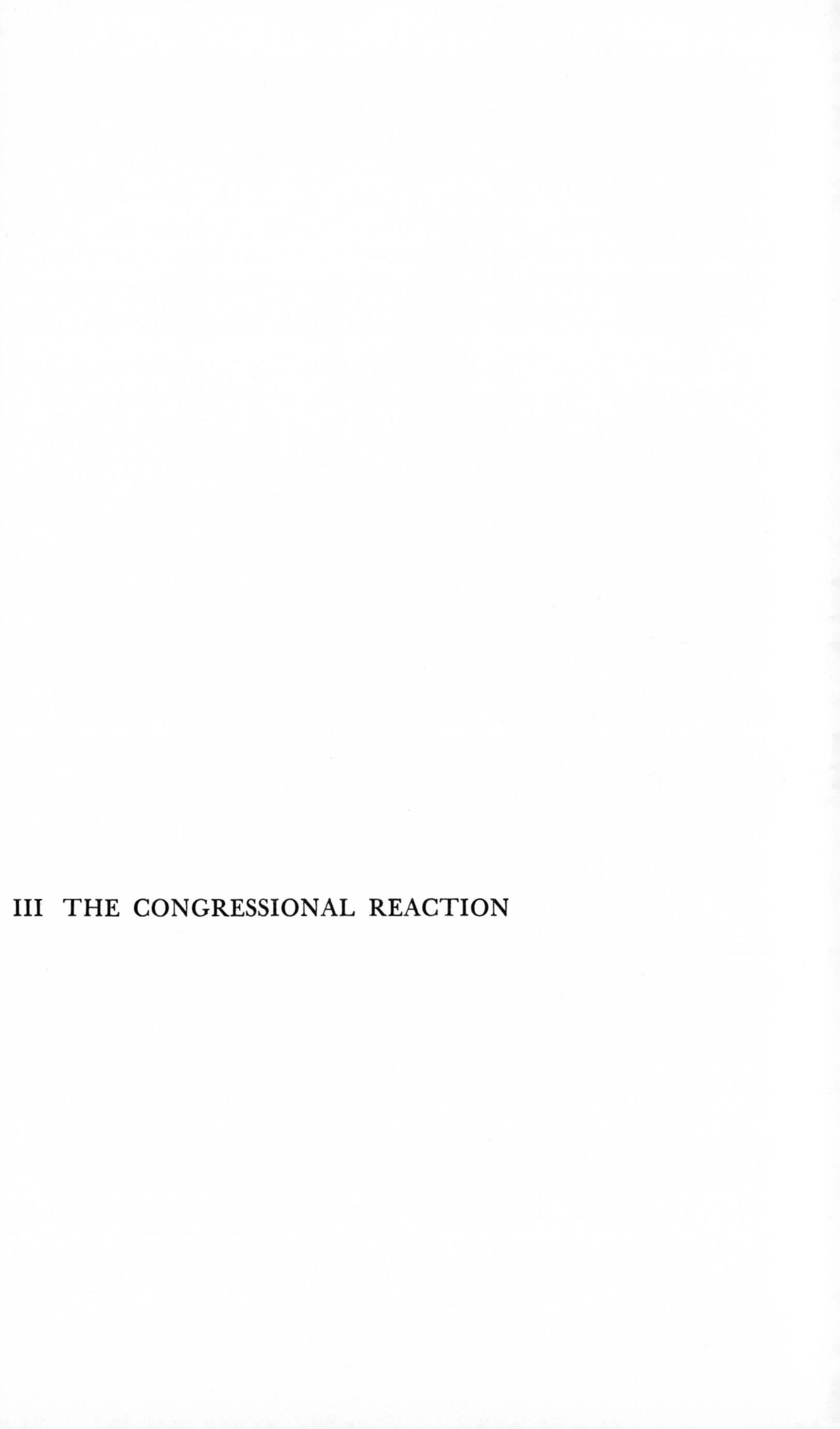

III THE CONGRESSIONAL REACTION

6. THE JENCKS BILLS

While *Watkins, Yates, Sweezy, Service,* and the bar admission cases were all controversial as well as important decisions, newspaper,[1] congressional, and executive attention swiftly focused on *Jencks* v. *United States* as the most dangerous precedent of the lot. *Time Magazine* came up with a comment that typified the general evaluation in its statement that *Jencks* had knocked "over applecarts all across the U.S. security scene."[2]

Support for the decision came from a strange combination of sources. Liberal newspapers like the *Washington Post & Times-Herald* and the *New York Times* were pleased, as was the Communist press. To the embarrassment of the Court friends, the *Daily Worker* waxed eloquent over *Jencks* as "a blow at perjury." But the *Worker* dampened its enthusiasm with a warning: "J. Edgar Hoover is organizing a counterattack through his high-powered FBI publicity machine, newspaper and congressional friends. He well knows that if his informers can be cross-examined on their written reports, their tailor-made testimony will be discovered to be woven of shoddy frame-up thread."[3]

The third element in support of *Jencks* came from a portion of the business community. The *Wall Street Journal* had reservations about the decision and agreed that some clarifying legislation might be needed, but the *Journal* took the Attorney General to task for ordering an FBI agent not to obey a district judge's order for production of records.[4] The *Commercial and Financial Chronicle,* however, had no qualifications whatever in its lavish praise of the Court for the *Jencks* decision. The *Chronicle* stated that the majority opinion meant that federal agencies like the Securities and Exchange Commission could no longer refuse to allow inspection of their data when prosecuting businessmen. Clark's dissent was dismissed as "startling" and "not well reasoned." As for remedial legislation, the *Chronicle* said: "We believe this is unnecessary. As the Court pointed out, the interest of the United States . . . is not that it shall win a case, but that justice shall be done. In that framework, this seven to one decision constitutes a bulwark in the interest of the fair and impartial trial."[5]

Despite this curious blend of support, the reaction of most of the press was one of strong protest. David Lawrence described the decision as "Treason's biggest victory." Under a caption "A Blow at the FBI," the *New York Herald Tribune* discussed the "startling ramifications" of Brennan's majority opinion and concluded that the "Supreme Court is in effect destroying the essence of the FBI."

The columnist Constantine Brown, writing in the *Washington Star,* alleged that Communists had "tried every trick and subterfuge to deal a fatal blow to our top investigative agency by forcing it to reveal its secret information sources. Now they appear to have succeeded." The *Washington Daily News* commented: "The time is short, the issue is vital, and therefore, it seems to us, Congress should move quickly to find out just how the United States Supreme Court's decision must be applied, or overruled, by a new law. . . . [I]t is better to make a new law quick, or find convincing evidence that the Supreme Court's ruling is not as dangerous as Justice Clark says it is."

The *Memphis Commercial Appeal* pleaded for congressional action on a "no time to lose" basis. "It is the function of the Congress to make the nation's laws. . . . It would almost seem, on the basis of one year's record, that the Supreme Court majority is attempting to make laws by the indirect method of frivolous interpretation. Congress cannot afford to ignore such a challenge." The *New York Daily News* condemned *Jencks* as a "Supreme Court blunder," and called on Congress to "reverse the High Court fast. . . . We hope Brownell and Congress will move as fast as they can to undo this latest Supreme Court favor to the Party of Traitors." William Randolph Hearst, Jr., in a signed editorial,[6] set the tone for his newspaper chain on the "extremely dangerous" Jencks case:

> Here is a situation in which Congress can act and should act quickly. . . . I think it could speed this thing up if you who read this took time to jog your own Representatives or Senators into some action. . . . [T]he thought occurred to me in plowing through some of the recent decisions that maybe the Soviet's TV glamor boy, Khrushchev, had been reading them, too, and that they formed the basis for his prediction that our grandchildren would grow up under socialism.

The *Atlanta Constitution* commented that "if the Court ruling stands, it is difficult to see how it will be possible to maintain internal security, combat enemy agents or control interstate criminals and mobs." The *Cincinnati Enquirer* agreed: "The Supreme Court decision would breach the dike against Communist intrigue, and the breach should be repaired speedily." The *Fort Lauderdale Sunday News* rebuked "our Alice-in-Wonderland Supreme Court," and noted: "The dope peddlers are smiling, and so is Uncle Nikita."

In an editorial entitled "Change It Now!" the *Detroit Times* charged that *Jencks* had struck a "devastating blow" at the FBI. In the body of the editorial the *Times* shouted in double-sized caps: "CONGRESS SHOULD ACT, AND ACT IMMEDIATELY." The *Albuquerque Journal* expressed the hope that remedial legislation would "be rushed with all speed." The *Houston Chronicle* said *Jencks* had created "a new and strange rule of evidence" which "seems to endanger national security as well as traditional court procedure." The *El Paso Times* stated that "Congress Must Act." Indeed, this Texas paper thought Congress "ought to go still further and pass a resolution calling for a constitutional convention at which the powers of the Supreme Court would be spelled out along with the rights of the 48 sovereign states."

The *St. Louis Globe-Democrat* branded *Jencks* "an astonishing decision," while the *Boston Daily Record* and the *Los Angeles Herald and Express* echoed an accusation made by George Sokolsky[7] that

> it is not only a matter of FBI files that Mr. Justice Brennan put in peril, but all police files and all police activities. . . . Those who tell must be protected or the law-enforcement agencies had better close up shop and forget all about murderers, sex deviates, kidnappers and other horrors who beset our lives. Open the files of every police department in the country to every shyster lawyer who works for a hood and we might as well hand law-enforcement over to Lucky Luciano and let him run the show.

BIRTH OF A BILL

Much congressional reaction was only barely more restrained than the newspaper comments. In the House of Representatives Kenneth Keating of New York interrupted debate on the civil rights bill to announce in an ominous voice the news of the *Jencks* ruling:

> If this decision stands and nothing is done by the legislative branch it may well result, as Justice Clark has indicated in his minority opinion, in our investigative agencies having to close up shop. . . . I have asked the Attorney General to assist me in the preparation of legislation which can immediately be studied by the Judiciary Committee in order that we can come to grips with this serious threat to our security.[8]

Representative Davis of Georgia accused the High Bench of having "in great measure destroyed the effectiveness of the Federal Bureau of Investigation,"[9] but, by and large, southern congressmen allowed northern and western Republicans to carry the burden of criticizing *Jencks*. Usher Burdick of North Dakota claimed that the Court, "[f]or all practical purposes," had "[put] the FBI out of business. . . . This decision encourages crimes. It encourages the underworld, and it is a blow to law enforcement."[10] Harold Collier of Illinois declared that the FBI files had become "sitting ducks in an open hunting season. . . . [The Court] has created and compounded confusion not only among the law enforcement officers of the executive branch, but among the jurists of the lower courts as well."[11] Paraphrasing the remark of the *Jencks* trial judge that the Supreme Court's decision was "the greatest comfort to guilty defendants in many a year,"[12] Donald Jackson of California called *Jencks* and *Watkins* "a victory greater than any achieved by the Soviet on any battlefield since World War II."[13]

The executive department had been thrown into an uproar by *Jencks.* Within a few days of the decision, the Attorney General's office had begun to receive the first of what would grow into dozens of telegrams and letters from regional district attorneys and other law enforcement officials informing the department of serious *Jencks* problems and requesting advice, assistance, and if possible new legislation.

At his press conference on June 19, the President told reporters that the Justice Department was studying the Court's June decisions to determine whether additional legislation was necessary.[14] Two weeks before this announcement, James O. Eastland, chairman of the Senate Judiciary Committee, had written the Attorney General inviting suggestions for a new statute to protect the FBI. The implications of *Jencks,* Eastland said, "are even more frightening than the decision itself."[15]

Justice Department lawyers had started to work almost as soon as Brennan's opinion was published, and on June 24 a department bill, largely drafted by Assistant Attorneys General Warren Olney III and Wilson White, was introduced in the House by Kenneth Keating and in the Senate by Joseph O'Mahoney, with Eastland, Kefauver of Tennessee, Butler of Maryland, Dirksen of Illinois, Neely of West Virginia, Potter of Michigan, and Wiley of Wisconsin as cosponsors.[16] Three days later the President conferred with GOP legislative leaders and Attorney General Herbert Brownell. After the meeting, Press Secretary Hagerty announced that the administration would "urge" passage of Jencks legislation.[17]

The Senate bill, S. 2377, was sent to the Judiciary Committee, and Eastland assigned the bill to O'Mahoney's Subcommittee on Improvements in the Federal Criminal Code. Although Eastland's vitriolic Court criticism and advocacy of white supremacy might well have made his managing S. 2377 a kiss of death, O'Mahoney* was in many ways an ideal choice to lead the fight for this legislation.

* Joseph Christopher O'Mahoney (1884—–) was born and reared in Boston. After a brief stint at Columbia University, he went into journalism, and in 1908 he moved to Boulder, Colorado, to become city editor of the *Herald.* In 1916, he went to Cheyenne, Wyoming, where he took over the same position on the *State Leader.* Shortly thereafter, the owner of the paper, Senator John B. Kendrick, brought O'Mahoney to Washington as his secretary. While working for Kendrick, O'Mahoney got a law degree from Georgetown University. During the 1920's he stayed on Kendrick's staff and also held a number of positions with the Democratic party, helping to write the party platform in 1932. FDR appointed him Assistant Postmaster General, but O'Mahoney resigned within six months to accept an appointment to fill out Kendrick's unexpired term in

The senator from Wyoming had been battling for liberal ideas and ideals during most of his seventy-three years. He was more conservative in 1957 than he had been in 1912, when he supported Theodore Roosevelt, or during the 1930's, when he fought for Teddy's young cousin on almost all measures except Court-packing; but O'Mahoney still had a solid claim to the halo of progressivism. To back up this liberal reputation, he was known as a stickler on matters of constitutional law, with a fine knowledge of and a deep respect for Supreme Court decisions. If his imprimatur on the Jencks bill did not allay all the doubts of Senate liberals, at least it helped to dispel the aroma of reaction and racism which Eastland's leadership would have created.

O'Mahoney insisted that if he was to manage the Jencks bill, he was to be the spokesman for the group. Eastland and the others were to avoid public statements attacking the Court on this issue. With a touch of irony that passed unnoticed, O'Mahoney and the Justice Department wanted the bill to be pushed as a reform in and a codification of judicial procedure and not as a Court curb. The other sponsors agreed to follow this line, or at least O'Mahoney thought they had. The leadership matter reached a quick crisis within a week after the bill was introduced when Senator Potter of Michigan castigated the Court for having made life immeasurably easier for traitors by turning "Government records into a free peepshow for alien powers."[18]

O'Mahoney's staff was furious, and one of his aides wrote the senator from Wyoming a blistering memorandum:

> This is unrestrained demagoguery, and is a serious enough breach of the courtesy afforded [Potter]—when he asked to join on the bill —to suggest that he withdraw his name from among the sponsors. The reason is obvious: he does not possess the seriousness of purpose, the objectivity, the reasoning, and the restraint of the other Senators who are sponsors of the measure.
>
> While other Senators—such as Senators Eastland and Butler—have strong opposing views on the subject, they recognize that you, as Chairman, are calling the shots and, therefore, refrain from making statements which serve only to confuse and complicate your task.[19]

---

the Senate. In 1952, O'Mahoney was swept under by the Eisenhower tidal wave, but in 1954 he came storming back to win another Senate seat after a long and especially dirty campaign. O'Mahoney's penchant for speech-making earned him the title of "the most deliberative member of the world's most deliberative body." In the summer of 1959 he suffered a serious stroke and retired from the Senate the following year.

O'Mahoney was angry, though less so than his staff, and he let Potter know about his anger; but he did not follow the suggestion that the senator from Michigan be asked to withdraw as a sponsor. There were, however, no more such outbursts. Even southern senators not officially connected with S. 2377 generally laid off the Court on the Jencks issue.

JENCKS BILL #1

As drafted by the Justice Department, S. 2377 provided that no statements or reports of a witness or "person" other than the defendant in the possession of the United States would be given to the defense in a criminal trial except under the narrow terms prescribed in the bill. After a witness had testified, the defense could petition the court for reports or statements of that witness bearing on the events as to which he had just testified. The trial judge would then order the government to turn over to the court all such reports "as are signed by the witness or otherwise adopted by him as correct." The judge would inspect these documents *in camera,* decide what portions, if any, related to the testimony, and give those portions, and only those portions, to the defendant. In the event the United States chose not to comply with a court order for the production of such reports, the judge was authorized, in his discretion, to strike the testimony of the witness from the record and allow the trial to proceed, or "if the interests of justice require," to declare a mistrial.

O'Mahoney's subcommittee promptly held hearings on S. 2377.[20] On June 28, Attorney General Brownell and Assistant Secretary of the Treasury David Kendall appeared and offered brief testimony. Kendall merely stated that passage of the bill would greatly aid law enforcement, but Brownell went into some detail. Taking the approach which the Justice Department had agreed upon with O'Mahoney, the Attorney General explained that the executive branch accepted the Supreme Court's principle that a defendant was entitled to see FBI files containing data relevant to the testimony of a prosecution witness. What the Justice Department feared, Brownell emphasized, was lower court misinterpretations of the Supreme Court decision, not the decision itself.

Citing a number of specific examples of trial court orders for production of government records, the Attorney General pointed to three basic problems. First, "the insistence by some courts that entire reports of the F.B.I. or other federal investigative agency be handed over to defense counsel, even though but a small part of the report relates to the testimony of the witness." This exposed not only confidential sources of information but also patterns and techniques of federal investigations. Second, the Jencks case had ordered the government to turn over oral reports; but the Justice Department thought the Court had meant only those reports which the witness had signed or approved, and it wanted this spelled out by a statute. The third problem area was that of pre-trial discovery. The government wished to restrict a defendant's use of official files to the period after the witness had testified, a limitation which, Brownell felt, was fully in keeping with the facts of the Jencks case.

JENCKS BILL #2

With these two statements by administration spokesmen the hearings were closed on the same day they opened, and the proceedings were never published. The subcommittee held a three-minute discussion at the end of the hearings and approved the bill as introduced. Three days later the full Committee on the Judiciary reported S. 2377 with minor amendments.[21] The only significant change was the inclusion of the terms of a bill[22] introduced by Bricker of Ohio to require the government, in the event of conviction and appeal, to make the documents, together with any material excised by the trial judge, available to the appellate tribunal.

The committee report emphasized that the proposed legislation

> is not designed to nullify, or to curb, or to limit the decision of the Supreme Court insofar as due process is concerned. . . . On the contrary, the proposed legislation, as reported, reaffirms the decision of the Supreme Court in its holding that a defendant on trial in a criminal prosecution is entitled to reports and statements in the possession of the Government touching the events and activities as to which a Government witness has testified.

Stressing that there had been widespread misunderstanding and misinterpretation of *Jencks,* the Committee stated that the purpose of S. 2377 was merely "to establish a procedural device that will provide such a defendant with authenticated statements and reports of Government witnesses which relate directly to his testimony."

COMMITTEE ACTION IN THE HOUSE

In the lower chamber, the House Judiciary Committee acted almost as speedily. The bill went to a special subcommittee headed by Edwin O. Willis of Louisiana. Brownell and Kendall submitted the same statements as they had to the Senate group. In addition, the general counsel of the Post Office Department sent a five-paragraph letter to the committee chairman. No opposition witnesses were heard, and the hearings were not printed. The Judiciary Committee rejected a bill by Francis Walter of Pennsylvania, which would have flatly overruled *Jencks* and given the Attorney General a virtual blank check to refuse to permit inspection of documents in the possession of the government. Instead, the committee substituted the text of Keating's administration proposal and on July 5 reported this bill as H.R. 7915,[23] the number originally assigned to the Walter bill.

OPPOSITION IN THE SENATE

In going from introduction of S. 2377 to hearings, to subcommittee action, to committee vote, to committee report in exactly seven days, the Senate was acting with unaccustomed speed; and the bill's foes hammered at the theme that the administration was trying to ramrod the measure through the Senate without debate or thought. Wayne Morse of Oregon warned his colleagues that they were "dealing in too much haste with a precious right in criminal jurisprudence."[24] Senator Joseph Clark of Pennsylvania also tried to persuade the Senate to slow down. "We should not be panicked into action because, in a hurry, the Attorney General comes forward and asks, on a scare basis, for a piece of legislation designed to accomplish a purpose which, in my judgment, could be far better accomplished . . . by the orderly procedures of the Federal courts."[25]

The *Washington Post & Times-Herald* picked up this cry on its editorial page and chided the bill's supporters:[26]

> Congress has been in such a hurry . . . that it has not even found time to grant a hearing to opponents of the bill. Yet there is serious opposition from men of high reputation and great legal learning who see no need for such legislation. Dean Erwin O. Griswold of the Harvard Law School, for example, says: "There is absolutely nothing in the [*Jencks*] opinion giving the public access to secret files of the FBI. It simply blueprints procedures used right here in Boston in every criminal court." . . . Nothing will be lost by taking a little time for study. The Senate is supposed to be a deliberative body, and this is a problem which calls for the most careful deliberation.

Editorial attacks and sniping on the Senate floor were means of persuasion, but even more important was the work going on behind the scenes. Clark* was opposed to any legislation, strong, moderate, or weak, at least until there had been some appellate review of the lower court decisions which had so frightened the Justice Department. If he was going to lead the fight to preserve as much of the Supreme Court decision as possible, Clark's first problem was one of staff assistance. His administrative assistant and legal adviser, James Quigley, was in Europe that summer, and Bernard Norwitch, his other assistant, was not a lawyer. Knowing that the Jencks bill was going to be largely a wrangle over minute technicalities, Norwitch recruited three bright young men who were skilled lawyers to advise his chief. Senator Matthew Neely of West Virginia was in Bethesda Naval Hospital dying of cancer, and his administrative assistant, George Arnold, son of Thurman Arnold, was more than willing to help Clark. Norwitch also secured the assistance of one of Senator Javits' aides, Sidney Kelley, and one of Wayne Morse's staff, Merton Bernstein. Arnold was particularly influential since he was not only a close adviser to Clark, but as administrative assistant to the highly respected Neely he could also speak as to the views of the senator from West Virginia.

George Arnold's father was also deeply concerned by the Jencks

* Joseph Sill Clark (1901—), B.S. Harvard, 1923 (*magna cum laude*), LL.B. University of Pennsylvania, 1926, had broken with his family's long Republican tradition to support Al Smith in 1928. In 1934–35 he served as deputy attorney general of Pennsylvania. He left his law practice shortly before Pearl Harbor to accept a commission as a captain in the Army Air Corps. Mustered out as a colonel, Clark went back to his law practice until 1949 when he successfully ran for city controller of Philadelphia. Two years later, with the aid of Labor's League for Political Education and the support of the *Philadelphia Inquirer*, he was elected as the city's first Democratic mayor in sixty-seven years. He came to the Senate in January, 1957.

issue, and his law firm sent several memoranda to O'Mahoney in an effort to help Clark persuade him to loosen the terms of the Administration bill.[27] Two interest groups which were always active in civil liberties matters, the American Civil Liberties Union and the Americans for Democratic Action, also contacted Clark and offered to assist him. Although both organizations submitted drafts of amendments to S. 2377, Clark depended more on his newly formed staff than on outside help.

At the opposing staff level, O'Mahoney also had able assistance. He relied primarily on C. Aubrey Gasque, general counsel for the Subcommittee on Improvements in the Federal Criminal Code. Gasque in turn was aided by Samuel A. Culotta, associate counsel, and Francis Rosenberger of the Judiciary Committee staff. Gasque was firmly convinced of the immediate need for legislation and was distrustful of the motives of some of the people around Clark. On the other hand, Gasque, like O'Mahoney, realized that many of the bill's supporters were only interested in pursuing a vendetta against the Court, and that getting equitable legislation was going to be a most difficult task.

JENCKS BILL #3

Armed with the information that Arnold, Bernstein, and Kelley had given him, Clark was able to approach O'Mahoney and make a convincing argument that, as it stood, the Jencks bill was a distinct threat to civil liberties. O'Mahoney had the reputation as one of the greatest "half-loaf men" in the Senate. He pictured himself in the role of a compromiser, a role which would involve him in considerable difficulty during the following weeks. And, as a liberal, O'Mahoney had no desire to harm the cause of civil liberties at this, the final stage of his career. Accordingly, against Gasque's advice, O'Mahoney announced on July 8 that because several senators had objected to various portions of S. 2377, he was now, under authorization of his subcommittee, submitting to the Senate an amended version of the bill.[28]

Although the form of S. 2377 remained generally the same, there were three sets of major changes in substance. First, rights of defendants were safeguarded by dropping the reference to "person" and restricting application of the law to statements or reports of a "witness." Since in legal parlance a corporation is a "person," this change meant that the government would not be able to invoke the Jencks law to deny a defendant the right to examine business records seized in a tax, antitrust, or similar prosecution. As an additional protection—one aimed more specifically at shielding any existing rights to pre-trial inspection—relevant reports in the possession of the government could be ordered produced not only in accordance with the bill's terms but also as provided in the Federal Rules of Criminal Procedure.

Second, relevant statements or reports were to be turned over *directly* to the defendant unless the United States claimed that the documents contained "privileged information, the disclosure of which would be prejudicial to the public interest or national security. . . ." Where the government invoked this claim of privilege, the trial court would follow the procedure in the original bill, that is, obtain the material from the prosecutor, examine it *in camera,* excise those portions not relating to the witness' testimony, and deliver the remainder to the defense.

The third change enlarged the scope of the reports which were to be made available to the defendant. Now the defense could obtain not only such statements "as are signed by the witness, or otherwise adopted or approved by him," but also those documents which "contain a recitation or the substance of any oral or written statement previously made by the witness."

Gasque found this last change particularly objectionable, and he had pleaded with O'Mahoney not to compromise. A week before Clark had suggested this enlargement, Gasque had warned O'Mahoney that such a proposal would be made and had sent him a long memorandum explaining why it should be rejected:

> The only purpose of making any statements of the witness available to the defendant is to help him in cross-examination, i.e., to assist his efforts to impeach the witness. It would be grossly unfair to use for this purpose any statement purporting to be that of the witness but not in fact actually approved by him. This would be substituting someone else's idea or understanding of what the witness had said, for the witness' own understanding thereof.[29]

Clark, however, countered this by saying that the FBI could evade the intention of Congress and the Court by simply dropping the practice of having informants sign their reports, and, for the time, his argument persuaded O'Mahoney.

THE FBI LOBBY

Liberal opposition was only one of the obstacles in the path of Jencks legislation. It was commonly expected on Capitol Hill that the Senate was going to have to spend most of what was left of the session in a drawn-out debate of the civil rights bill which the House had passed on June 18. Both in private and on the Senate floor, O'Mahoney had tried to persuade Majority leader Lyndon Johnson to bring S. 2377 up before the debate on the merits of the civil rights bill began; but the most O'Mahoney was able to obtain was a statement from Johnson, who even then was looking ahead to the 1960 National Convention, that he was sure the Senate would want to consider the Jencks legislation prior to sine die adjournment.[30]

The prospect of a long delay delighted opponents of the bill. Pat McNamara of Michigan praised the "protracted and repetitious" civil rights discussion for serving "to forestall what might have been panicky adoption of S. 2377. . . ."[31] The bill's supporters, however, were frustrated and irritated. Mundt of South Dakota denounced Johnson's refusal to schedule the Jencks proposal ahead of civil rights legislation. While the Senate talked, Mundt declared, "the Communists, crooks, kidnapers, and cheaters continue to function. I do not think the Senate can expect the parade of history to stand still. . . ."[32]

In the House of Representatives, a number of congressmen expressed fear that no action would be taken on the Jencks bill until the next session. The forthcoming trial of the Russian spy, Colonel Rudolph Ivanovich Abel, was frequently cited as an example of the pressing need for immediate legislation lest Abel's lawyer carry out his announced intention of subpoenaing the whole FBI file in the case. Representative Hosmer of California typified these fears in his comment: "Every moment we delay enacting laws to stop the FBI's secret weapons against subversion from being disclosed to friends and enemies alike, we are playing Russian roulette with American security."[33]

To keep Congress interested and anxious to get at the Jencks bill while the civil rights issue pre-empted the publicity scene, the FBI was putting on quiet but intense pressure.* Led by Louis B. Nichols, the congressional liaison people in Hoover's office maintained a steady campaign, and local agents sent long letters to their representatives in Washington, or, when in town, found time to go up to Capitol Hill and explain the imperative need for new legislation. The National Society of Former Special Agents of the FBI, with a membership of 3,500, made certain that Congress was informed of its active interest in the passage of the administration measure.[34] In addition, third parties who had influence with an individual legislator would contact that congressman or senator, ostensibly on another issue, and then steer the conversation to the Jencks bill. As a final means of persuasion, the FBI was easily able to start a snowball effect with newspaper editorials urging quick passage and suggesting that readers write their congressmen to demand speedy action.

On July 17, Eisenhower made his strongest and clearest statements regarding his own feelings about a judicial decision. After supporting Brownell's earlier explanation that the administration was opposed only to "widespread opening of FBI files," not production of specific papers relating to a witness' testimony, the President added: "You could do incalculable damage, to my mind, just by opening up the FBI files. It would be terrible."[35]

It was not until late July that J. Edgar Hoover made his first public statement regarding the *Jencks* decision. In submitting his annual report to the Attorney General, the FBI chief took pains to point up the importance of confidential information; he stated that such tips had led to 1,400 arrests by his organization in the previous year. "The very basis of our success is the F.B.I.'s assurance to this country's citizens that the information they give will be maintained in strictest secrecy in our files."[36]

Two weeks later, with his lobbying activity in full swing, Hoover

* Compare the comments of V. O. Key in his general analysis of "Administration as Politics": "In one respect administrative agencies are like the associations we have called pressure groups: they operate continually, in Republican and Democratic administrations alike, to advance their interests. . . . Often with a personnel distributed over the nation, it is sometimes able to stir up, by discreet measures, pressure from home to bear on Congress. With almost a monopoly of information in its sphere of interest, the administrative organization is able to release or withhold data in such a fashion as to influence the course of legislative action." *Politics, Parties, and Pressure Groups* (3d ed.; New York: Thomas Y. Crowell Co., 1953), p. 722. See also Arthur Maas's book-length treatment of the Army Engineers: *Muddy Waters* (Cambridge, Mass.: Harvard University Press, 1951).

dropped all efforts at subtlety and sent a "Dear Joe" letter to House Minority leader Joseph Martin. Linking the FBI's effectiveness directly to its ability to secure information, Hoover complained that since the *Jencks* ruling his agents had been faced with increasing reluctance on the part of citizens to co-operate. The need to remedy this situation by means of the administration legislation, Hoover said, was "urgent." "Its enactment is vital to the future ability of the Federal Bureau of Investigation to carry out its internal security and law enforcement responsibilities."[37]

COMPROMISE: JENCKS BILL #4

While J. Edgar Hoover was pressuring Congress and the Senate talkathon on civil rights was droning on, the supporters of S. 2377 were having internal difficulties. O'Mahoney's July 8 draft had partially placated Clark and his liberal coterie; but this third version of the Jencks bill had not been cleared with the Attorney General's office, and the Justice Department was strongly opposed to several of the new provisions.

Caught between the two groups, O'Mahoney and his staff arranged a conference on August 12 in the District of Columbia room in the Capitol Building. Acting Attorney General William P. Rogers represented the Justice Department, Senators Dirksen and Butler and an aide of Senator Bricker could speak for those who wanted a strong bill, and Clark and Merton Bernstein—who was present in a double capacity as an agent of Wayne Morse and an adviser to Clark—represented those senators who wanted no bill at all that summer. Dirksen could stay for only a few minutes, but the others stayed in session for almost two hours.

Rogers outlined the department's objections to the July 8 bill, emphasizing his opposition to the inclusion of the reference to the Federal Rules of Criminal Procedure. This, he feared, might be construed to allow pre-trial examination of FBI files, something the Supreme Court had explicitly avoided. His second principal objection was lodged against permitting examination of unsigned oral or written reports of witnesses. Clark and Bernstein listened to Rogers and then injected their objections to the Justice Department's position. At this point Clark and Rogers got into a quarrel, but when

O'Mahoney adjourned the meeting he thought he had found enough common ground to work out an acceptable compromise. He and Clark talked the matter over in private, and Clark left with the impression that he had obtained a promise from O'Mahoney that the essence of the liberal position would be maintained and only minor concessions made to Rogers.

After the meeting O'Mahoney instructed Gasque to make a few changes in the July 8 bill. Gasque had been working closely with Warren Olney III, and he was convinced that the administration's position was far sounder than Clark's. Accordingly, the draft went beyond O'Mahoney's instructions, but he explained this to O'Mahoney and argued that the new wording was necessary if the measure was to protect both the integrity of the FBI files and the rights of defendants. O'Mahoney carefully read over Gasque's draft and conceded it was the best solution yet offered. Later in the afternoon of August 12, O'Mahoney introduced this fourth version of the Jencks bill as a substitute for S. 2377.[38]

As in the original Justice Department proposal there was no reference to the Federal Rules of Criminal Procedure, and Rogers' objection to unsigned oral reports was met by another change in wording. Returning to the June 24 and July 1 versions, the August 12 bill provided that to be available to the defense written statements of a witness had to be signed or "otherwise adopted or approved" by him, and the use of oral statements was restricted to "transcriptions or recordings."

The necessity of the government to invoke a claim of privilege to avoid giving the documents directly to the defense was also eased; it would now be sufficient for the government to assert that material unrelated to the testimony was in the reports in order to require the trial judge to examine the files *in camera.* As a last change, this one suggested by Senator Clark, the discretion of the trial judge was broadened. In the event that the United States would not produce the reports, the judge could strike the witness' testimony from the record and proceed with the trial, declare a mistrial, or "take such other action as [he] deems appropriate."

Three days later, Mike Mansfield of Montana, speaking on behalf of O'Mahoney, asked unanimous consent of the Senate to withdraw the Judiciary Committee's report of July 1 and to submit a new report incorporating the August 12 amendments as the committee proposal.[39] Clark interrupted Mansfield to ask sarcastically: "I wonder what is the purpose of this motion? This is a most important bill. I wonder why we are going to have a fourth version of it. . . . I would like to have the record show that in my judgment this ill-considered legislation is being rushed through the Senate without adequate opportunity for all Senators to understand its real purport."[40]

LIBERAL PRESSURE INCREASES

Without objection, the new report was substituted, but this acceptance did not solve any of the basic problems. The civil rights debate had reached a temporary truce with the passage the previous week of a weak bill; but since it was clear that the House would reject at least some of the Senate changes, the armistice would probably be short-lived. And Clark's barbed remarks indicated that O'Mahoney's latest effort at compromise had failed and that the liberals were alienated again. Equally impressive as the liberal votes was the fact that Majority leader Lyndon Johnson did not wish to call up the Jencks bill until both sides had settled their major differences.

The August 12 Jencks bill had in fact deeply irked the liberals. Clark sent O'Mahoney a memorandum on August 13,[41] stating that although the fourth version of S. 2377 had met a number of his earlier objections, it still "goes considerably further than either clarification of the Jencks decision requires or Assistant Attorney General Rogers told us yesterday he intended to go." Although this memorandum was mild in tone, Clark was actually hopping mad. Arnold, Bernstein, and Kelley had warned him that these latest changes practically brought the bill full circle to its June 24 form. Clark believed that Gasque had taken O'Mahoney in and was working to give the Justice Department and FBI everything they were asking for and a little more besides.*

Clark followed up his memorandum by going to see O'Mahoney and informing him in strong language that the August 12 version was simply unacceptable. Then, applying the heaviest kind of pressure one senator can put on another, Clark said: "Joe, you *promised*

* The American Civil Liberties Union had exactly the opposite reaction. Irving Ferman, head of the ACLU's Washington office, wrote O'Mahoney a letter on August 12 stating that the fourth version of the Jencks bill had his "wholehearted support." Subcommittee Files, Box 8.

me!" Caught in the middle once more, O'Mahoney gave in and assured Clark that when the bill came up for floor action the changes in wording Clark wanted would be incorporated.

When told of these plans for a new change, Gasque was as angry as Clark had been. He had been present at several O'Mahoney-Clark meetings and was certain in his own mind that O'Mahoney had never promised Clark that he would write a bill which Clark could vote for. O'Mahoney, Gasque believed, had only agreed to safeguard the rights of defendants in criminal trials. Gasque felt that Clark did not fully understand the issues and was inadvertantly acting as a front man protecting defendants in antitrust and tax prosecutions, a conclusion reinforced by the communications from the law firm of George Arnold's father which had quite candidly expressed concern over these more specific kinds of cases. At this point, Gasque—torn between personal devotion to O'Mahoney and the principle as he saw it—offered his resignation as subcommittee counsel, but O'Mahoney refused to accept it.

With a fifth version in draft form, O'Mahoney talked over the telephone with Warren Olney III and persuaded Olney that this new bill was the only possible legislation which could get through the Senate at that session. Hoover's advisers, however, disagreed with Olney's decision to go along with O'Mahoney. They felt that bill #5 did not afford their files sufficient protection, and Hoover immediately protested to Rogers. The day after the Olney-O'Mahoney telephone conversation, Rogers called O'Mahoney to say that the Justice Department would have to fight for a stronger measure than bill #5, even if it meant the loss of liberal support.

Since Hoover's firm policy had won out in the Justice Department and Olney had taken a position at odds with this line, his role became less influential. Wilson White, who was thought to be ready to back a stronger bill, was called in to work with Olney. Rogers explained to Olney that because the *Jencks* matter really concerned White as Assistant Attorney General in charge of the Office of Legal Counsel as much as it did Olney, White's advice should be sought and utilized.

The Justice Department's opposition made O'Mahoney's work more difficult, but he had now pledged his word to Clark and there was no turning back. In spite of his troubles with the people "downtown" and the Senate liberals, O'Mahoney had one trump card. He had been one of the principal sponsors of the jury trial amendment to the 1957 civil rights bill, a provision which the southerners considered an absolute necessity if any civil rights legislation were to be allowed to pass without an extended filibuster. Because of his strong and successful fight for this amendment, the southerners owed O'Mahoney an immense debt. Practically any Jencks bill O'Mahoney might write would automatically have the vote of every southern senator. With northern liberals placated by the concessions to Clark, and Lyndon Johnson delighted that someone else had done the dirty work of reconciling liberals and conservatives within the Democratic party, O'Mahoney felt reasonably certain that he could get his latest Jencks measure through the Senate without the Justice Department's approval. There was even some doubt as to whether the administration would officially oppose his latest compromise. On August 14, Vice-President Nixon had issued a statement[42] that Congress should not adjourn without adopting a bill to protect the FBI files, but the Vice-President had voiced no public objections to any specific bill and no preferences, for that matter.

PASSAGE OF JENCKS BILL #5

On Thursday, August 22, Jencks bill #5 was circulated.[43] It reversed the August 12 concessions to the Justice Department and went back to the July 8 version by including a reference to the Federal Rules of Criminal Procedure. In addition, the "oral statements" restriction was loosened. The August 12 compromise had limited production orders to "transcriptions or recordings" of oral reports, but bill #5 changed the word "recordings" to "records."

The next day Lyndon Johnson called up the Jencks bill for debate. Sticking to their bargain, Sam Ervin of North Carolina and Olin Johnston and Strom Thurmond of South Carolina spoke in favor of O'Mahoney's moderate measure. Although Thurmond almost ruined the plan by not being able to pass up the opportunity to blast the Warren Court, Johnston and Ervin were particularly effective. Johnston urged the Senate to adopt O'Mahoney's bill now, and wait until January to see if a more stringent statute were necessary. Ervin, a former justice of the North Carolina Supreme Court, stated that careful study of the majority opinion in *Jencks* had made him sympathetic to its objectives. Indeed, he thought it "essential to the proper administration of justice."[44] Returning to the O'Mahoney–Justice Department theme, Ervin said that it was lower court misinterpretation and not the Supreme Court decision which was dangerous. And he laid much of the blame for this misunderstanding on the flamboyant language of Justice Clark's dissent.

The liberals had been afraid that with the civil rights legislation out of the way, a stiff Jencks bill might be pushed through the Senate. This fear had made it easier for them to bargain with O'Mahoney and to be satisfied with modifying the administration measure. A bitter exchange of words between O'Mahoney and Pat McNamara of Michigan gave evidence of serious misgivings among the liberals, but as Wayne Morse said in indorsing the fifth version of the Jencks bill: "I still would prefer to let the whole matter rest for the operation of the judicial process. . . . [However,] I am also a realist, I hope. I know that legislation is going to be enacted. Therefore I shall try to do what I can to help enact legislation which will be good."[45]

The Friday debate threatened to go on late into the night, as Morse,* holding a fat manuscript in his hand, obtained the floor. Few senators were in a mood for another extended discussion, and Morse yielded to O'Mahoney to allow him to secure unanimous consent for limited debate on S. 2377 the following Monday, August 26. To confirm the wisdom of this action, Morse proceeded to deliver a two-hour oration on the Jencks case, the mayor of Portland, Ore-

* Wayne Lyman Morse (1900—–), Ph.B., University of Wisconsin, 1923, A.M., 1924, LL.B., University of Minnesota, 1928, J.D., Columbia University, 1932, began teaching as an assistant professor at the University of Oregon in 1929; by 1931 he was full professor and dean of the law school. Morse achieved national prominence because of his skill as a labor mediator. During World War II he served first as chairman of the President's Railway Emergency Board and then as a member of the War Labor Board. After resigning from the latter post in 1944 because he thought the board was kowtowing to John L. Lewis, Morse was elected to the Senate for a six-year term beginning in January, 1945. He started his career as a liberal Republican, but in the middle of the 1952 presidential campaign he ended this uneasy alliance, resigned from the party, and, proclaiming himself an Independent, openly supported Adlai Stevenson. In February, 1955, Morse officially became a Democrat. A hard-nosed, unyielding liberal whom William S. White has characterized as "saturnine and salty," Morse has constantly spurned compromise on any issue of principle as a betrayal of the people's trust. His moralistic attitude, hypersensitive personality, and explosive temper have brought the senior senator from Oregon into bitter feuds with conservatives, liberals, and moderates alike, and have kept him out of the select Senate "inner club." But these same traits have caused senators to recognize Morse as an adroit parliamentarian and stout-legged orator who will not hesitate to filibuster—in all, a dangerous and courageous foe.

gon, the Public Works bill, and the construction of a military base at Bethel, Minnesota.

As an indication of the Justice Department's concern, on Monday night Rogers was in the Vice-President's office, just off the Senate floor, and Warren Olney was up in the gallery. After the discussion got underway, Rogers sent out notes to Everett Dirksen, who was acting as administration floor leader, and to other Republicans, suggesting arguments and questions or occasionally asking a senator or an aide to come off the floor for a quick conference.

The debate itself, in contrast to that Friday, was crisp and pointed. O'Mahoney outlined the bill's complex history, and after explaining its purpose answered a number of thoughtful, probing questions. Dirksen, an old-fashioned Chautauqua orator, was at his booming, evangelical best. He went into several detailed discussions of the Justice Department's objections and proposed two amendments to bring the bill more nearly in line with the original committee report of July 1. The first would have eliminated the reference to the Federal Rules of Criminal Procedure, and the other would have changed the "records" of oral statements to "recordings," a modification, O'Mahoney claimed and Dirksen admitted, which would have limited the production of oral statements to those transcribed on tape recording machines or similar mechanical devices.

When the vote was taken on Dirksen's amendments, O'Mahoney's southern allies stood firm. Not one southern senator supported either attempt to strengthen the bill; and, with the help of a handful of liberal Republicans, the changes were defeated 30–45 and 37–43.[46]

After handing the opposing forces this double defeat, O'Mahoney accepted a pair of amendments.[47] One, proposed by Roman Hruska, Republican from Nebraska, cut back the trial judge's discretion to that of the original bill. If the United States would not produce previous reports of a witness, the judge could only strike that witness' testimony and proceed with the trial or declare a mistrial; he could not dismiss the indictment or take other action. The second amendment was suggested by Jacob Javits of New York. This provided that when the government claimed there was irrelevant matter in records which a court had ordered produced, the documents were to be given to the trial judge for his *in camera* inspection and editing, no matter whether the production order was issued pursuant to the Jencks statute or the Federal Rules of Criminal Procedure.

With these two changes, O'Mahoney's bill #5 was passed by a voice vote.[48]

THE HOUSE PASSES THE JUSTICE DEPARTMENT'S BILL

On the same day the Senate was debating S. 2377, Howard Smith of Virginia, chairman of the House Rules Committee, reported a pair of rules to the House. The first regulated debate on the revised civil rights bill; the second allowed one hour of debate,[49] to be equally divided, on the FBI files bill.

On the following day, August 27, immediately after the final version of the Civil Rights Act was passed, the special rule for H.R. 7915 was adopted, and the Jencks bill became the subject of a short, sharp debate. The lower chamber had been spared the Senate's confused parade of Jencks measures, and the proposal before the House was essentially that which the Senate and House Judiciary Committees had approved in July. Kenneth Keating was the bill's floor manager, and the leader of the opposition was Emanuel Celler, chairman of the Judiciary Committee. Celler was an outspoken civil libertarian, and, as his fight against H.R. 3 had shown, he was opposed not only to reversing any specific Court decision, but even more so to the idea that Congress should in any way give segregationists reason to believe the High Bench was being censured.

During the debate Celler met the pleas that new legislation was urgently needed with the same arguments against haste that had been used in the Senate. He excoriated the Justice Department for "deliberate and purposeful" misinterpretation of *Jencks* designed to insure passage of its legislation. "This hullabaloo about opening up the FBI records so that spies, traitors, and saboteurs could have those records . . . is ridiculous. That argument has emanated from the Department of Justice because it does not like the Jencks decision."[50]

Celler spoke with conviction, but he spoke almost alone. The question, both sides knew, was not whether the House would pass a bill, but how strong a bill. Keating was in far better shape in the House than Dirksen had been in the Senate. First, the Democratic party had been badly divided over the civil rights issue, and Celler was not the man who could heal the breach. The conservative Southern Democrats were the natural enemies rather than the allies of the liberal New York Jew who had sponsored and fought for so many civil rights bills. Nor was the party leadership willing to help Celler. John W. McCormack, the Majority leader, was in favor of the administration proposal, and Speaker Sam Rayburn had no serious objections. Furthermore, both men knew that the anger of southern representatives at the Warren Court and the imminent enactment of civil rights legislation made any effort to work for a softer Jencks bill futile. Not even O'Mahoney, who went onto the House floor and tried to trade on his recent support of the jury trial amendment to the civil rights bill, could persuade Southern Democrats to compromise.

Second, congressmen, subject to biennial elections, were more sensitive than most senators to charges of being soft on communism. It would take only a mild Red scare to send members scampering into line. As leverage Keating and his associates were able to cite lower court extensions of *Jencks* as well as to reiterate the dangers to the FBI files lurking in the pending spy trial of Colonel Abel. In addition, the relentless pressure from the FBI lobbyists was difficult to resist; and as a clincher for the record the Justice Department supplied a memorandum from J. Edgar Hoover:

> It is my considered judgment that the enactment of this legislation . . . is vital to the future ability of the Federal Bureau of Investigation to carry out its internal security and law enforcement responsibilities. The FBI certainly cannot continue to fulfill its responsibilities unless the security of its files can be assured as has been the case prior to June 3, 1957. . . . Since the Jencks decision, however, we have faced one obstacle after another. We have experienced instance after instance where sources of information have been closed to our agents because of the fear that the confidence we could once guarantee could no longer be assured.[51]

Keating had other support which might have been more helpful had it been quieter. Several southern representatives leaped at the opportunity to attack the Warren Court. Howard Smith had started it when, in discussing the rule his committee proposed, he had explained: "The purpose of the bill is to correct the decision of the Supreme Court in the so-called famous Jencks case."[52] Forrester of Georgia claimed that along with H.R. 7915, the Department of Justice should have submitted an apology for nominating a man like

William J. Brennan for the High Bench. "I want it recorded here and now," Forrester continued, "that I do not think it was the sense of the Committee on the Judiciary to come out with any expression whatsoever that we are endorsing the principles laid down by the Supreme Court. Under no circumstances will I do it. Nor do I think the House Judiciary Committee will do it."[53]

Cramer of Florida and Poff of Virginia, both Republicans, tried to keep the discussion on the misinterpretation track, yet even Cramer could not resist calling the *Jencks* ruling "inconceivable"[54] and putting full blame for any misunderstanding on the vague and loose language of the majority opinion. This southern outburst against the Court caused O'Hara of Illinois to allege that there was a two-package deal going on; as reparation for their civil rights defeat the southerners were being permitted to rebuke the Court by means of a stringent Jencks bill.

This charge, however, had little effect. In fact, northern and western representatives joined the southerners in criticizing the Justices. Bosch of New York spoke[55] of "a long series" of decisions "more legislative than judicial" of which *Jencks* was the most outstanding example of "usurpation" of congressional authority. Burdick of North Dakota claimed that "all the commotion about finding fault with the Supreme Court has risen from the fact that they have very few lawyers on that Court. . . . " Burdick pictured the alternatives before the House as defeating the bill or bringing the law back "where it was before the Supreme Court forgot their duty as interpreters of the law and started to legislate."[56]

The hopelessness of liberal opposition had been apparent before the debate began, and when Celler proposed to substitute the Senate bill for the administration measure, his motion was beaten down by a three to one margin.[57] Then, when the vote came on the passage of the Jencks bill, the House approved it by an overwhelming 351–17,[58] with all the nays cast by northern Democrats.

COMPROMISE IN CONFERENCE

Since the two houses had passed different bills, a conference committee had to be appointed to iron out the differences. The five House members were Emanuel Celler, Kenneth Keating, Edwin Willis of Louisiana, Laurence Curtis of Massachusetts, who had spoken and voted in favor of the administration bill, and Jack Brooks of Texas, who had taken no part in the debate but had voted for the bill. This selection gave the proponents of the Justice Department measure a 4–1 majority.

The choice of Senate conferees caused more trouble. O'Mahoney, who had been maneuvered pretty much into the ranks of the liberal opposition, was ready to bypass his subcommittee and to select himself, Alexander Wiley of Wisconsin, a liberal Republican, and Sam Ervin of North Carolina. O'Mahoney would have been easily able to control this group in a fight for a soft bill; but Eastland got news of O'Mahoney's maneuver and intervened. As chairman of the Judiciary Committee, it was his responsibility, not that of a subcommittee chairman, to recommend Senate conferees. Both to accommodate protocol and to insure that a tough bill would come out of conference, Eastland selected himself, O'Mahoney, and Everett Dirksen,* all members of the Subcommittee on Improvements in the Federal Criminal Code.

The Justice Department's concern, of course, had increased with Senate passage of O'Mahoney's bill #5, and its last hope of attaining its ends through legislation rested in the conference. To make the department's final plea, Wilson White and Warren Olney had lunch with O'Mahoney, Eastland, Dirksen, Keating, and several of the other House conferees. Although Gasque was also asked to attend, Emanuel Celler was pointedly overlooked. In the noisy clattering of the small Senate restaurant in the Capitol Building, Olney emphasized that there were only a few major points of disagreement and tried to get Keating and O'Mahoney to discuss a middle ground between the House and Senate bills which would meet the Justice Department's goals. After lunch Olney, White, and Gasque got together, and the three worked out the specific language of a compromise proposal.

When the conferees met officially, they were in session for less than an hour. Almost without discussion the Olney-White-Gasque draft was accepted as the conference bill.[59]

In form, the measure was couched in the language of the Senate version, but there were two significant changes which met the Justice Department's objections to O'Mahoney's bill #5. First, all reference to the Federal Rules of Criminal Procedure had again been elim-

* Eastland had intended to appoint John Marshall Butler, another member of the subcommittee and an outspoken critic of the Warren Court, but Butler had to leave town. Dirksen, as administration floor leader, was Eastland's second choice.

inated; and it was explicitly stated that no statement or report of any witness in the possession of the United States would be the subject of subpoena, discovery, or inspection until after that witness had testified in a criminal prosecution. Second, a compromise was reached on the problem of production of oral reports. The body of the bill required production of "statements"; and in the last subsection "statement" was defined as: "(1) a written statement made by said witness and signed or otherwise approved by him; or (2) a stenographic, mechanical, electrical, or other recording, or a transcription thereof, which is substantially a verbatim recital of an oral statement made to an agent of the Government and recorded contemporaneously with the making of such statement."

Shortly after 9:00 P.M. on Thursday, August 29, J. Strom Thurmond of South Carolina ended his one-man civil rights filibuster, a long-winded twenty-four hours and eighteen minutes which had broken the tacit Senate bargain of no southern filibuster in exchange for weakening the civil rights bill. Two hours later, the 1957 Civil Rights Act was on its way to the President. Then, after a half-hour devoted to a compromise foreign aid measure, the Senate turned to the Jencks legislation.

O'Mahoney delivered the conference report and told his colleagues that these modifications did not change the basic design of his bill #5. With this assurance, as well as the blessings of the Justice Department, imparted by Everett Dirksen, the Senate at 12:27 on the morning of August 30 approved the conference proposal by a 74–2 majority.[60]

The next afternoon, Emanuel Celler boasted to the House of Representatives that the conference committee had virtually adopted the substitute he had proposed three days earlier. Kenneth Keating flatly contradicted Celler and asserted that the conference bill was even stronger than H.R. 7915. With both sides thus pleased, the House immediately accepted the conference report 315–0.[61]

THE JENCKS ACT

The Warren Court's friends claimed that the Jencks law actually was no more than a codification of the High Bench's decision.[62] The Court critics, on the other hand, claimed that they had slapped the Justices, lightly but meaningfully, across their robed wrists. Both sides were right to a degree.

The new statute[63] did go a long way toward codifying the *Jencks* decision, although it followed more closely the procedures suggested in Burton's concurrence than in Brennan's majority opinion. With the exception of a few southerners and a handful of conservative Republicans in the House, almost all of the bill's supporters had taken great care to point out that they were not attacking the Warren Court. Mark Antony, of course, had disavowed criticizing Brutus, but the final bill would hardly have received the votes of almost every liberal Court defender in both houses of Congress if such a legislative purpose had been widely accepted.

All through the summer O'Mahoney had been deeply worried about Court-curbing implications, and his office undertook to elicit the views of the Justices on the bill. Because of the Court's taboo against advisory opinions, this probing had to be done most delicately and through several reliable and tactful intermediaries. In late August, after several unsuccessful attempts, O'Mahoney received rather vague word that his informants had not been able to discover any serious objections among the Justices regarding bill #5. While this was in no sense even an off-the-record indorsement. O'Mahoney was still pleased with the news as a means of reassuring the liberals.

The effect of the Jencks act on the Court's prestige is difficult to judge. In contrast to the decision itself, the Jencks legislation was not generally headline news. The *Philadelphia Inquirer* merely reported the story on page three in a short, unemotional article.[64] The *Chicago Tribune* did not even list it among the principal achievements of the Eighty-fifth Congress' first session, though the *New York Journal American* did, expressing regret that the bill had been watered down.[65] The *New York Daily News* spoke editorially of the new legislation as an effort to "protect [FBI] files from Earl Warren's Supreme Court's pro-communist decision."[66] The *New York Herald Tribune* referred to the act under the heading of "FBI Rescued,"[67] while the *New York Times* was coldly factual—though in a separate article Anthony Lewis speculated whether some of the publicity over the decision might not have been the work of Justice Department officials.[68] The *Washington Post & Times Herald* kept to its position that Congress had acted too hastily.[69] All in all, it would seem that while *America*'s comment[70] that the bill was "universally" thought to be a rebuke to the Court was overstated, a considerable portion of the public probably did so interpret the new statute.

7. THE ATTACK GAINS MOMENTUM

On *July 26, 1957,* in the middle of the Senate debate on the civil rights bill, William E. Jenner* of Indiana obtained the floor. In a flat Hoosier voice he began to read a long speech, a verbal assault on the High Bench which could have competed in intensity with any made by his southern colleagues. "The Supreme Court," Jenner charged, "has dealt a succession of blows at key points of the legislative structure erected by Congress for the protection of the internal security of the United States. . . . The Court has become, for all practical purposes, a legislative arm of the Government; and many of its feats are subject to no review."

* William Ezra Jenner (1908——), A.B. (1930), LL.B. (1932), University of Indiana, got his first taste of politics in 1930 when he worked as an elevator operator in the House Office Building while going to George Washington Law School at night. He quickly took up politics with a professional's zeal. In 1934 he was elected to the state senate, serving as minority leader from 1937 to 1939, and majority leader and president pro tem from 1939 to 1941. In 1942–44 he was on active duty with the Army Air Corps. When he returned from military service in 1944, Jenner won the right to serve out the remaining two years of the late Senator Van Nuys' term and became the first

Jenner had strong words for each of the political offender decisions, although it was *Watkins* which apparently had struck the deepest blow to the senator's sensibilities. That case, he stated, "severely cripples, if it does not wholly smash, the Congressional power to investigate. By so doing it multiplies the danger of constitutional imbalance. . . ." As for *Mallory*, Jenner asked: "How many more . . . girls will be raped in 1957 because the United States Supreme Court was so zealous a protector of Andrew Mallory's rights as an individual?"[1]

All in all, this speech was probably the most searing attack on the Warren Court any northern senator—with the exception of McCarthy —had made in public. Jenner was angry, and when angry he was known as a man who did not pull his punches. In 1950 he had branded General Marshall as "not only willing, [but] eager to play the role of a front man, for traitors." And in 1951 he had lashed out at Harry Truman: "I charge that this country today is in the hands of a secret inner coterie which is directed by agents of the Soviet Union. . . . Our only choice is to impeach President Truman and find out who is the secret invisible government. . . ."[2] Whether or not Jenner had earlier only been engaging in rough and tumble name-calling, in July, 1957, he intended to carry through his attack. His speech was an explanation of the reasons behind the introduction of S. 2646, a bill to curb the Court by striking at its weakest point, that of appellate jurisdiction. Utilizing the assistance of Robert Morris and J. G. Sourwine of the staff of the Internal Security Subcommittee, Jenner had drafted a bill which would have removed the authority of the Supreme Court to review five types of cases: (1) contempt of Congress; (2) the Federal Loyalty-Security Program; (3) state antisubversive statutes; (4) regulations of employment and

---

World War II veteran elected to the Senate. Re-elected in 1946 and 1952, in 1958 he retired from politics and went back to private life. In Washington Jenner was not, William S. White claims, a true Senate type. He was, rather, as Telford Taylor put it, one of those legislators "clustered at the extreme right end of the political color spectrum, where purple deepens into black." (*Grand Inquest: The Story of Congressional Investigations* [New York: Simon & Schuster, 1955], p. xiii.) An isolationist and extreme Anglophobe, Jenner feuded with Dean Acheson almost as vehemently as with President Truman. Jenner combined his foreign policy views with the militant type of anticommunism usually associated with Joseph McCarthy; and in 1953 under Jenner's leadership, the Senate Internal Security Subcommittee grew to be a serious headline competitor both to McCarthy's investigations and to the House Un-American Activities Committee as well.

subversive activities in schools; (5) admission to the practice of law in any state.

Jenner's proposal was soon to grow into the most fundamental challenge to judicial power in twenty years, but in the summer of 1957 few people took S. 2646 seriously. Perhaps it was because of the focus of attention on the civil rights bill, or perhaps it was because several similar bills had been introduced in the Eighty-fifth Congress only to be duly pigeonholed. Whatever the reason, the Jenner bill raised little furor either in the Senate or in the press. And on the afternoon of August 7, when hearings were held before the Internal Security Subcommittee, only Eastland, the chairman of the subcommittee, Jenner, Morris, Sourwine, and one other member of the subcommittee staff appeared. Two witnesses offered testimony, William E. Jenner and Benjamin Mandel, director of research for the subcommittee. The proceedings lasted less than half an hour.

For the record Jenner repeated his castigation of the Warren Court and explained the purposes of his bill, taking special pains to outline the authority of Congress under Article III of the Constitution to enact such a statute. When Jenner had begun his criticism of the separate political offender decisions, Eastland interrupted:[3]

> THE CHAIRMAN: "Well, now, in these decisions, as you know, they have been using the expression 'freedom of association.' What is the basis for that in the Constitution of the United States?"
>
> SENATOR JENNER: "Well, there is none, I am afraid, Mr. Chairman. The expression 'freedom of association' appears nowhere in the Constitution of the United States. I first heard about it in statements that the Communists have issued before the subcommittees, and before our committee, and before other committees, for years. . . ."
>
> CHAIRMAN: "In other words, isn't that expression, and those holdings, an amendment to the Constitution? That is what they are doing, is it not?"
>
> JENNER: "That is exactly right."
>
> CHAIRMAN: "Amending the Constitution."
>
> JENNER: "Judge-made law."
>
> CHAIRMAN: "And doing that in violation of their oaths of office."
>
> JENNER: "That is right."
>
> CHAIRMAN: "Do you believe that?"
>
> JENNER: "I believe that."

The Jenner bill went through the Internal Security Subcommittee without a hitch, and the following week Eastland made S. 2646 one of the first orders of business for the full Judiciary Committee. Senator John Carroll of Colorado, who had been appointed to the committee in place of Senator Neely of West Virginia, read over the legislation and told the chairman that it was a complex bill which needed considerable study, and that it had come up as a surprise. Eastland replied that as a matter of courtesy any committee member was privileged to ask that a bill be held over for a week. Carroll was reluctant to appear obstructive or overly aggressive at his first committee meeting, and he said he would have to think about it for a few minutes.

At this point Hennings put the embarrassing question to the chairman: How many witnesses had appeared at the hearings? Eastland answered truthfully. Hennings then proposed that the bill be held over until the next session so that complete public hearings could be held with the bar, the law schools, and other interested groups invited to express their views. Jenner objected and tried to force the bill through the committee by moving to table Hennings' proposal. When Jenner's motion failed by one vote, the committee agreed to postpone a decision on S. 2646 until after full-scale public hearings.

THE 1958 JENNER HEARINGS: PROPONENTS OF THE BILL

Neither Jenner nor Eastland was willing to let S. 2646 drop, and on February 3, 1958, shortly after the opening of the Eighty-fifth Congress' second session, the Judiciary Committee ordered the Internal Security Subcommittee to hold "intensive" hearings on the Jenner bill. The subcommittee carried out this command with efficient dispatch. In nine days more than fifty witnesses appeared to testify and thirty-seven more filed formal statements. In addition, the subcommittee staff collected and printed as an appendix to the *Hearings* shorter communications from several hundred other individuals and organizations.[4]

The proponents of S. 2646 turned out en masse. Besides a parade of individual citizens, two senators, one state judge, and thirty-nine organizations went on record as indorsing Jenner's bill. These groups ranged in importance from the Veterans of Foreign Wars, the Dames of the Loyal Legion, the Duval County (Florida) Federation for Constitutional Government, the Ladies of the GAR, the Independent Farmers of Indiana, and the National Sons of the American Revolution to the Iowa State Society of the National Society of the Daughters of 1812, the Indiana Property Owners Association, and numerous chapters of the Massachusetts Committees of Correspondence. Despite this gathering of organizational support, a number of groups were conspicuously absent. The Director of the American Legion's national legislative committee wrote that the legion had taken no position on the bill, and the American Farm Bureau Federation, the U.S. Chamber of Commerce, and the National Association of Manufacturers were, officially at least, silent.

Some of the Jenner witnesses, like the SPX Research group which attempted to prove via a curious brew of algebraic symbols mixed with Roman numerals and world maps that the Supreme Court was an instrument of international communism, were obvious cranks. But many supporters were serious and intelligent people. Although there was a noticeable segregation undercurrent, the bond which seemed to unite the pro-Jenner witnesses was a common fear that the Supreme Court was destroying the nation's barriers against internal subversion.

Francis J. McNamara, assistant director of the National Legislative Service of the Veterans of Foreign Wars, told the subcommittee that his organization had been gravely worried by the trend of recent Supreme Court decisions and had voiced this concern in resolutions urging Congress to reverse the *Yates, Cole,* and *Jencks* decisions. Turning to the role of the Supreme Court in the American system of government, McNamara asserted:

> The judiciary is one of the three branches of the Federal Government. As such it is part of the Federal power. If we are to have real self-government, all of the Federal power, not just part of it, must be responsive to the people. Legislation represents the will of the people. The Court's function, in other words, is that of interpreting the people's will. If the Court does not serve the people in this way, it becomes an agent of autocracy, not democracy.

R. Carter Pittman, lawyer and writer from Georgia, filed a statement amplifying the need for the Jenner bill. "Nine men in black robes ride herd over the Congress and the people. Their horses are phantoms but that can make no difference to a defenseless people if their Representatives in Congress are in headlong flight."

The Secretary of the American Coalition of Patriotic Societies, claiming to represent some three million members of various organizations, presented for the record a resolution deploring the tendency of the Supreme Court to override constitutional limitations on its power. T. David Horton, chairman of the executive council of the Defenders of the American Constitution and the Arlington (Virginia) Federation of Home Owners, quoted Representative Wint Smith of Kansas to the effect that the Justices had committed "impeachable" offenses. Speaking of Court "depredations," Horton fully indorsed Jenner's proposal: "S. 2646 . . . is a wise move, consonant with the congressional duty to balance irresponsible judicial power through the limitation of appellate jurisdiction—a move that at its worst will remove tyranny from its inaccessible and centralized seat in Washington."

Senator George Malone of Nevada was unable to appear at the hearings, but he sent a memorandum declaring that it would be "a waste of time" to recite the many instances in which the Court had disregarded the ancient safeguard of individual rights, *stare decisis,* and that the time "has already passed" for Congress to put the Court back in its proper place.

Senator J. Strom Thurmond of South Carolina offered testimony in person and told the subcommittee that Congress had to face up to the "alarming" trend of Court decisions and call a halt to "this unconstitutional seizure of power." Plugging his own bill to take away Supreme Court jurisdiction to review school litigation as well as Jenner's proposal, Thurmond echoed James F. Byrnes's 1956 plea: "The Supreme Court must be curbed. If it continues in the direction it is headed, we shall all become the victims of judicial tyranny.

Edgar C. Bundy, president of the Abraham Lincoln National Republican Club, appeared as a witness. Although claiming his organization had members in forty-six states and Alaska, Bundy refused to give any membership figures because "there are so many left wing, pseudoliberal groups that would like to find out just how strong we are." Then, referring to the "inexcusable and intolerable" Supreme

Court decisions, Bundy accused the Justices of giving "aid and comfort and protection to individuals who seek to destroy one of the grandest and noblest forms of human government ever devised in the history of the world."

Judge William Old of Chesterfield County, Virginia, widely credited with resurrecting Calhoun's doctrine of interposition in white southern efforts to halt integration by "nullifying" the Supreme Court's school decisions, testified as to the "desperate necessity" of S. 2646. Judge Old explained that "it is now clearly apparent, from a long list of revolutionary decisions by the Supreme Court, headed by Chief Justice Warren, that the Court is determined to destroy our dual system of government under the Constitution, and create, by judicial usurpation and encroachment, a judicial oligarchy of unparalleled proportions."

L. Brent Bozell, editor of the *National Review,* developed what was probably the most systematic argument for S. 2646. First, Bozell asserted that the bill was constitutional, being clearly authorized by the provisions of Article III granting Congress power to make exceptions to the appellate jurisdiction of the Supreme Court. Second, he attempted to demonstrate that the Jenner proposal grew from deeper roots than mere displeasure with specific decisions. Basing his position on belief in and support of the Court as an institution, Bozell nevertheless claimed that the present Justices' frequent misuse of discretion, constant expansion of power, "gratuitous abuse of congressional investigating committees," and "dishonesty" in handling precedents had placed recent decisions beyond the realm of reason. "Therefore, the Court needs to be disciplined quite aside from the impact of its decisions on our constitutional system and quite aside from the effect of its decisions on our internal security. Our society must deal with the Court as it deals with many other transgressors of law and order. *We must teach the Court judicial responsibility.*"

One of the most damaging pieces of testimony against the Court came from Edward S. Corwin, professor emeritus of Princeton University and long recognized dean of American constitutional scholars. Although not indorsing the Jenner bill because he feared it was too drastic, Corwin wrote the subcommittee that he was in sympathy with "the general purpose" of S. 2646. A month later Corwin sent a caustic letter to the editors of the *New York Times:* "There can be no doubt that on June 17 last the Court went on a virtual binge and thrust its nose into matters beyond its competence, with the result that (in my judgment at least) it should have its aforesaid nose well tweaked. . . . The country needs protection against the aggressive tendency of the Court."[5]

THE COURT DEFENDERS TESTIFY

The anti-Jenner witnesses were heavily outnumbered. On the other hand, while only a few of the supporters of S. 2646 were recognized legal authorities and only the VFW was a widely known national organization, the anti-Jenner forces lined up such well-known liberal groups as the American Civil Liberties Union, the NAACP, the Americans for Democratic Action, the American Jewish Congress, and the Committee on Federal Legislation of the Association of the Bar of the City of New York. Labor's political power was not at a peak, but the AFL-CIO sent a representative to speak against the bill.

To add prestige to their cause, the Jenner opponents were able to get testimony or statements from people like Jefferson Fordham, dean of the University of Pennsylvania Law School; Roscoe Pound, dean emeritus of Harvard Law School; the eminent attorney John Lord O'Brian; Thomas McBride, attorney general of Pennsylvania; and Whitney North Seymour, Assistant Solicitor General for Herbert Hoover. To reinforce the liberals still further, the Justice Department officially recommended that the bill be shelved. The subcommittee had invited Attorney General Rogers to testify, but instead—Jenner claimed that Rogers was afraid to face cross-examination—the Attorney General wrote a strong letter describing S. 2646 as a "retaliatory measure" which "threatens the independence of the judiciary."

Senator Hennings pulled off a major coup by writing the dean of almost every large law school in the United States, as well as partners in some of the leading law firms in various sections of the country, asking for their views on S. 2646. Every practicing lawyer who replied opposed the bill as either "unwise," "dangerous," "utterly lacking in merit," "unfortunate," or "ill-advised."

The law school replies, while not unanimous, constituted an

equally resounding blast of Jenner's proposal. Only three deans and two professors favored S. 2646, and three of these five indorsements were qualified. The other forty-eight answers were decidedly negative. Dean Miller of Catholic University wrote:

> The case on the merits against the bill is one-sided. It seems so obvious that restrictions through legislation on any functions of the Supreme Court are inconsistent with judicial independence. However, the people who are interested in this legislation have axes to grind. They do not adjust themselves to any arguments except those which relate to the immediate effects of decisions they do not like.

Dean Snodgrass of the University of California called the bill "a shocking thing." Dean O'Meara of Notre Dame termed it "vicious." Duke and Southern Methodist reported that every member of the law faculty opposed Jenner's measure. Even the reply from the University of Alabama, though mild, was unequivocal in stating that "S. 2646 is an unwise proposal."

SUBCOMMITTEE COUNSEL

Countering in part the array of names allied against the Jenner bill was the work of J. G. Sourwine, who had succeeded Robert Morris as subcommittee counsel. A heavy-set, graying man with small, square, rimless glasses, Sourwine was a tight-lipped lawyer who firmly believed in Jenner's views on internal security. But his emotional attachment to S. 2646 did not affect Sourwine's intellectual agility, and his incisive cross-examination could be formidable, as hostile witnesses as able as Dean Fordham and Joseph Rauh of the Americans for Democratic Action discovered. Rauh, in particular, ran into difficulty when he lumped the bill's proponents into two categories, segregationists and "security-mad politicians." Sourwine immediately interrupted: "So that we may know what you are talking about, what is a security-mad politician?"

> Mr. Rauh: "I would say it is one who, in large measure, caused the actions which the Supreme Court reversed in the eight decisions to which I will come. I would put in that category the actions which the Supreme Court—and I would like to come to that in detail and show the unanimity of the Supreme Court on this—which the Su-

preme Court reversed in the eight decisions, which I understand S. 2646 opposes. Now, it seems to me—"

MR. SOURWINE: "You mean a security-mad politician would include anybody that had anything to do with the decisions that the Supreme Court reversed?"

RAUH: "No, I didn't say that, Mr. Sourwine. I said that I thought it was a type of person who had been in on the general conduct which the Supreme Court reversed. I don't say that every person in every situation would be in that category. And I am sure reasonable men could differ on some of them.

"Some of the cases were close, though most of them were not."

SOURWINE: "You mean some explicitly approved the conduct that the Supreme Court in its decision reversed?"

RAUH: "Yes, I think so."

SOURWINE: "Would that include the members of the courts of appeal who wrote decisions which the Supreme Court reversed?"

RAUH: "No. I think the members of the courts of appeal were making a deference to Congress in that respect. I don't think any of them agreed with what was going on. I think they felt—and it is not unusual for courts of appeal and district courts to feel that they ought not reverse action of Congress, let's say, and I think that the Supreme Court, composed of men who have been Senators, governors, and so on and so forth, has a little less temerity about that kind of action."

SEARCH FOR A COMPROMISE

At the conclusion of the hearings, Jenner summed up the arguments for his bill. He denied that his intention had been to punish the Court. Rather, his purpose had been remedial: to check the drift to judicial supremacy and to push the Supreme Court out of areas of state and congressional authority. "I introduced this bill not out of any spirit of retaliation, but out of a deep concern for the preservation of the Constitution of the United States as it was meant to be, and our American way of life as we used to know it." Then, broadly hinting at the possibility of compromise, Jenner stated that he was not wedded to a single line of S. 2646, that he took no pride in authorship, and that if the committee could come up with a similar or different measure to achieve the same end of restoring the constitutional balance, he would support such a proposal.

Jenner's compromise offer was necessary. Even while the hearings were in progress, the defeat of S. 2646 had become evident and inevitable unless the measure were dramatically revised. Not only had Hennings' poll of the legal profession and the failure of important conservative groups to speak out damaged S. 2646's chances, but other voices from the right joined the liberals in opposition. The *Chicago Tribune,* archetype of the standpatter, warned that "a conservative must be very shortsighted, indeed, to uphold the Jenner bill."[6]

Most significant was the action of the American Bar Association,[7] the lawyer group which more than any other legal association represented the bedrock of conservatism. Meeting in February in Atlanta, the ABA's House of Delegates had before it a resolution from its board of governors to have the association go on record against S. 2646. A strange and fascinating debate ensued, with the lawyers struggling to avoid the sharp horns of an ethical and political dilemma. On the one hand, many members felt obliged to rally to the defense of the Court as an institution, if for no other reason than to appear consistent with their 1937 opposition to FDR and their later support of the constitutional amendment to freeze the size and jurisdiction of the Supreme Court. On the other hand, a great number of lawyers, especially those from the South, were totally out of sympathy with the Warren Court's jurisprudence and, in fact, could be much harsher in their criticism of the High Bench than Jenner had ever been.

The result of this cross-pressure was a compromise resolution drafted by a Mississippi lawyer:

> *Resolved,* That, reserving our right to criticize decisions of any court in any case, and without approving or disapproving any decisions of the Supreme Court of the United States, the American Bar Association opposes the enactment of Senate bill 2646, which would limit the appellate jurisdiction of the Supreme Court of the United States.

Those who wanted a firm indorsement of the Court called this resolution "whining," but the argument was also made that such a stand, supported as it was even by those who wholly disagreed with the present Justices, would mean far more than if the association pretended to agree with recent decisions. After a brief debate the proposal was carried by a voice vote.

The Bar acted on February 25, and six days later Senator John Marshall Butler of Maryland introduced a simpler version of the Jenner bill which would have removed the Supreme Court's appellate jurisdiction only in state bar admission cases.[8] Meanwhile, with the hearings completed, the Senate Judiciary Committee had to deal with Jenner and the Court. The fifteen-man committee was divided into several mutually antagonistic camps. A four-man bloc—consisting of two Southern Democrats, Chairman James O. Eastland, and John McClellan of Arkansas, as well as two conservative Republicans, Jenner and Butler—was dedicated to curbing the Court in any way possible and at almost any price.

At the opposite extreme were two liberal Republicans, Alexander Wiley of Wisconsin and William Langer of North Dakota, and two Democrats, Thomas C. Hennings of Missouri and John Carroll of Colorado. This group stood solidly behind the recent Court decisions and would fight doggedly against any attempts to curb the Court or to reverse specific decisions. Estes Kefauver of Tennessee was close to the Court defender bloc, although he was less opposed to legislation to reverse individual decisions.

Arthur Watkins of Utah, Roman Hruska of Nebraska, and Everett Dirksen of Illinois were conservative Republicans, worried by the effect of the Warren Court's security decisions. Although closer to the wing of their party represented by Jenner and Butler than by Wiley or Langer, none of the three could have felt comfortable being publicly identified with Eastland's militant white supremacy, and Watkins must have been embarrassed by some of the McCarthy overtones running through the anti-Court bloc.

Olin D. Johnston and Sam Ervin were Southern Democrats, but both had the reputation of being as liberal as their constituencies would allow. Johnston, who had gone to work in a textile mill at the age of eleven, had in 1944 ousted "Cotton Ed" Smith from the senatorial seat he had held for thirty-four years. Johnston had had a checkered career of defeats and victories in gubernatorial and senatorial campaigns. Able to carry the piedmont region with its large mill-worker population, he had often been beaten by the tidewater aristocracy in and around Charleston. Citing this "upper class" bias against him, Johnston had played the role of a New Deal reformer, and one of his first acts when elected governor in 1934 had been to secure passage of a forty-hour work week law for textile mills. In a parallel move, soon after coming to the Senate, he had introduced a bill to raise the minimum wage from fifty to sixty-five cents an hour.

Johnston's liberalism had been expressed in other ways as well. Through his position first as a member and later as chairman of the Senate Post Office and Civil Service Committee, he had fought a long, hard battle to establish a loyalty-security program which would provide maximum government protection along with absolute fairness to federal employees. In this regard he had helped stifle early efforts to reverse *Cole* v. *Young*.

Ervin, a former Justice of the North Carolina Supreme Court, had been one of the leaders of the southern senators fighting for a jury trial amendment to the 1957 civil rights bill. Quiet, scholarly, and judicious, he could have little sympathy with Eastland's professional race-baiting. Nevertheless, neither Ervin nor Johnston could openly fight for the Warren Court; and Ervin's 1957 remarks in defense of the *Jencks* decision had been politically risky. Indeed, each was obliged to attack the "judicial oligarchy" at regular intervals, and Johnston was especially adept at stump speeches before cheering White Citizens Council audiences. Both men might work behind the scenes for something more moderate than S. 2646, but if a public showdown were forced they would be compelled to vote in favor of almost any legislation which might undermine the Court's prestige.

Joseph O'Mahoney of Wyoming was the last member of the committee. O'Mahoney could hardly have fully approved S. 2646, but, as his work on the Jencks bill showed, he was concerned with the political offender decisions and he could and would support legislation to reverse specific Court decisions. In light of O'Mahoney's view of his role as a mediator and compromiser, it was not unexpected that he would suggest the first compromise on the Jenner bill. What O'Mahoney proposed was an arrangement by which the Judiciary Committee would make it a standing practice to administer a special oath to judicial nominees, asking them to swear belief in the limited role of the courts under the separation of powers doctrine. On March 26, 1958, this oath was first put to George H. Casswell, nominated by Eisenhower to be a federal district judge in Florida. During the hearings, Eastland asked Casswell to stand and to give a sworn reply to the following question:[9]

> Do you, in contemplation of the necessity of taking an oath to support and defend the Constitution of the United States understand that such oath will demand that you support and defend the provisions of Article I, Section 1, of the Constitution, that "all legislative power herein granted shall be vested in a Congress of the United States . . ." and that therefore you will be bound by such oath not to participate knowingly in any decision to alter the meaning of the Constitution itself or any law as passed by the Congress and adopted under the Constitution?

Apparently taken by surprise, Casswell meekly complied, but the Justice Department reacted vigorously. In a press conference the next week, Attorney General Rogers branded the oath either "silly" or "unwise."[10] If its only purpose was to have the nominee repeat his oath of office, Rogers said, then it was "silly." If the oath were intended to single out one part of the Constitution as imposing a greater obligation on a judge, then, the Attorney General thought, the process was "unwise." The following day O'Mahoney fired back at Rogers and defended his extra oath as a necessary protection of the Constitution against executive and judicial encroachments on congressional power.[11]

Yet even aside from executive displeasure, the O'Mahoney oath was not satisfactory to any of the Judiciary Committee factions. The Court foes thought it a futile gesture, and the liberals echoed Rogers' criticism. At the next hearings on the confirmation of judicial nominees, held late in April, the oath was toned down to a question asking if the nominees would support Article I's allocation of legislative power to Congress. At subsequent hearings, the oath matter was either soft-pedaled or omitted, although there was no slackening of efforts to interrogate potential judges on their views of current court problems.

THE JENNER-BUTLER BILL

It was John Marshall Butler* rather than O'Mahoney who came up with a compromise on which a majority of the committee could

* John Marshall Butler (1897—) served in the AEF in France in 1917–19. When he returned, he entered Johns Hopkins and stayed for two years, playing right tackle on the football team. In 1922 Butler had to leave school because of financial reasons, but

agree. Butler was as vehement in his criticism of the Warren Court as either Jenner or Eastland, and he sorely regretted his earlier efforts to protect the Court's jurisdiction. He and Jenner were close personal friends, and Butler had helped polish S. 2646. While both men would have preferred to keep all the provisions of the original bill, they realized after the hearings that no such legislation would survive a floor fight, if, in fact, it could even get out of committee. Butler got the germ of an idea for a modified bill from the testimony of former Maryland State Senator Frank Ober in favor of S. 2646,[12] and he and Jenner formulated a new five-point proposal which might soothe the misgivings of some conservatives and still be a potent rebuke to the Warren Court. The Jenner-Butler bill would have revoked the Court's appellate jurisdiction only in bar admission cases, but several decisions would have been reversed by other clauses of the measure.

On April 21, the Judiciary Committee voted on three of Butler's proposals. The first two, to remove appellate jurisdiction in bar admission cases and to reverse *Watkins* by making the presiding officer of an investigation the judge of the pertinency of a question,[13] were approved by identical 9–6 votes. In each instance the three conservative Republicans, Hruska, Dirksen, and Watkins, as well as Olin Johnston and Sam Ervin, joined Jenner, Butler, Eastland, and McClellan to support the Court curb. A third Butler suggestion, that *Cole* v. *Young* be reversed by extending summary dismissal legislation to all federal jobs, was beaten when Johnston, Ervin, and Watkins switched their votes. McClellan did not vote on this question.

---

he did continue his education at night, obtaining an LL.B. from the University of Maryland in 1926. He stayed in private practice until 1947 when he served for two years with the Baltimore City Service Commission. In 1950 Butler got the Republican senatorial nomination even though he did not win a majority of the votes cast in the primary. With the aid of Senator McCarthy, Butler campaigned vigorously against Senator Millard Tydings and the Tydings Committee's "whitewash" of the State Department against McCarthy's charges of Communist infiltration. One of the methods used to defeat Tydings was the now famous composite picture showing Tydings and Earl Browder talking together. After the election, a Senate committee investigated the campaign and, while deploring such tactics, found no valid grounds to refuse to seat Butler. The Justice Department also announced that its own inquiry had revealed no basis for criminal prosecution. In the Senate, Butler joined the right wing of the Republican Party, consistently urging economy in government and advocating more stringent means of dealing with Communists. Except for one investigation of communism in labor unions, Butler's only previous legislative notoriety had come with his sponsoring the proposed constitutional amendment to freeze the Supreme Court's size and jurisdiction.

Nine days later the committee by a 10–5 vote—O'Mahoney sided with the right wing—approved S. 2646 with four amendments. All the jurisdiction clauses but one had been eliminated, and in addition to the *Watkins* change, *Nelson* was specifically reversed by the re-institution of state sedition statutes. The last two provisions modified the *Yates* decision. First, the Smith Act's definition of "organize" was broadened. Second, another clause declared that not only had the Court's distinction between incitement to action and advocacy of abstract doctrine "never [been] intended by the Congress," but such a distinction infused the statute with "uncertainty" and was highly "undesirable." Therefore, the Smith Act was to be amended to apply to the advocacy of violent overthrow of the government "without regard to the immediate probable effect of such action. . . ."

The five liberals on the committee filed three sets of minority views protesting against the bill. The Court defender bloc stressed that aside from the withdrawal of jurisdiction clause, no part of the amended bill had been the subject of hearings or investigations by the committee. To make up for this omission, the minority appended to their report[14] letters or telegrams from the Justice Department; the president of the American Bar Association; the deans of Harvard, Yale, Notre Dame, Indiana, and Pennsylvania law schools; the Association of the Bar of the City of New York; the St. Louis Bar Association; the Missouri Bar Board of Governors; the State Bar Association of Connecticut; the board of managers of the Chicago Bar; and, in their personal capacities, the chairmen of five other bar associations, including that of the state of Arkansas. All of these communications disapproved the amended bill. In addition, the Americans for Democratic Action, the American Veterans Committee, the NAACP, and in this strange company the *Chicago Tribune* and the board of governors of the ABA got themselves on record as being equally as opposed to the Jenner-Butler bill as to the original S. 2646.

Hennings scored another coup by writing retired Circuit Judge Learned Hand. In February, 1958, Hand had delivered the Oliver Wendell Holmes Lectures at Harvard,[15] and he had there continued his lifelong critique of the doctrine of judicial review. As always, Hand's remarks were pungent and quotable, and segregationists as well as other Jenner-Butler supporters had immediately boasted that the most revered of American jurists was on their side in the Court fight. A careful reading of the Holmes Lectures would have demolished this claim, but Hand exploded the myth himself by replying to a request for clarification from Hennings. Hand offered the opinion that a statute removing Supreme Court jurisdiction "if enacted would be detrimental to the best interests of the United States."

Despite these objections, the Jenner-Butler bill had overcome its first hurdle. S. 2646 had been approved in committee on April 30, although the formal report was not filed until May 15 to give the minority time to formulate their dissenting views. This left three full months before normal adjournment time for maneuvering, debate, and possible passage.

BARRIERS TO PASSAGE

There were three major obstacles now confronting the Jenner-Butler forces. The first was executive power and influence. The Justice Department had taken a resolute stand against S. 2646 in both its original and modified versions; but William S. White, writing during the critical period of committee debate in April, reported that for all its talk the White House was making no effort to line up party strength against the bill.[16] And when the vote came, five of the seven Republicans on the Judiciary Committee supported the amended measure.

When questioned at his news conference about the defection of supposed stalwarts like Watkins and Dirksen, Eisenhower confessed that he had not heard about the committee's division. Then commenting on the Jenner-Butler bill in general, the President explained his position in his own inimitable prose: "I do believe most emphatically in the separation of powers. But, let's not be too didactic, you might say, in exactly what the meaning of that expression is. . . . But on the other hand when we get down to this, just law interfering with the constitutional rights and powers and authority of the judiciary, I think that that will have to take a lot of studying, and by very fine lawyers, before I could see the justification of any law."[17]

A presidential veto was a major threat to the Jenner-Butler coalition; but the ambiguity of Eisenhower's remarks and his failure to utilize party machinery against the bill were taken by anti-Court senators to mean that the executive department would follow the same laissez faire attitude toward congressional action which had characterized much of the previous five years of the Eisenhower administration.

The House might be stampeded into approval by the Red Specter, but the Senate liberals would be more of an immediate problem. Carroll, Hennings, and Wiley were respected men in the Senate, and they were already working in close co-operation with other liberals like Paul Douglas, Hubert Humphrey, Wayne Morse, and Jacob Javits. On May 1, Javits had attempted to counter the S. 2646 blow by introducing, with seven cosponsors, a constitutional amendment freezing the Court's appellate jurisdiction.[18] But no such amendment was likely to pass, as no one knew better than Butler. Moreover, through southern control of key Senate committees, plus the personal prestige of senators like Richard Russell of Georgia, the Jenner-Butler people could hope to more than offset liberal strength, particularly since liberal leaders like Morse and Douglas were not members of the Senate's inner circle.

The third barrier was Lyndon Baines Johnson, the astute, hard-working, fifty-year-old Texan, who was thought by some observers to be the shrewdest Senate Majority leader of the century. A one-time fire-eating New Dealer who had headed the Texas branch of the National Youth Administration, Johnson had been elected to Congress in 1937 on a platform indorsing FDR's Court-packing plan. Eleven years' experience in the House and ten additional years in the Senate had mellowed Johnson into a liberal conservative or a conservative liberal.* His middle-of-the-road ideology plus his coming from a partly southern, partly western state had put him in an excellent position to parlay his natural diplomatic talents into a means for keeping the Democratic party together and the Senate running smoothly. Furthermore, Johnson's success in building up a reservoir of personal power had encouraged him to think of himself as a logical candidate for the 1960 presidential nomination. Because of his influence and ambitions, Johnson would have a crucial role in determining the fate of S. 2646—or any other Court legislation.

* In his detailed case study of the Eighty-first Congress, David Truman notes that Johnson's voting position placed him in the center of his party. *The Congressional Party* (New York: John Wiley & Sons, Inc., 1959), p. 113. See also Truman's comments on Johnson's personality and leadership, pp. 116 n., 307 ff., 314 ff.

H.R. 3 AGAIN

In its annual report, James O. Eastland's Internal Security Subcommittee reinforced the attack of S. 2646. Lacing into the June, 1957, political offender decisions, the report, drafted largely by J. G. Sourwine, accused the Court of "semantic obtuseness" and "sophistry" in *Yates*. *Watkins* was described as a "grasping [of] the power to declare not the acts of Congress, but the official *activities* of the Congress to be unconstitutional." At the end of its section on legislative problems, the report concluded: "Decisions of the Supreme Court during 1957 operated to continue the undermining of official efforts at effective anti-Communist activity in the United States."[19]

The Warren Court was faring no better in the other wing of the Capitol. Fresh anti-Court bills and fresh anti-Court speeches were swelling the *Congressional Record*. Wint Smith of Kansas spoke for many of those concerned with problems of internal security when he said that the "Warren Court has now thrown its protective cloak around fellow travellers and Communists. The Court is simply blind to the reality of our time."[20]

The segregation people were willing to carry more than their share of the oratorical burden. Howard Smith of Virginia stated: "To put it plainly and bluntly, the Supreme Court has seized the power to write 'the law of the land' contrary to and in defiance of the Constitution."[21] Colmer of Mississippi begged for strong congressional action. "[T]here is a real impelling and urgent need to curb this Court if any semblance of the United States Constitution, the sovereignty of the several States of the Union, and the basic principles and institutions of this free land are to be preserved for posterity."[22]

Far more important than these verbal attacks was the proposed anti-Court legislation. Emanuel Celler had sat on H.R. 3 during 1957. In 1958, however, Howard Smith, as chairman of the House Rules Committee, had been able to force Celler to hold additional hearings, this time on H.R. 3 and eight similar bills.[23] Only two witnesses appeared at this third set of hearings, Howard Smith and a former federal district judge, Lawrence Walsh, now Deputy Attorney General. Walsh set out once more the executive department's disapproval of the misty scope of H.R. 3, and suggested that in its place

Congress pass specific legislation giving the states authority to re-enter the field of sedition against the national government.

Smith repeated his arguments for the bill, and under questioning he made it quite plain that his proposal was intended to apply not only to future laws but to every statute in the Federal Code:

> SMITH: ". . . Let me say very emphatically that if you are going to talk about prospective legislation, let us drop the whole subject now because Congress can always do that."
>
> CELLER: "You say that your bill is retroactive, covers all past laws?"
>
> SMITH: "It covers existing law, yes. It merely says to the Supreme Court, 'If we intend to take jurisdiction away from the States, we are going to say so.' "
>
> . . . .
>
> CELLER: "Would that not put a different construction on this, different from what the Court interpreted Congress intended, and, therefore, it might unsettle many, many cases that have been settled?"
>
> SMITH: "I hope to goodness it will unsettle some of them. That is what I am trying to do."

The fight for H.R. 3 went on within the House Judiciary Committee. Celler had hoped that holding the hearings would stall Smith, but the Virginian wanted his bill to reach the floor as soon as possible. He put triple pressure on Celler by delaying a rule on legislation which Celler considered important and by making a veiled but unmistakable threat to exercise the Rules Committee's authority to take a bill out of the hands of a standing committee.[24] Most effectively of all, Smith worked on other members of the judiciary group, letting them know that not only Celler's bills but theirs as well would have a tough time getting a rule if H.R. 3 did not come out of committee soon.

With the added pressure from southern committee members who wanted to see the measure passed, Celler had no choice but to call his group together for a vote. On June 13, the bill, in a slightly amended form, was reported favorably,[25] although ten of the thirty-two committee members dissented. The committee version of H.R. 3 contained the essence of Smith's original proposal; the change consisted mainly in compressing Smith's two-sentence bill into a single sentence:

> No Act of Congress shall be construed as indicating an intent on the part of Congress to occupy the field in which such Act operates, to the exclusion of all State laws on the same subject matter, unless such Act contains an express provision to that effect, or unless there is a direct and positive conflict between such Act and a State law so that the two cannot be reconciled or consistently stand together.

Led by Celler, nine members of the committee signed a minority report charging that H.R. 3 would "take us back to the Articles of Confederation." The minority added: "Seldom has the House had before it a bill so productive of chaos, in the legal relationships governing substantial areas of American economic and political life. Ironically, there has seldom been a bill which is more likely to prove a disappointment to its advocates. . . . H.R. 3 is a horse-and-buggy formula applied to an atomic age."

Kenneth Keating of New York filed a separate set of views. Although expressing sympathy with the majority's desire to "correct a number of recent Supreme Court decisions based on misinterpretations of congressional intent," Keating seriously doubted whether H.R. 3 would perform that function. Indeed, he flatly stated that the bill would not curb "judicial law-making." Quite the contrary, by its very vagueness "it virtually enjoins the Court to act as a quasi-Congressional body set up to reexamine the legislative intentions of enactments going back in some instances more than 100 years."

COLE V. YOUNG: THE REACH OF THE SUMMARY SUSPENSION ACT

After more than thirty-eight months of maneuvering and feuding, H.R. 3 had finally cleared the Judiciary Committee, and with Howard Smith as chairman of the Rules Committee, a favorable decision there was a foregone conclusion. H.R. 3 was the second piece of anti-Court legislation ready for House action. Immediately after the 1956 decision in *Cole* v. *Young,* a number of bills had been introduced in both houses to extend the coverage of the Summary Suspension Act of 1950 to "non-sensitive" as well as "sensitive" jobs. Senate proposals sponsored by McCarthy, Mundt, and Eastland were reported out by the Internal Security Subcommittee,[26] but had never got past the full Judiciary Committee. Companion measures in the House,[27] although indorsed by the Justice Department and the Civil Service Commission, had met a similar fate.

In the summer of 1957, the Senate Post Office and Civil Service Committee approved S. 1411,[28] a mild bill sponsored by the administration. The Justice Department had changed its mind in the months since *Cole* v. *Young*. S. 1411 did not attempt to reverse the Court; rather it softened existing law by easing the provision which made mandatory the suspension of employees suspected of being security risks. For this requirement the administration bill substituted an arrangement which would have allowed the head of a federal agency, at his discretion, to retain such people pending a hearing and final determination of their status.

In August, 1957, the Senate took time out from the business of civil rights and the Jencks case to pass S. 1411 with no more floor discussion than a brief explanation of the measure by Post Office and Civil Service Committee Chairman Olin Johnston.[29]

The House Post Office Committee acted swiftly. Tom Murray, Johnston's opposite number in the House, was the author of the Summary Suspension Act of 1950, and he had been incensed at the *Cole* decision as a violation of congressional intent. At the time S. 1411 was passed by the Senate, Murray had been holding hearings on legislation to reverse the Court, and he seized on the opportunity presented by the Senate. Retaining only the enacting clause of S. 1411, Murray's committee substituted the text of Francis Walter's measure to extend summary suspension provisions to all federal jobs.[30]

The House committee report expressed agreement with the dissenting opinion of Justices Clark, Reed, and Minton that *Cole* v. *Young* had "stricken down the most effective weapon against subversive activity available to the government." Explaining that this decision had created a "grave situation," the committee stressed that the need for new legislation was "urgent." In support, the report cited earlier letters from the Justice Department as well as Civil Service Commission statements from the previous year that, until and unless Congress acted, 80 per cent of federal employees would be outside the reach of the loyalty-security program.

THE GREAT WRIT

A third old-timer among anti-Court bills was a piece of habeas corpus legislation.[31] Under Supreme Court interpretations of existing statutes, a prisoner convicted in a state court had two successive avenues of access to review in the federal courts. First, he could appeal through the state judicial system and then petition the U.S. Supreme Court for certiorari. If he were unsuccessful in this effort, he could seek a writ of habeas corpus in a federal district court, and, if this were denied, appeal to the Court of Appeals and finally to the U.S. Supreme Court again.

This double review had been galling to state officials who disapproved of a single-judge federal court sitting in judgment on a decision of the highest state tribunal. As the 1952 Conference of State Chief Justices said: "Orderly Federal procedure under our dual system of Government should require that a final judgment of a State's highest court be subject to review only by the Supreme Court of the United States."[32] Striking from a different angle, police officials had condemned the delays which the second avenue of appeal had caused in the administration of criminal law. In addition, many federal judges had expressed displeasure with the Supreme Court's interpretation of the habeas corpus statutes in that over a seventeen-year span it had piled more than 8,500 cases onto already overcrowded dockets. And most of these petitions were merely frivolous, dilatory efforts to postpone executions. In fact, the federal courts were granting less than 2 per cent of these requests. As one judge noted in an official opinion: "[O]ur sphere of superintendence should not extend to state police activities; there the state courts should have the burden, subject only to certiorari in the Supreme Court in the few cases where needed."[33]

After extensive hearings, the House Judiciary Committee in 1955 favorably reported[34] a measure drafted by a special committee of the Judicial Conference of the United States, headed by the late Judge John J. Parker, in co-operation with the Conference of State Chief Justices. The Parker bill, the first piece of legislation ever drawn up by the joint action of these two judicial organizations, would have allowed state prisoners to seek habeas corpus in federal courts only where all three of the following conditions were met: (1) a question of federal constitutional rights had not previously been "raised and determined" in the state proceedings; (2) the petitioner had not had a fair opportunity in the state courts to raise the federal issue; and (3) that issue could not be subsequently raised in the state courts.

The Parker bill, supported by the Justice Department, the National Association of Attorneys General, the American Bar Association's section on judicial administration, and, of course, the Judicial Conference and the State Chief Justices, passed the House in 1956 almost without debate. The Eighty-fourth Congress, however, adjourned while the measure was still pending in the Senate Judiciary Committee. Reintroduced in the Eighty-fifth Congress, the bill was not acted on during 1957, but in January, 1958, the House committee again reported the measure out with the recommendation that it "do pass."[35]

The habeas corpus changes provided a particularly attractive means of attacking the Warren Court. Not only did this bill enable the anti-Court bloc to identify itself with respected groups of judges who were seeking more efficient judicial administration, but the Parker proposal could be cited as further evidence that the Justices had been abusing their power in creating loopholes through which convicted criminals were escaping punishment. Most basically, the philosophy of the Supreme Court habeas corpus decisions, in preferring strict scrutiny of constitutional rights of individuals to state autonomy in criminal procedures, ran counter to much of the philosophy uniting the Court foes. Thus to an extent which went far beyond the terms of the actual bill, the habeas corpus changes became significant symbols of underlying differences on public policy.

MALLORY AND POLICE DETENTION

Mallory v. *United States* had made a fresher wound in the field of criminal law. This decision had provoked a series of bills similar to those *McNabb* had elicited fourteen years earlier. The proposal which caught the public spotlight was that of Kenneth Keating. It provided simply that a delay in arraignment would not of itself invalidate a statement or confession otherwise admissible in evidence in a federal court.

In the summer of 1957, a special subcommittee of the House Judiciary Committee was appointed to study the controversial cases of the 1956 Term. Chaired by Edwin Willis of Louisiana, the hearings[36] opened within a few weeks after the Court had adjourned. With attention centered on *Mallory*, a number of law enforcement officials were called on to testify. The U.S. attorney for the District of Columbia, the Washington police chief, the chief of detectives for the District of Columbia, two representatives from the Post Office Department, the acting chief of the U.S. Park Police, and the Los Angeles police chief, all stated unequivocally that the Supreme Court had created an emergency situation which demanded immediate remedial action to save the capital from a crime wave.

Robert Murray, chief of the Metropolitan police, told the subcommittee that *Mallory* would "in my opinion, cause a complete breakdown in law enforcement." Edgar Scott, chief of detectives, testified that "if we work under the Mallory ruling, there will be thousands of guilty persons that will be freed. . . . This rule encourages the criminal." William H. Parker, Los Angeles police chief and more famous as the technical adviser to the TV drama "Dragnet," appeared as a representative of the International Association of Police Chiefs and tried to establish a direct link between recent court decisions protecting defendants' rights and the rising crime rate. Fearful that the Supreme Court would extend the *Mallory* doctrine to state as well as federal officers, Parker warned that such a move "would destroy modern law enforcement as practiced and as preached today."

Testimony was also given by George M. Hart, Jr., then a Washington lawyer and chairman of the Law Enforcement Commission of the District of Columbia. Hart, who was soon to be appointed a federal district judge, praised the Keating bill as establishing the proper balance between the public interest in efficient police work and the protection of citizens' constitutional rights.

Warren Olney III, Assistant Attorney General in charge of the criminal division of the Justice Department, appeared as a witness, but he made it clear that he would be speaking largely for himself since he had not had time to consult at any length with the Solicitor General or other officials. The Justice Department, Olney stated, would not oppose bills modeled along the lines of Keating's proposal. In offering his personal opinion, Olney was much more emphatic. He not only warmly approved the Keating bill but advocated quick passage as well. "It seems to me that the application of this decision . . . shows that there is a plain and immediate necessity for some kind of action if we are not going to have a very serious condition result."

Opposing any new legislation were three Washington lawyers, Myron Ehrlich, chairman of the committee on criminal rules and procedure of the District of Columbia Bar, James J. Laughlin, and Albert Ahern. All three were critical in varying degrees of the past conduct of the Metropolitan police force, and each urged that Congress undertake a full study of the situation and delay any legislative action until a reasonable operation of the *Mallory* rule would allow a calm evaluation of the dire warnings of the law enforcement officials.

In February, 1958, the special subcommittee received a pair of communications. The National Society of the Sons of the American Revolution strongly criticized the *Mallory* decision and recommended swift corrective action. On the other hand, the American Civil Liberties Union, the American Veterans Committee, the Americans for Democratic Action, the Friends Committee on National Legislation, the International Union of Electrical, Radio & Machine Workers, The United Auto Workers, and the Workers Defense League signed a joint letter defending the Supreme Court's decision:

> The Mallory case forced the Supreme Court to choose between sending a man to his death on the basis of a confession obtained in flagrant disregard of our most cherished traditions, and holding that the United States did not need to base its convictions upon tainted evidence. . . . It is vital to understand how little the Court actually did in the Mallory case. The Court did not hold that Mallory should go free. It only reaffirmed its previous decision that in the Federal courts one cannot be adjudged a criminal on the strength of damaging statements drawn out of him in the sinister circumstances of illegal, incommunicado detention. . . . Significantly, the Government did not avail itself of its second chance to convict Mallory because, apart from the admissions that were illegally obtained from him, there was not even sufficient evidence to go to trial, let alone to convict.

The Willis subcommittee recommended to the House Judiciary Committee that new legislation should be adopted to "clarify" the *Mallory* rule, but just as with the other anti-Court bills, there were deep divisions within the parent committee. On May 27, 1958, a majority of the judiciary group reported out a compromise measure,[37] H.R. 11477, dubbed the Keating-Willis bill. H.R. 11477 would have added two subsections to Title 18 of the *U.S. Code*. The first would have held that evidence "otherwise admissible" should not be deemed inadmissible "solely because of delay" in bringing an accused before a magistrate. The second section would have made inadmissible as evidence any statement to a law enforcement official unless the accused were first advised of his constitutional right to silence and warned that anything said might be used against him.

In March, 1958, before the House Judiciary Committee had reported the Keating-Willis bill, Senator Hennings' Subcommittee on Constitutional Rights also conducted hearings on *Mallory*.[38] Hennings, of course, supported the *Mallory* decision and secured testimony from a number of witnesses, including three law school professors from Harvard and Georgetown universities and representatives from the ACLU, the ADA, and the National Bar Association, all opposing any revision of the Federal Rules of Criminal Procedure which might reverse or modify the *McNabb-Mallory* rule.

On the other hand, Judge Alexander Holtzoff told the subcommittee that the advisory group which had helped draw up Rule 5(a) had considered and rejected wording that would have been open to the interpretation the Court had applied in *Mallory*. The *McNabb-Mallory* doctrine, the federal district judge stated, "often unnecessarily blocks the work of the police and other investigative agencies and at times leads to acquitting the guilty. It is not necessary for the proper and legitimate protection of the accused and it may seriously hamper the administration of justice and interfere with the protection of the public."

Edgar Scott, chief of the District of Columbia detective force, was more blunt in his criticism. Asserting that *Mallory* would be "disastrous" to law enforcement, Scott turned on the defenders of the Court:

> Now, some people who seem to be afraid of remedial legislation have been screaming about the Constitution, due process of law, the Bill of Rights, and probable cause, and so forth, but the truth is, of course, that none of these things are involved in the Mallory decision. . . . Such references to rights which we all hold sacred become excellent tools in the hands of those who would throw up a smoke-

screen to obscure the real issue here. I, personally, think it would be well to examine some of these persons to see what selfish interest they might have in seeking to make it easy to get criminals off.

The Hennings hearings assembled a great deal of useful background material on the whole problem of police detention and law enforcement difficulties. This work, however, served no immediate purpose since the hearings were not printed until after adjournment, and because, as Hennings well knew, Eastland would not give the Constitutional Rights Subcommittee jurisdiction over any anti-Court legislation which he wanted adopted.

THE MEANING OF "ORGANIZE"

Much later in the summer, the House Judiciary Committee recommended another proposal aimed at a specific Supreme Court decision. Four bills to reverse the *Yates* decision's narrow definition of the term "organize" in the Smith Act had been introduced in the Eighty-fifth Congress,[39] and Willis' special subcommittee had heard brief testimony[40] from the attorneys general of New Hampshire and Idaho and the assistant attorney general of Wisconsin advising adoption of an amendment to the Smith Act so as to include under proscribed activities the forming of new units or the expansion of existing units of a group aiming at violent overthrow of the government. Without any other formal investigation except a letter from Deputy U.S. Attorney General Walsh supporting such a bill, the Judiciary Committee favorably reported Francis Walter's H.R. 13272.[41]

Referring to the *Yates* decision's "deleterious effect upon the Government's efforts to combat the Communist conspiracy," the report stated: "From a study of the legislative history of the Smith Act, and as a matter of common sense, the committee is of the opinion that the term 'organize' was intended to mean a continuous process of organizing groups and cells and recruiting new members and not merely the original organization of the Communist Party or some other party. . . ."

The Court supporters had been backed into the untenable position of having to advocate easing restrictions on Communists to defend the Court; and, although Willis rather than Chairman Emanuel

Celler presented the report, no committee member filed any minority views on the Yates bill.

THE HOUSE APPROVES THE ANTI-COURT BILLS

The Court-curbing stage had been set by the favorable committee reports, and Howard Smith supplied the necessary rules to clear the bills for the floor. With these roadblocks eliminated, the House quickly approved all the reported bills. The habeas corpus proposal was adopted on March 18.[42] On July 2, the Mallory bill received a thumping 294–79 majority;[43] eight days later, the *Cole* v. *Young* measure was passed by an even more impressive margin of 298–46.[44] On July 17, H.R. 3 received a 241–155 indorsement;[45] and on August 12, the bill to broaden the definition of "organize" in the Smith Act passed by a voice vote.[46]

The roll calls showed a solid conservative Republican–Southern Democratic coalition opposing a demoralized aggregate of northern Democrats and a few liberal Republicans. Voting for the Mallory bill were 169 Republicans and 125 Democrats, 75 of whom were from the South* and 21 from border states. The Justice Department had expressed no objections to changing the *Mallory* rule (in fact Olney had personally backed Keating's bill), but it had voiced militant opposition to H.R. 3. Indeed, on July 15 Kenneth Keating had read a statement to the House that the President had serious doubts about the bill as it then stood.† Nevertheless, 140 Republicans voted for the measure, joined by 101 Democrats, 88 of whom were from the South* and 10 from border states. Only 46 Republicans voted against Smith's bill.

There was an even more resounding Republican repudiation of

* Texas is counted as southern in these figures.

† Keating was careful not to say that the President would veto the bill. In light of future developments in the Senate, Keating's statement should be quoted: "At this point, I think I should read into the RECORD a statement I am authorized to make which was given to me this morning and from which I give you my understanding of the position of the President of the United States. Both he and the Attorney General are for the objectives of this bill. . . . However—and I have written this down because I want to be accurate—the President has serious questions about the generalities of the bill. On the advice of the Attorney General, under its present provisions, he feels it would cause serious difficulty." 104 *Congressional Record* 13854.

the administration on the *Cole* v. *Young* measure. The Department of Justice had asked that the bill be shelved until a full study of the loyalty-security program could be completed. In spite of this request not a single GOP representative voted against the bill, and only Burdick of North Dakota was paired against it. The sole concession made to the executive branch was a clause specifying that the measure was meant to be a temporary rather than a permanent solution. Apparently the Red label had instilled fear in most congressmen. Only 46 Democratic votes could be mustered against the *Cole* reversal.

THE "INDIRECT APPROACH" IN POLITICAL STRATEGY

House passage of five of the anti-Court bills and the Senate Judiciary Committee's action on Jenner-Butler brought the legislative attacks on the Warren Court close to a climax. Unlike the Jenner-Butler bill, none of the House measures struck directly at judicial power, but collectively they were classic examples of the "indirect approach" in political strategy. They were symbols, symbols of congressional repudiation of the moral authority of the Warren Court to lead the nation. And lacking either means of physical coercion or control of money, the Court's power teeters on its moral authority far more precariously than that of either Congress or the President. If Jenner-Butler or all or most of the House bills were enacted into law the resurgence of judicial power would come crashing down.

8. OCTOBER TERM, 1957

While the anti-Court people in the House of Representatives were persuading a majority of their colleagues to go along with their efforts to undermine judicial power, the 1957 Term was drawing to a close. The Justices might have looked as serenely indifferent to worldly cares as ever, but neither the thick marble of the Court's exterior walls nor the velvet tapestries of its inner sanctum could insulate Warren and his brethren from the effects of the storm that was raging on Capitol Hill. This year, as usual, the Court docket contained important cases, and decisions in those cases would further embroil the High Bench in the legislative struggle.

FREEDOM OF ASSOCIATION

In the race relations field, *NAACP* v. *Patterson* temporarily frustrated Alabama's efforts to drive the Negro organization out of the state by demanding the names and addresses of all members of the association. For a unanimous Court, Harlan recognized that the purpose of Alabama's action was to expose these Negroes to private and possibly public sanctions because they had dared to exercise their constitutional rights. "We hold that the immunity from state scrutiny of membership lists which the Association claims on behalf of its members is here so related to the right of the members to pursue their lawful private interests privately and to associate freely with others in so doing as to come within the protection of the Fourteenth Amendment."

ALIENS AND CITIZENS

In two other civil liberties sore spots the Court worked within the interstices of existing law to increase individual security. It had long been settled that Congress could deport an alien for any reason it chose, since a foreigner had no constitutional right to be in the United States in the first place. In 1954 *Galvan* v. *Press* had reaffirmed this doctrine in its harshest form by allowing, under the Internal Security Act of 1950, the deportation of a Mexican because of Communist party membership between 1944–46. The Court had ruled, with Black and Douglas dissenting, that it was not even necessary under the statute that Galvan have had knowledge of any illegal aims of the Communist party; it was enough that he had joined the group of his own free will.

Despite this decision, the Warren Court had generally been more solicitous of the rights of aliens than had the Vinson Court.[1] As in other fields of cold war litigation, the High Bench had not limited the substantive power of Congress, but had taken a narrow interpretation of existing statutes and had insisted that the Justice Department observe strict procedural standards in deportation actions. And, early in the 1957 Term, *Rowoldt* v. *Perfetto* cut sharply into the value of *Galvan* v. *Press* as a precedent. Writing the majority opinion, Frankfurter—who had also been the author of the *Galvan* opinion—held that even though the petitioner had admitted being a member and a functionary of the Communist party for about a year in 1935, this admission was insufficient to justify deportation:

> Bearing in mind the solidity of proof that is required for a judgment entailing the consequences of deportation, particularly in the case of an old man who has lived in this country for forty years, we

> cannot say that the unchallenged account given by petitioner of his relations to the Communist Party establishes the kind of meaningful association required by the alleviating Amendment of 1951. . . .

Dissenting for himself, Burton, Clark, and Whittaker, Harlan pointed out that the "alleviating Amendment of 1951" to the Internal Security Act had been "motivated solely by the problems of aliens who were being *excluded* from entry into the United States because they had joined totalitarian organizations in foreign countries." Harlan expressed sympathy with Rowoldt's plight, as well as regret at his inability to concur in Frankfurter's opinion. "The difficulty is that in order to reach its result the Court has had to take impermissible liberties with the statute and the record upon which this case is based."

An unbroken line of cases had established, over dissents from libertarian judges, that the citizenship of a naturalized citizen could be canceled if it were later shown that there had been fraud in the naturalization proceedings.[2] Here, too, the Warren Court had insisted on strict standards. In 1958 two cases[3] held that questions asked by the government during the 1930's concerning the membership of prospective citizens in organizations advocating the violent overthrow of the government had been ambiguous and that membership in the Communist party in this period did not of itself provide "clear, unequivocal, and convincing" evidence that the applicants had not been attached to the principles of the Constitution.

CRUEL AND UNUSUAL PUNISHMENT: A PERTINENT DEBATE

In *Trop* v. *Dulles* a bare majority put aside statutory interpretation and struck directly at congressional power. For the third time since Warren had become Chief Justice, the Court declared an act of Congress unconstitutional,[4] and, as in each of the other two instances, the statute involved delegation of authority to military tribunals. Warren, for himself, Black, Douglas, and Whittaker, held that a law establishing loss of citizenship as a penalty for wartime desertion was a "cruel and unusual punishment" forbidden by the Eighth Amendment. Such punishment did violence to civilized standards by taking away "the right to have rights." Brennan concurred in a separate opinion in which he denied the authority of Congress under its war powers to enact a statute wreaking "naked vengeance." Frankfurter, joined by Burton, Clark, and Harlan, disputed the judgment that loss of citizenship was a penalty forbidden by the Constitution. The dissenters deemed this question a matter left to the determination of Congress.

Trop v. *Dulles* had implications which, in light of the Court crisis of 1958, went far beyond the problems of constitutional rights of deserters. In their opinions Warren and Frankfurter engaged in a pertinent debate regarding authority of the Supreme Court vis-à-vis Congress. Frankfurter extolled the virtues of self-restraint and respect for co-ordinate agencies of government:

> Rigorous observance of the difference between limits of power and wise exercise of power—between questions of authority and questions of prudence—require the most alert appreciation of this decisive but subtle relationship of two concepts that too easily coalesce. No less does it require a disciplined will to adhere to the difference. It is not easy to stand aloof and allow want of wisdom to prevail. . . . But it is not the business of this Court to pronounce policy. . . . That self-restraint is of the essence of the judicial oath, for the Constitution has not authorized the judges to sit in judgment on the wisdom of what Congress and the Executive Branch do.

Warren replied in equally forceful language and demonstrated why his concept of the role of the Court and his leadership had brought the Justices into conflict with Congress:

> We are oath-bound to defend the Constitution. This obligation requires that congressional enactments be judged by the standards of the Constitution. . . . We cannot push back the limits of the Constitution merely to accommodate challenged legislation. . . . We do well to approach this task cautiously, as all our predecessors have counseled. But the ordeal of judgment cannot be shirked. In some 81 instances since this Court was established it has determined that congressional action exceeded the bounds of the Constitution. It is so in this case.

FREEDOM TO TRAVEL: THE PASSPORT PROBLEM

Trop v. *Dulles* provided an excellent platform for display of conflicting judicial philosophies, but it was the Passport cases[5] which brought the biggest headlines of the 1957 Term. The State Department had denied Rockwell Kent and Weldon B. Dayton passports to travel abroad because of their connections and associations with the Communist party. The lower courts had sustained the department's action, but the Supreme Court, with Frankfurter joining the liberal bloc, reversed both decisions by identical 5–4 votes. Douglas, for the majority, took a surprisingly middle-of-the-road position and employed the standard tactics of the Warren Court. First, he rattled the big stick of the Bill of Rights, warning that "the right to travel" was protected by the due process clause. Then, after pointing to this constitutional protection, Douglas declared that it was unnecessary to decide such issues since the Secretary of State had relied on erroneous statutory interpretation. Congress had never authorized a denial of passports because of beliefs or associations.

In their dissents, Clark, Burton, Harlan, and Whittaker did not reach the constitutional question either, but they were convinced that Congress had delegated authority to the Secretary of State to deny passports in such cases. Indeed, they claimed that the Court had decided this issue in 1939.[6]

COLD WAR MISCELLANY

In several other decisions related to the cold war, the Warren Court continued to antagonize the security-conscious. *Sacher* v. *United States* reaffirmed the *Watkins* rule by reversing, without oral argument, a contempt of Congress conviction. In two state cases,[7] the Court, without reaching basic constitutional issues, ruled that California constitutional and statutory provisions which made tax immunity for religious and charitable institutions dependent on loyalty oaths did not meet requirements of procedural due process.

Harmon v. *Brucker* held that Congress had not authorized the army to give other than honorable discharges to draftees dismissed from military service because of pre-induction activities which affected their security status. This case caused a minor explosion in the usually placid atmosphere of the courtroom when, after considerable oral argument, counsel for the government conceded that the Justice Department agreed with the draftees on the substantive question and had so informed the Department of the Army. Not only did the government lawyer's admission provoke probing, and at first angry, questions from the Bench, but, as the argument closed, Warren and Frankfurter broke into a bitter bicker over whether the Chief Justice had authority to dispense the Solicitor General from the Court's traditional requirement of confessing error in writing.[8] Earlier in the term, Warren had caustically reprimanded Frankfurter for interrupting him while he was questioning an attorney; and late in the term a third Warren-Frankfurter exchange caused observers to wonder if a new intra-Court feud were developing.[9]

JUDICIAL STRAWS IN THE POLITICAL WIND

While the Court seemed to be following the general trend of its two previous terms, there were four cases which might have been construed as hints of an impending shift in judicial policy-making. Over dissents by Warren and Douglas (Black did not participate), *International Association of Machinists* v. *Gonzales* held that the Wagner and Taft-Hartley Acts did not pre-empt the field of labor relations to the extent of precluding state jurisdiction to entertain damage suits against a union by union members who had been expelled from the organization.

The backers of H.R. 3 might possibly have seen *Gonzales* as a break in the dike of pre-emptive federalism, as in fact Warren and Douglas did. Even more encouraging to those whose primary concern was internal subversion were two 5–4 decisions, *Beilan* v. *Board of Education* and *Lerner* v. *Casey*. Herman Beilan, a Philadelphia public school teacher, had been discharged as "incompetent" after he had refused to tell school authorities whether he had served in 1944 as press officer for the professional section of the Communist Political Association. Speaking for a majority composed of himself, Frankfurter, Clark, Harlan, and Whittaker, Burton disposed of the issues in an unusually brief opinion. The gist of his reasoning was that competency to teach was not restricted to classroom performance but depended on a broad range of factors. When Beilan had undertaken a public teaching job, he had assumed obligations of frankness and candor to his superiors, and the school board had found him remiss in these duties. Under such circumstances, his discharge violated no provision of the federal Constitution.

In the other case, Max Lerner, a New York subway conductor, had been fired because he had invoked the Fifth Amendment when city authorities had asked if he were currently a member of the Communist party. Harlan, speaking for the same five-judge majority in the *Beilan* decision, did a better job than had Burton in distinguishing the Court's reasoning in the 1956 Slochower case. That earlier decision, Harlan explained in his usual precise manner, had involved loss of state employment rights because of use of a federal constitutional right before an agency of the *federal* government. Lerner had lost his state job because he had refused to give a frank answer to questions posed by *state* authorities. New York law allowed dismissal when a person was found to be of doubtful loyalty—a classification the majority did not find arbitrary. And since the Fourteenth Amendment did not include protection from self-incrimination in a state proceeding, there was no constitutional bar to New York's action.

Douglas, with the concurrence of Black, filed a single dissent for both cases, asserting that the Court was permitting an inference of wrongdoing from the invocation of a constitutional right. Equating possible party membership with "belief," Douglas claimed that in effect Beilan and Lerner were being punished for their beliefs:

> Anyone who plots against the government and moves in treasonable opposition to it can be punished. Government rightly can concern itself with the actions of people. But it's time to call a halt to government penalizing people for their beliefs. . . . When we make the belief of the citizen the basis of government action, we move toward the concept of total security. Yet total security is possible only in a totalitarian regime—the kind of system we profess to combat.

In *Beilan* Warren wrote his own dissent, claiming that the situation was identical to that presented by *Slochower* in 1956. For thirteen months after his refusal to answer the school board's questions, Beilan had been retained as a teacher; he had been fired five days after he had utilized the Fifth Amendment before a subcommittee of the House Un-American Activities Committee. In *Lerner,* Warren joined Brennan's dissent, which charged the majority with being blind to the fact that Lerner had been dismissed for disloyalty on a record "wholly devoid" of evidence necessary to support such a finding.

Frankfurter's position in these cases was crucial. In *Lerner* and *Beilan* he represented the fifth vote, and in all three he had been the senior majority judge, responsible for assigning the opinion of the Court. In *Gonzales* he wrote the opinion himself; and in spite of his choice of Burton and Harlan to do the writing in the other two, he still felt constrained to append a short concurring opinion warning the dissenters of the dangers on the road they were traveling:

> The argument runs, in essence, that because such an inquiry may in certain instances lead to a determination of disloyalty, the refusal to answer any question in this process and dismissal therefor themselves establish disloyalty. To make such an attribution to the State from a carefully limited exercise of power . . . is a curbing of the States through the Fourteenth Amendment that makes of that Amendment an instrument of general censorship by this Court of state action.

In another decision, this one far quieter than any of the political offender cases, the Court refused to review a Pennsylvania ruling sustaining an evasion of the High Bench's 1957 decision in the Girard College litigation.[10] After the 1957 decision that the school was a state institution in terms of the Fourteenth Amendment's prohibition against racial discrimination, the trustees of Girard College had divested themselves of all state affiliation and had continued to bar Negroes. The Court's denial of certiorari could have been seen as an implication, at least, that southern efforts to thwart the effects of the school segregation decisions via "private" educational systems might not run into insuperable constitutional difficulties.

NO RESPITE

Gonzales, Beilan, Lerner, and the refusal to review the Girard College case might have been omens of future changes in Supreme Court policy; but, if so, they did not yet foretell shifts of the same magnitude as had the *Parrish* and *Jones & Laughlin* decisions in 1937. Nor were they tactically similar. In 1937 Hughes had led the Court in its withdrawal from the field of constitutional battle. In 1958, if the Court were about to retreat, the Chief Justice had been left behind in command of a hold-at-all-costs rear guard.

The critics of the Warren Court might have been able to take some encouragement from these four decisions, but they did not. The Court was still formulating public policy, and doing so in areas which many congressmen viewed as their own private preserve. The *NAACP* decision was an advance toward rather than a withdrawal from integration, and the Court's refusal to review the Girard case could be dismissed as meaningless since the Justices themselves often stated that denial of certiorari did not imply any views on the merits of a case.

The tenor of the other civil liberties decisions, especially those involving alien and citizenship questions, more than outweighed any "benefit" from *Beilan* and *Lerner*. Nor did *Gonzales* bring wild cries of delight. After all, it did not repudiate the pre-emptive doctrine. And the most far reaching decisions of the term, the Passport cases, were interpreted as another blow at national security. Senator Jenner described them as "the latest havoc wrought by the United States Supreme Court. . . . As a result of these decisions, Communist conspirators are being dispatched abroad on treasonous errands."[11]

The executive department also intervened at this point. All matters of the Court struggle aside, the President and his advisers were worried about the effects of the Passport decisions; and on July 7 Eisenhower sent a formal message to Congress requesting immediate legislation to give the Secretary of State authority to refuse passports for reasons of national security. "I wish," the President wrote, "to emphasize the urgency of the legislation I have recommended. Each day and week that passes without it exposes us to great danger."[12] The House reacted with moderate haste—by congressional standards —and passed a slightly modified administration bill on August 23,[13] but by that time affairs in the upper chamber had grown too complex for quick action.

9. SHOWDOWN IN THE SENATE

House passage of the Court bills poured the struggle over judicial power into the saucer of the Senate; but unlike George Washington's famous cup of tea, there would be no cooling effect, at least not immediately.[1] For here the battle would be fought far more savagely than in the lower chamber, though the manner of combat would be radically different. Concealed behind trappings of elegant debate and complex parliamentary rules would be the peculiar political ethic of a most peculiar political institution. The Senate of the United States, William S. White has eulogized, "is an odd, mixed place. It is hard and efficient, and it is soft and dawdling. It is harsh, and it is kind. It is dignity, and it is disorder. It is arrogant, and it is humble."[2] It is, above all, a place where institutional history and tradition dominate. It is a place which has as much, perhaps, in common with the marble temple across the plaza as with the other wing of the Capitol building.

THE JUDICIARY COMMITTEE ACTS

The Senate showdown got off to a quiet beginning. On July 29, on the motion of Olin D. Johnston, the Senate rejected the House amendments to S. 1411, the *Cole* v. *Young* bill, and appointed five conferees to meet with the House managers.[3] The major portion of the Court proposals, however, went directly to James O. Eastland's Judiciary Committee.

The Jenner-Butler bill had brought out the divisions within the judiciary group, and the best the liberals could hope for was to slow the progress of the Court bills. But there were limits to the delay that could be obtained, and in late summer Eastland began forcing the Court measures out of committee. On August 5, S. 654 was favorably reported.[4] This was a proposal to reverse *Pennsylvania* v. *Nelson* by reinstating state sedition laws. Originally introduced by Styles Bridges of New Hampshire, its twenty cosponsors included the late Joseph McCarthy, William Jenner, Senate Minority leader William Knowland, and Irving Ives of New York, as well as liberals like Alexander Wiley of Wisconsin and Jacob Javits of New York.

The next day, the Parker bill to revise habeas corpus proceedings came out of committee,[5] together with S. 337,[6] the Senate companion to H.R. 3, introduced by John McClellan of Arkansas for himself, ten other Southern Democrats, and four midwestern Republicans. The liberals did secure one significant change from H.R. 3. At the suggestion of O'Mahoney, S. 337 was amended to be prospective rather than retroactive in effect. As reported, the bill would have excised the pre-emption doctrine only from future congressional legislation.

The Mallory bill caused more immediate complications. Hennings' subcommittee hearings in the spring had led to no action. And knowing Hennings' feelings on the matter, when the House bill came to his committee Eastland had assigned it to O'Mahoney's subcommittee rather than Hennings' group.* This was the same subcommittee which had handled the Jencks legislation in 1957; the only change in membership had been the replacement of the late Senator Neely of West Virginia by John Carroll of Colorado.

* This was perfectly proper since the Federal Code Subcommittee had at least as much of a jurisdictional claim as the Constitutional Rights Subcommittee.

Eastland and Butler were clearly out to strike at the Warren Court and *Mallory* was as good an instrument as any. Dirksen was vacillating, though he tended to side with Eastland and Butler on this particular issue. Carroll was a pro-Court liberal who, while opposing the Keating-Willis bill, was willing to concede that legislation to clarify *Mallory* would not necessarily be harmful, though he wished to restrict any legislation to the District of Columbia rather than include general federal law enforcement. This line-up permitted O'Mahoney to clear the House bill for full committee action, but with a promise to Carroll that he would work out an amendment to make the measure more palatable to the liberals.

In the full Judiciary Committee meeting on August 4, the matter of an amendment was thrashed out. Carroll did not pursue his plan to restrict the legislation to Washington, and instead proposed that the Keating-Willis bill be changed to provide that confessions obtained during "necessary delay" should not be excluded from evidence. O'Mahoney offered "reasonable" as a substitute for "necessary." Then Kefauver tried to incorporate both changes by suggesting "reasonably necessary." After some dicussion, the committee agreed on O'Mahoney's proposal.[7]

As amended, H.R. 11477 retained the clause declaring that to be admissible a confession or statement had to be preceded by advice to the suspect of his right to silence and a warning that anything said might be used against him. But the opening section now read:

> Evidence, including statements and confessions, otherwise admissible, shall not be inadmissible solely because of *reasonable* delay in taking an arrested person before a commissioner or other officer empowered to commit persons charged with offenses against the laws of the United States.

Only the old Non-Partisan League campaigner from North Dakota, William Langer, was unwilling to go along with this compromise. In committee, Langer had stopped chewing his cigar—as always, the cellophane wrapper had been left on—long enough to spit out his disgust at what he considered to be a farcical procedure by which the Court's foes would be given an apparently anti-Court bill which the Court's friends had drained of all substance. And, as printed, his official minority views were only slightly less tart. He stated that with the "reasonable" amendment, the bill made no change whatever in the Supreme Court decision and was therefore a "meaningless gesture." More basically, Langer believed that the *Mallory* rule was a desirable one. "In arriving at this decision," he wrote, "the Supreme Court followed a sound and well-established rule of evidentiary exclusion based upon the highest considerations of public policy."[8]

THE ANTI-COURT LEADERSHIP

By the end of the first week in August, the Senate had divided into three factions; none was well defined, though the pro- and anti-Court groups were more easily identified than the dwindling number of uncommitted senators. On the right, the leaders were Jenner, Butler, Eastland, McClellan, and Thurmond, with several other senators like John Bricker of Ohio and Styles Bridges willing to lend their influence to anti-Court recruiting. Richard Russell of Georgia, who has been frequently called the most powerful man in the Senate, was in favor of several pieces of anti-Court legislation, but he was more restrained than some of his compatriots. He preferred to move behind the scenes, designating individual southern senators to lead a particular atack, while he himself stayed apart as a good commander in chief should.

All of these people were veterans of many Senate campaigns, and they had evolved a loose but workable strategy. The Jenner-Butler bill was to be the stalking horse. Despite prodding, Lyndon Johnson had refused to call it up for debate, and now the time of the Eighty-fifth Congress was running out. The first task was thus to force Johnson to permit the bill to come up for floor action. The anti-Court group wanted a vote on S. 2646, even though they knew that the measure would probably be defeated. They were hoping for a show of strength which would frighten enough senators to insure a compromise that would entail passage of as much other Court legislation as possible. The Southern Democrats had a second reason for a vote: they wanted a chance to let their constituents know how intensely they opposed the Warren Court.

LIBERAL LEADERSHIP

The pro-Court faction was also coalescing. Paul Douglas of Illinois, Thomas Hennings of Missouri, Frank Church of Idaho, William Proxmire of Wisconsin, John Carroll, Jacob Javits, Joseph Clark, Wayne Morse, and Hubert Humphrey formed the core of this group, with perhaps another dozen senators strongly sympathetic. Liberal leadership was divided among three men, Carroll, Hennings, and Humphrey. Hennings, and more particularly Carroll, assumed responsibility for keeping the group united around a minimum plan of action, while Humphrey was to maintain liaison with the Majority leader.

Choice of leadership of a Senate faction is an informal affair, more a matter of gravitation than official election. But in this instance, at least, the selection had been quite rational, however informal. Humphrey,* as a close personal friend of Lyndon Johnson, was the obvious man to work with the Majority leader. Both he and Hennings†

* Hubert H. Humphrey (1911——), graduate of the Denver School of Pharmacy, 1933, A.B. University of Minnesota, 1939, A.M. Louisiana State University, 1940, had a varied career as a pharmacist, professor of political science, WPA official, Minnesota Director of Adult Education, assistant director of the War Manpower Commission in Minnesota, and news analyst for a radio station before settling down to politics as a profession. In 1945 he was elected mayor of Minneapolis, and after two vigorous reform years which included establishment of an FEPC commission, he was re-elected by the largest majority in the city's political history. In the 1948 Democratic Convention Humphrey was one of the northern liberals responsible for the strong civil rights plank in the party platform, a plank which caused the defection of a number of southerners and the creation of the States' Rights party. Elected in 1948 as Minnesota's first Democratic senator, Humphrey at first continued his free-swinging fight for civil rights. In spite of his youth and apparent brashness, he quickly though painfully learned the ethic of the Senate, and the Senate in turn recognized his talents. Humphrey lost none of his liberalism, but he did manage to be less abrasive toward conservatives. In time, and with Lyndon Johnson's friendship and help, Humphrey became a member of the Senate's inner circle.

† Thomas Carey Hennings, Jr. (1903–60), A.B. Cornell, 1924, LL.B. Washington University at St. Louis, 1926, got his start in politics at the age of thirteen when he was a page boy at the 1916 Democratic National Convention. After serving as assistant district attorney for St. Louis from 1929 to 1934, he was elected to the House of Representatives for three terms. In 1940 he chose to run for district attorney in St. Louis—a post to which he returned after service with the navy in World War II. In 1950, over the opposition of the President of the United States, the governor of Missouri, the mayor of St. Louis, and the CIO, he secured the Democratic nomination for U.S. senator and won in the general election by 93,000 votes, the only Democrat to unseat a Republican senator that year. In the Senate, Hennings soon became an open and articulate foe of Joseph McCarthy. He also opposed the Tidelands Oil legislation, the Butler amend-

were accepted and established members of the Senate's "inner club"; and, although Carroll* was only serving his freshman term, he had already managed to impress his liberal colleagues, as well as the Majority leader, without having yet alienated the older conservatives. Carroll and Hennings were on the Judiciary Committee, where they had been able to watch much of the enemy's battle plan develop, and Hennings was also secretary of the Democratic Policy Committee, a vantage point from which he could try to block floor consideration of the Court bills.

In the second week of August, Carroll began calling the group together for occasional strategy conferences. These meetings were held in the basement of the Old Senate Office Building, and Paul Douglas commented that the liberals were beginning to look like the Christians in the catacombs. At one of these gatherings some fifteen senators showed up, but usually only five or six were present. Yet, no matter how small or large the conclave, it was obvious that the liberals—like the anti-Court faction—were divided in their degree of opposition to the Court bills as well as in their ideas of how best to cope with the legislative situation. They could agree on only the most general and obvious plan of battle.

As in the Jencks fight, the pro-Court faction had an advantage in the fact that the end of the session was near, as well as an additional asset in that 1958 was an election year and a large number of senators could not tolerate an extended session. Again as with the Jencks bill, none of the measures had had full hearings in the Senate except Jenner-Butler, and, as the minority of the Judiciary Committee had pointed out, all the Jenner hearings had centered on revocation of jurisdiction, not the four clauses added in committee.

---

ment to the Constitution freezing the size and jurisdiction of the Supreme Court, as well as Hubert Humphrey's 1954 proposal to make Communist party membership a crime. His most important fight was waged against the Bricker amendment. More than any single senator, Hennings was responsible for the defeat of this measure in the great debate of 1954. He died suddenly in 1960.

* John Albert Carroll (1901——) enlisted in the army during World War I; after the war he worked as a riveter's helper and later as a laborer in a tire factory. He attended Westminster Junior College in Denver and then financed his way through Westminster Law School at night by working as a city policeman. Admitted to the Colorado bar in 1929, he quickly became active in state politics. In 1933, he was appointed assistant U.S. attorney; in 1936, he was elected district attorney in Denver; but in 1940 he was defeated in the Democratic gubernatorial primary. During World War II Carroll served in the army. On his return from active duty he re-entered politics and won a seat in the House of Representatives in 1946. Re-elected in 1948, he was later beaten in bids

It was clear, then, that the first liberal tactic would be to charge haste and panic and to plead for postponement until the next session. The second tactic agreed upon tied in with the first: to talk at great length on the floor, to be ready to talk at greater length, and then to press for motions to table or to recommit rather than allow a vote on final passage. When their quasi-filibuster was going on, the liberals could approach the Majority leader and caution him not to bring up more Court bills lest the Senate never adjourn. If all of this failed, they agreed to resort to dentistry and by amendment try to pull some of the teeth of the anti-Court measures.

THE MAJORITY LEADERSHIP

While the liberals could not view Lyndon Johnson as their full ally, they did plan to co-operate with him as far as possible. As party chief, Johnson[9] was caught up in the Court tornado. His critics often drew an exaggerated picture of him as omnipotent in the Senate. Johnson was powerful, but he had to work with other powerful and equally strong-minded colleagues. A Majority leader can reward and even to some extent punish, but generally he must trade, swap, and bargain. And Johnson, whose diplomatic talents had made him the chief broker between the two wings of the Democratic party, could bargain and compromise as well or better than any man in the Senate. The key to Johnson's success lay in his instinctive ability to gauge what would be acceptable to his own party, the opposition, and the White House. To facilitate his quiet probing he had for all practical purposes abolished the Democratic caucus. This allowed him to talk to senators individually or in small groups, to feel out alignments and common ground without exposing ideological divisions and causing deep rifts before real discussion had begun. Johnson would seldom risk intraparty strife, or even a veto, on a measure which might be better in the abstract than a workable compromise; but once he

---

for the Senate in 1950 and 1954. These frequent defeats at the polls earned Carroll the nickname "Jinx." In 1956, however, he nosed out former Secretary of Agriculture Charles F. Brannon for the Democratic senatorial nomination, and in the general election defeated Governor Dan Thornton by the slim margin of 2,730 votes. By pressing for a change in Senate rules to curb filibustering and by opposing the jury trial amendment to the 1957 Civil Rights Act, Carroll immediately established a reputation as a fighting liberal.

had found common ground acceptable to a substantial majority of his party—and enough of the opposition to insure passage—he would fight doggedly to achieve this limited goal.

The Court bills put Johnson in an embarrassing position. S. 2646, even in its amended form, was unacceptable to him. Even had he approved of its provisions—which he did not—it would have been objectionable. First, it would have caused a breach, perhaps irreparable, within the Democratic party, and Johnson was intensely loyal to his party. Moreover, the Majority leader felt that his own presidential ambitions could be best advanced if he could present himself to the 1960 national convention as a western (not a southern) moderate whose political talents could both unify the party to win an election and then get meaningful party legislation through Congress. It would have been as damaging to Johnson's prestige as Majority leader to have the Democrats splinter over a Republican-sponsored bill as it would have been disastrous to his 1960 plans to become identified with either the McCarthy wing of the Republican party or the segregation wing of his own party. Second, his presidential ambitions aside, Johnson loved the Senate. Like many of his colleagues, he was sure that passage of such a bill would not reflect credit on the judgment of the upper chamber; and he was concerned that, if enacted into law, the bill might upset the balance of power within the federal government, perhaps in the long run to the detriment of the Senate.

With liberal opposition so aroused, Johnson could see that the political implications of H.R. 3 were different in degree rather than in kind from those of S. 2646. And, on the merits of the bill, Johnson believed H.R. 3 would have thrown federal-state relations into a morass of confusion and would have further fragmented political power. The only advantage of Smith's proposal over the Jenner measure was that it had been sponsored by a nominal Democrat.

The Majority leader was less opposed in principle to the other bills cleared by the Judiciary Committee, but he was still afraid that any facet of the Court issue could tear the Democratic party to pieces, just as it had in 1937. Under the circumstances, Johnson's tactics were to delay as long as possible and use the time to persuade the two wings of the Democratic party to agree on a compromise. He had held up action on the Jenner-Butler bill for three months, and he was in no hurry to bring up the other Court bills. Johnson had been trying to persuade several southerners who were pushing H.R. 3 and S. 2646 that it was useless to try to force through these measures in the face of stiff liberal opposition, but he had had little success. To maximize their bargaining power, the hard core of anti-Court senators was determined to keep heavy pressure on Johnson to bring up every one of the Court bills.

Some senators on the liberal side were quite ready to trade passage of a few of the less objectionable bills, like Mallory or habeas corpus, in exchange for defeat of Jenner-Butler and H.R. 3. But there were also people on the left who were unwilling to discuss compromise. Men like Douglas, Morse, and Clark saw the Court bills as a matter of principle, a struggle between the forces of light and darkness, liberalism and reaction. They were girding themselves for Armageddon to do battle for the Lord, the Constitution, and the Warren Court. When Johnson tried to persuade Clark that the habeas corpus bill had to be harmless since it had been approved by the judicial conference over which the Chief Justice had presided, Clark stubbornly answered that he and his friends would still have to insist on thorough floor discussion of the measure. And Paul Douglas later publicly announced that, as far as he was concerned, the Senate could stay in session all fall; he was not running for re-election and saw no reason to rush through doubtful bills.[10]

On the twelfth of August, the liberals put their opposition to the Court bills in writing. Hubert Humphrey personally delivered a letter to Johnson signed by himself and nine other senators, Paul Douglas, John Carroll, Wayne Morse, Joseph Clark, Thomas Hennings, Pat McNamara, Richard Neuberger, William Proxmire, and John Kennedy:

> We are deeply concerned that, in the last minute rush to adjourn, one or more decisions of the United States Supreme Court may be overruled by hasty legislation enacted without adequate consideration. . . . We are not opposed to a full debate on the recent decisions of the United States Supreme Court. In such a debate we will be prepared to give our reasons for supporting the Supreme Court's decisions requiring desegregation and to point out why the Senate should adopt legislation implementing these decisions. . . . A great debate on the recent decisions of the Supreme Court has much to recommend it, but we do not believe that the last days of the Congress are the appropriate time for such a debate.

> A bill to overrule a decision of the Supreme Court cannot be considered in isolation. Just as our opponents desire to override the Court for its symbolic effect, so we desire to present fully the symbolism involved in supporting the Court and particularly in having the free world know that America is proud of the humanitarian decisions of its highest court. We urge you to announce this great debate for the next session of Congress rather than bringing up legislation to reverse isolated decisions in this last stage of the Congress.

The liberals knew that they had hit Johnson in a vulnerable spot. The last thing in the world he wanted was to rip the party apart by a full debate on segregation. The next day the liberals pressed their advantage by deliberately leaking to the Majority leader their plan to tack an amendment onto either the habeas corpus or Nelson bill:

> This section shall not apply in any State engaged in subversion against the Government or Constitution of the United States by maintaining in effect or enforcing laws which deny the equal protection of the laws to any person by reason of race, color, or religion.

THE GROUP STRUGGLE

While Johnson was searching for a compromise which could keep the Democratic party from civil war and still allow the Senate to finish its business with reasonable dispatch, the various groups interested in the anti-Court bills stepped up their activity. Leading the fight for H.R. 3 were the Chamber of Commerce and the National Association of Manufacturers, assisted by the American Farm Bureau Federation.

To supplement its regular Washington lobbying, the Chamber of Commerce tried to create a grass-roots campaign by which local member organizations would put pressure on their own senators. The chamber's peculiar economic interest was indicated by the fact that the campaign was under the direction of its labor relations section. But other broader business interests were also involved. The national office explained to its local chapters that agricultural areas would benefit by sharing control over production and distribution; western states would preserve their proprietary rights in water control; natural gas regions would be saved from "future encroachment" by federal authority; truckers and shippers would gain from a clarification of local control. Not least:

> All members of Congress who recognize the need to preserve state authority in the field of labor relations support H.R. 3 as a constructive step toward this objective. States which are now able to regulate mass picketing, violence, personal injuries, safety standards, minimum wage and maximum hours will—if H.R. 3 is enacted—also be able to regulate employee elections and unfair labor practices to protect both unions and employers, provided there is no direct conflict with federal law.[11]

In midsummer this special flyer was sent to all member units urging that they dispatch telegrams and letters to Lyndon Johnson and James O. Eastland, with copies to local senators, strongly advocating that H.R. 3 be brought to a vote. To give such communications more weight, the national office suggested use of an assortment of data and doctrine, including a statement from Representative Colmer of Mississippi.

The NAM was trying to stir up a similar grass-roots movement, but its campaign was more co-ordinated and concentrated. Working closely with Thurmond* and McClellan†—who had assumed joint

* J(ames). Strom Thurmond (1902—–), B.S., Clemson College, 1923, second cousin to Georgia's Senator Herman Talmadge, was born and reared in Edgefield County in the upcountry of South Carolina not far from the home of John C. Calhoun. After graduation from college Thurmond taught in high school and took law school correspondence courses at night. He was admitted to the bar in 1930, shortly after becoming county superintendent of education. In 1933 he was elected to the state senate and five years later was appointed to the state circuit bench. After Pearl Harbor he joined the army, serving in the Normandy invasion with the 82d Airborne Division. When he returned from the army Thurmond resigned his judgeship and ran for governor on a platform which included an anti-poll tax plank. As governor (1947–51) he urged the legislature to appropriate more money for Negro schools—a proposal which the legislature did not take seriously until after the School Segregation cases had been instituted. In 1948 Thurmond earned national notice by his efforts to bring to justice the white men who had lynched a Negro in Greenville; that same year, however, Thurmond led the anti-civil rights bolt from the Democratic National Convention. Chosen as the Dixiecrat presidential candidate, Thurmond was able to carry only those four southern states on whose ballots he was listed as the official Democratic nominee. In 1954 Thurmond was elected to the Senate as a write-in candidate—the first senator so chosen. In the Senate Thurmond has tended to be a lone wolf, not accepted as a member of the inner clique even by his southern colleagues. Perhaps the most extreme example of Thurmond's go-it-alone attitude was his refusal to honor the tacit Senate agreement not to filibuster against the 1957 Civil Rights Act—a refusal which angered both supporters and opponents of the bill.

† John Little McClellan (1896—–) finished high school in 1913; in the same year the Arkansas legislature passed a special act allowing him to practice law even though he

responsibility for H.R. 3—the NAM had a stream of influential local businessmen contact their own senators regarding H.R. 3. Replies were turned over to the Washington headquarters of the organization and examined and compared until something bordering on a commitment in favor of the bill was forthcoming. This information would be given to Thurmond and McClellan, and either or both of them would then approach the senator and invite him to become a cosponsor of H.R. 3. At very least they would try to get a firm promise to vote for the bill. The NAM kept a daily check of tally sheets with Thurmond's office, and by mid-August they could count forty-eight votes definitely pledged with five more probables. This strength was built around a solid nucleus of thirty-four cosponsors, nineteen more than the bill had had when originally introduced.

While business and farm groups were officially pushing only H.R. 3, the NAACP, the Americans for Democratic Action, the American Civil Liberties Union, and the American Veterans Committee were openly fighting to defeat all of the Court bills. They were joined by the AFL-CIO, which was trying to kill both H.R. 3 and the Jenner-Butler measure. At this stage, however, the operations of the pro-Court groups were of limited effectiveness. The ADA was still under the stigma of being a "bleeding heart" organization; and this prevented it from having a broad appeal to the Senate, although its counsel, Joseph Rauh, was acting as an adviser to several of the liberal senators. The AVC and the ACLU were small groups which

---

was four years under the minimum legal age. After military service in World War I, McClellan went into politics and at the age of twenty-four became city attorney of Malvern, Arkansas. Seven years later he became a state prosecutor. In 1934 and 1936 he was elected to the House of Representatives, but was defeated for the Senate in 1938. Blaming his defeat on the "captive vote" of 50,000 WPA workers in Arkansas, McClellan came roaring back to win a Senate seat in 1942. In the Senate he continued to practice his conservative, states' rights, pro-segregation philosophy; in 1948 he was one of the few southern senators to publicly support the Dixiecrat ticket and for a time after the party split he listed himself as an "Independent Democrat." It was not until attrition and the seniority system left him as the ranking Democrat on McCarthy's investigating subcommittee that McClellan attained national recognition. His dignity and disgust at the army-McCarthy spectacle won him much favorable acclaim, and in 1957 he teamed up with John Kennedy's bright young brother, Robert, to conduct a series of investigations into labor racketeering that made national figures out of McClellan, Kennedy, Dave Beck, Jimmy Hoffa, and an assortment of thugs. McClellan's personal life has been deeply marked by the tragic deaths of his wife and each of his children. Cabell Phillips has described him as having "the astringent, disapproving demeanor of a stern man of the cloth. His mere glance can convey a chilling sense of barely controlled outrage."

had consistently been more effective in the judicial than in the legislative process. The labor movement was in the midst of internal wrangling and housecleaning as well as an external struggle for its life. With Dave Beck and Jimmy Hoffa the current popular symbols of unionism, the AFL-CIO had its hands full with its own problems, though H.R. 3 was a bread-and-butter issue.

The NAACP's public image was in far better shape than labor's, but Clarence Mitchell, the association's chief Washington lobbyist, had little reason to cheer as he viewed the situation from his office in the old red brick building on the edge of the Negro slums around Union Station. Preservation of the Supreme Court's power and prestige was vital to the continued achievement of NAACP goals; and, while the Negro vote was beginning to become a real factor which legislators had to weigh, the NAACP was, in this fight, suffering from a political fact of life which besets many interest groups. Those members of Congress most likely to listen to its arguments were the ones already persuaded to defend the Court; the major Court opponents, especially those from the South and even the Midwest, were almost immune to the sanction of the colored vote. Confronted with this situation, Mitchell concentrated his efforts on Lyndon Johnson's office and on buttonholing midwestern Republicans whose favorable attitude on Negro civil rights might be used to soften hostility created by the political offender decisions of the Warren Court.

JOHNSON'S HAND IS FORCED

Lyndon Johnson continued to delay a decision on floor action for the Court bills, and southern pressure increased as time went on. Russell of Georgia told reporters that he had "used every kind of poker on Johnson I could, cold poker and a hot poker."[12] Finally, at the meeting of the nine-man Democratic Policy committee[13] on Saturday, August 16, Russell bluntly stated that if the Majority leader wanted to get the Mutual Security Administration appropriation through the Senate, at least some of the anti-Court legislation would have to be brought up first. Hennings and Johnson warned that this would touch off a fiery debate which might wreck the party; but Russell stood firm, and the policy committee cleared the Nelson, habeas corpus, and Mallory bills. After the meeting, Johnson told newsmen that he would call up the first of these bills on Monday and predicted quick passage.[14]

On Monday, the Attorney General sent a lengthy letter to Eastland to clarify the stand of the Department of Justice before the debate began.[15] Rogers said that the department supported the Nelson and habeas corpus measures as well as the bill to redefine "organize" in the Smith Act—though this last was still bottled up in committee. The Attorney General had no objections to the Mallory bill with the "reasonable" amendment, but Rogers repeated his objections to S. 2646 and set out a detailed argument against H.R. 3 and its Senate companion.

Although Saturday, August 23, was the target date for adjournment, and in spite of his earlier announcement, it was not until Tuesday, August 19, that the Majority leader could get the Senate to consider the first of the Court bills. Liberal opposition had caused a number of shifts in Johnson's plans. He had intended to start with the Nelson proposal, but quickly changed his mind and decided on the habeas corpus bill. Then, after talking to Clark, and remembering the antisegregation amendments, Johnson concluded that since the addition of "reasonable" to the Mallory legislation had made that the least controversial of all the measures, it would be best to consider that issue first.

THE MALLORY DEBATE

Johnson had hoped to get the bill through the Senate in a few hours, but his time schedule was immediately wrecked. O'Mahoney opened the discussion with a sketch of the history and aims of the measure and the purpose of the "reasonable" amendment. Then the liberals took the floor and began to debate with all the graceful courtesies and generous compliments for which the Senate is famous. First Carroll, then Hennings, then Javits and Proxmire, all assisted by leisurely interpolations and leading questions by Douglas, Church of Idaho, and Cooper of Kentucky, took up the bill in detail. When Ervin of North Carolina had finished the only formal speech opposing the "reasonable" amendment, more than nine hours of valuable Senate time had been consumed.

Shortly after 9:00 P.M. a roll call was taken on the O'Mahoney amendment, and the addition of "reasonable" was accepted, 41–39,[16] with six senators paired and ten others not voting, four of whom had expressed opposition to the "reasonable" amendment. In less than an hour the Senate rejected additional changes sponsored by Ervin and Morse, and the bill was passed, 65–12, in the same form in which it had left the Judiciary Committee.[17] John Marshall Butler had voted against the measure because he thought it too weak. This put him in the strange company of eleven liberals led by Douglas, Javits, Humphrey, Morse, and Clark, all of whom had decided to go on record against even the watered-down bill.

The next item of business was the appointment of conferees to meet with the House managers. Eastland selected himself, O'Mahoney, Dirksen, and Carroll from the Federal Code subcommittee, along with Alexander Wiley from the parent Judiciary Committee.

THE DEMISE OF JENNER-BUTLER

Although Mallory was disposed of for a time, Lyndon Johnson's position did not materially improve. Thurmond and McClellan were continuing their push for H.R. 3. They were confident that they had strength to pass the bill—if they could get it to a vote. To put more pressure on Johnson, Thurmond informed the Majority leader that he intended to offer H.R. 3 as an amendment to every bill remaining on the Senate calendar. Johnson knew Thurmond well enough to know that this was not a bluff; in an effort to keep the Senate from being shackled, the Majority leader agreed that when he called up the Nelson bill later in the week H.R. 3 would be offered as an amendment.

Facing similar pressure on Jenner-Butler, Johnson had to consent to the same sort of arrangement. And as soon as the final roll call on Mallory was completed, he brought up a noncontroversial bill affecting federal appellate procedure,[18] then by prearrangement yielded to Jenner who offered the Jenner-Butler bill as an amendment to the pending measure. The Majority leader had polled the Senate quietly but carefully, and he was certain that when Hennings moved to table S. 2646 there would be enough votes to bury the bill. Johnson's only request to both sides was to be brief.

Mallory had taken up Tuesday afternoon and a good part of the evening, and most senators were more than willing to wait until the next day to do further battle. When the Senate finished its morning hour on Wednesday, August 20, the Jenner-Butler bill was the first item of business. Jenner made a long speech, and then Butler made a much longer one. These were followed by shorter remarks by Thurmond, Stennis of Mississippi, and Eastland—who began with the comment that although many senators were sincere in their opposition to S. 2646, the Communist party and its front groups were the most bitter opponents of the bill.

The liberals were irked at Johnson for bringing up S. 2646 in the first place, but they were even more grateful for his help in corralling votes for them, so they took little time in debate. Wiley had only a few words, and Hennings carried the burden of the opposition. At the conclusion of his speech, Hennings moved to table the Jenner-Butler bill, and after quick comments by Olin D. Johnston, the roll was called. The tabling motion carried as expected,[19] but the 49–41 division was an impressive demonstration of anti-Court strength, considering that Joseph Robinson, with the full weight of FDR's political magic behind him, had never been sure of more than thirty Senate votes for the 1937 Court-packing plan.

THE DOUGLAS AMENDMENT

As soon as the votes had been tabulated, there was a scramble for recognition as Hennings, Douglas, and Johnson addressed the presiding officer. Douglas was shouting in the rear of the chamber, and Alan Bible of Nevada, in the chair, recognized him rather than Johnson. Douglas then dropped a bombshell into the Senate by introducing for himself, Morse, and Humphrey a one-sentence amendment to the harmless appellate procedure bill, which was still officially the business under consideration:

> The Congress hereby expresses its full support and approval of the recent, historic decisions of the Supreme Court of the United States holding racial segregation unlawful in public education and transportation as a denial of the constitutional right to the equal protection of laws.[20]

The Senate chamber was thrown into turmoil, and Bible pounded his gavel for order, but with such little success that he had to suspend all proceedings for a few moments to allow the furor to subside. The projected liberal amendment to the Nelson and habeas corpus bills had led Johnson to suspect that a move of this sort would be forthcoming, and he swiftly diverted attention by engaging in a short and obtuse debate on the propriety of a motion to table a motion to reconsider Hennings' successful motion to table the Jenner-Butler bill. When the chamber had calmed down, the Majority leader moved that the Senate proceed to take up S. 654.

Johnson's motion was carried by a voice vote; but, in a typical display of senatorial courtesy, the Majority leader asked that the vote be suspended when it became apparent that Douglas had been cut off before he had finished his speech in favor of his amendment. Allowed to continue speaking, Douglas chided those senators who had claimed it was not their function to judge Supreme Court decisions:

> I ask my colleagues, what have we been doing all afternoon? What has the Judiciary Committee been doing by passing on these questions? The amendment which was the so-called Jenner-Butler bill . . . was a thinly transparent effort to overrule no less than five Supreme Court decisions. . . . This is all part of a "reverse the Court" campaign which stems largely, although not entirely from the earlier decision in the Brown case. . . . I do not think we should ask the Court to be continuously on the receiving end of epithets or attempts to whittle down its authority, while at the same time and in the same process there are attacks on the integrity and patriotism of the Justices. . . . I think we must choose on whose side we stand. Do we stand on the side of Governor Faubus, or do we stand on the side of the Supreme Court. . . ?[21]

In the brief debate that followed not only the anti-Court people spoke against the Douglas amendment, but so did Kefauver, Javits, Carroll, and Neuberger of Oregon. Johnson let the discussion play itself out, then again put his motion to take up S. 654; once more that motion carried.[22]

Douglas' move was criticized as foolhardy by Johnson's supporters and by some liberals as well. From the liberal point of view, Douglas had taken a great risk. He had laid no groundwork for his proposal, and had a showdown been forced the votes might not have been forthcoming. From Johnson's viewpoint, Douglas had interfered with his plan to exploit the psychological effects of his victory over S. 2646 by immediately crushing the efforts he knew would be made to bring up H.R. 3. In addition, with the Court bills fought on the question of segregation, every southern senator would have been constrained to die fighting for any and all anti-Court measures.

On the other hand, Douglas' motion had also helped the liberal cause. By stating the issue so baldly, he had seriously embarrassed several Republicans who were intending to support H.R. 3 when it came up. Equally as important, Douglas' move had allowed Lyndon Johnson to say "I told you so" to his southern friends to strengthen his warning that if they pushed too hard to curb the Court, the whole affair might boomerang.

THE INITIAL VICTORY OF H.R. 3

But Johnson's warnings had gone unheeded. Styles Bridges had just completed his opening remarks on S. 654 when John McClellan obtained the floor. For himself and thirty-three colleagues, fifteen other Southern Democrats and eighteen Republicans, McClellan introduced an amendment in the nature of a substitute for S. 654. In effect, McClellan offered H.R. 3 with S. 654 as an appendage.

This dragged the Senate into another long debate. Ervin and McClellan spoke of states' rights, and Arthur Watkins of Utah outlined the need to restore local control of labor relations in order to curb union power. Eastland cut into the Warren Court in his customary ripsaw fashion: "The Smith Act was gutted by the Supreme Court. The Supreme Court in the Nelson case held that 42 state antisubversive statutes were unconstitutional. . . . Then it turned around a year later and destroyed the Smith Act. Mr. President, the people of the United States are today defenseless in the face of an internal Communist conspiracy to destroy us."[23]

Then the liberals answered. The ghosts of Calhoun and Webster returned to the Senate chamber to renew their old combat, as Carroll, Clark, and Church took on McClellan in a solemn theoretical debate on the nature of the Union.[24]

Johnson listened impatiently. McClellan's move, of course, had come as no surprise, and Johnson thought he had mustered enough votes to beat H.R. 3. The main thing, from his point of view, was to get on with the matter so that the Senate could consider the Mutual Security appropriation and the debt limitation bill. Late Wednesday night, the Majority leader interrupted the discussion to ask for unanimous consent to limit debate. His first proposal, to allow forty-five minutes more, failed when Gore of Tennessee objected; his second, to permit ninety minutes more of discussion, went down when Langer objected. Both sides, however, did promise that they would wind up as soon as possible.

The liberals, assured by Johnson that he had the votes to beat H.R. 3, cut short their speeches and had them printed for the *Record* rather than actually delivering them. Shortly after 11:00 P.M., Hennings made his motion to table the McClellan substitute, and the clerk began calling the roll. At this point the liberals suffered a stunning defeat. The quietness of the McClellan-Thurmond co-operation with the NAM had caused Johnson badly to underestimate H.R. 3's support; and when the count was completed, Hennings' motion had been defeated 39–46.[25]

The Senate was in a state of near pandemonium. Jenner, Butler, and McClellan were on their feet excitedly shouting, "Vote, vote!" Johnson was pale and visibly shaken. The prestige of his leadership was at stake. Not only had he just taken a drubbing from the southern wing of his party, but his usually tenuous relations with the party's ultraliberals had also suffered another damaging blow. Through his own efforts and those of Carroll, Hennings, and Humphrey, Johnson had convinced the Court defenders that they should not pursue the plan to bludgeon H.R. 3 to death in a brutal floor debate replete with embarrassing antisegregation amendments. In return for this, he had promised that he would gather the votes to table the bill, and he had failed. As the defeat of the tabling motion was announced several northern Democrats gathered in the back of the Senate chamber. They were undecided as to whether they should be more pleased that the Majority leader, who had so often in the past frustrated their liberal policies, had taken a licking, or more worried that H.R. 3 might pass. But whatever their emotional reactions, they were ready to utilize their amendments and prepared speeches to block further Senate action. Johnson, however, was not willing to relinquish his command. A series of parliamentary inquiries allowed him a moment to collect his thoughts. Then a leader of the southern conservatives walked up behind Johnson and told him, "Move for adjournment." The Majority leader interrupted Carroll, who was trying to make a motion to recommit the bill: "Mr. President, I should like the Senator to yield to me for the purpose of making a motion to adjourn until 12 o'clock tomorrow."[26]

Butler, McClellan, and Jenner were furious. They wanted to try to force an immediate vote on H.R. 3, although, since Douglas had the manuscript of a long speech in his hand, it is unlikely they could have done so. They hoped, however, that such a bold move just might succeed if they could strike before the confusion was over; and having seen Johnson preparing to spring something to block their plans, they leaped up and began, as Jenner said, "yelling at the chair." But Nixon had sized up the situation and blandly ignored their shouts. Johnson cut off their protests: "The motion is not debatable. I move the Senate adjourn." The Vice-President ruled that the question was on the Majority leader's motion, and the most Jenner could obtain was a roll call vote on the adjournment issue. The motion was carried 70–18;[27] only five Southern Democrats joined Jenner, Butler, Bridges, Bricker, Goldwater, and eight other Republicans to oppose the Majority leader.*

SCRAMBLE FOR VOTES

As the senators were leaving the floor, Johnson walked quickly over to the cluster of liberals and reasserted his command. Putting his arm around Hubert Humphrey's shoulder, he huddled the group together and in his most persuasive manner assured them that his indirect strategy would win the next day. Then he took Humphrey up to his office and discussed the tactics of the coming battle in great detail. Later, Johnson's real work began. He knew that H.R. 3 leaders would be trying desperately to close ranks to prevent defections; despite this resistance he would have to convert or neutralize seven votes.

Wednesday night and Thursday morning in his office and Thursday afternoon in the Senate chambers, Johnson talked to senators from both parties, arguing, cajoling, pleading, even threatening. He bargained with a few senators, others he frightened with the specter

* The reasons behind this support of the Majority leader were complex. See chap. 11 for a discussion.

of the resurrection of Douglas' amendment. He pleaded for the party, for the Senate, for the country, for speedy adjournment, for friendship. Several senators who were too deeply committed to change he asked simply to stay off the floor when the voting was going on.

The executive branch was also in the thick of the fight. Both Attorney General Rogers and Deputy Attorney General Walsh had expressed the Justice Department's unequivocal opposition to H.R. 3, but the cabinet was badly split over the bill. The H.R. 3 people had been encouraged by a rumor that three cabinet members had threatened to resign if the President vetoed the measure. This rumor was undoubtedly an exaggeration, but it did contain an element of truth. Postmaster General Arthur Summerfield was a staunch supporter of the bill, and he had been using his influence to line up votes. Moreover, Sinclair Weeks, Secretary of Commerce, and Robert Anderson, Secretary of the Treasury, were also backing H.R. 3. On the other hand, Sherman Adams and the Vice-President were both opposing the bill.

In light of this division, and because they knew Lyndon Johnson would be doing everything he could to swing votes, Rogers and Walsh decided not to try to make private contacts with individual senators. The executive process, they calculated, offered better prospects; and by Thursday morning a veto message for the President was substantially drafted. Rogers and Walsh realized that there would be a rough fight in the White House to get Eisenhower to veto the bill—assuming it passed—but they thought that with the help of Adams they could persuade the President, if for no other reason than that H.R. 3 concerned the Justice Department more immediately than any other executive office.

At this point labor for the first time put its full force into the fight. Lobbyists contacted a number of people who might listen sympathetically, but labor's main effort was concentrated on a few senators. Representatives from the United Mine Workers and the AFL-CIO went to see Senator John D. Hoblitzell of West Virginia and applied all the pressure they could muster. Both union men left the senator believing they had his assurance that he would change his vote and support Carroll's motion to recommit. Meanwhile, Walter Mason of the AFL-CIO called on George Malone of Nevada. Mason was unable to put the sort of pressure on Malone that his colleagues could on Hoblitzell, but the two men were old friends and Mason did his best to persuade Malone that H.R. 3 threatened to upset federal-state relations as well as union security.

The H.R. 3 people also had their antennae out. Senator Knowland, the Minority leader, was backing H.R. 3, but as a matter of principle he would not use Johnson's recruiting tactics; and Russell of Georgia was less interested in this bill than in some of the other Court measures. This caused most of the burden to fall on Thurmond, McClellan, and the NAM's Washington staff, although Howard Smith was also using his power to keep votes in line. Sensing uncertainty because of Tennessee's southern traditions, Thurmond coaxed Albert Gore to change sides. But overshadowing this gain of one vote was the fear that Lyndon Johnson might make mass conversions.

The first difficulty faced by the H.R. 3 leadership lay in discovering on whom Johnson was working so they might counter his moves. For a few hours on Thursday morning, they solved this problem by contacting an informant inside Johnson's office, and with this assistance followed swiftly behind—and sometimes even ahead of—the Majority leader and reapplied their original pressure. Some senators, like Hoblitzell of West Virginia, they were able to recapture even after the combined efforts of Johnson and labor. They helped other senators, like Thomas Kuchel of California, stand firm. Having learned that, because of pressure from people who had helped elect him, Kuchel had decided to oppose recommitting H.R. 3, if not to support the bill,[28] Thurmond and McClellan made sure that he would forget neither the debt nor the pledge. And in spite of fifty minutes of persuasion applied by Johnson and his assistant, Robert G. Baker, Kuchel stayed in the anti-Court camp.

THE FINAL VOTE ON H.R. 3

It was not long before Johnson realized that there had to be a leak in his office, and he quickly plugged it. With this source of intelligence denied the enemy, the Majority leader began to move quickly and effectively around the Senate. First, he completed his arrangements to insure that several opponents of H.R. 3 who had not voted the previous night would be on hand that afternoon. Then he contacted

Malone of Nevada and got a formal commitment on his agreement with the AFL-CIO. Later, Johnson got Milton Young of North Dakota and Joseph Frear of Delaware, two supporters of H.R. 3, to consent to be absent when the vote was taken. Shortly after this, the Majority leader found Frank Lausche of Ohio talking on the Senate floor. Playing one of the trump cards the liberals had given him, Johnson warned Lausche that the pro-Court people intended to ape Thurmond's tactics if their motion to recommit failed. They had over three hundred amendments prepared and were going to insist on full consideration of each one. Such an extended debate would, of course, paralyze the Senate. Presented with the dilemma of continuing to back H.R. 3 or to keep the Senate operating, Lausche agreed to change his vote.[29]

Despite all this, Johnson was still short of a majority, and one of his votes, Mike Monroney of Oklahoma, was out of town. On the other hand, Holland of Florida was back home campaigning for re-election, and he had arranged a pair for the Wednesday night vote. As an absentee, Holland was the logical pair for Monroney, but Johnson induced Smathers of Florida to agree to a "dead" pair with Monroney, and a possible pair for Holland somehow got lost in a very fast shuffle.

At this point the Majority leader's tally indicated that Carroll's motion would be defeated 42–40. Meanwhile, the Senate, which had convened at noon, had finished its morning hour; and as both sides were working behind the scenes, most of the senators wandered on and off the floor listening to remarks on national defense policy and exchanging congratulatory speeches on the retirement of Jenner and Martin of Pennsylvania.

Carroll waited for word from Johnson when to take up his recommittal motion again. He expected it at 1:00 P.M., but Johnson sent him a message to hold a while longer. A little after 2:00, when Carroll was eating lunch, the AFL-CIO called his office to tell him that they thought they had swung the necessary votes to carry his motion. Carroll checked with Johnson, but the Majority leader was not sure. It was not until just before 5:00 P.M. that Johnson was willing to go ahead.

He had been trying to convince Senator Robert Kerr of Oklahoma, one of his closest personal friends, to stay off the floor, but Kerr had refused to promise. Johnson then turned to Everett Dirksen of Illinois, who was slated to succeed Knowland as Senate Minority leader, and asked him to contact Wallace Bennett, Republican from Utah. Johnson explained that the vote on H.R. 3 would probably end in a tie—a highly optimistic prediction. A tie would put Nixon in an embarrassing predicament in terms of the 1960 nomination since the Taft wing of the Republican party was pushing the bill and the liberal wing was opposing it.* If Bennett switched his vote, the bill would be defeated, and Nixon would not have to alienate either party faction. To increase the force of this pressure, Johnson also used the same save-the-Senate-from-strangulation argument that he had employed on Lausche. The Majority leader also asked Dirksen to remind Bennett that since several H.R. 3 cosponsors had to leave Washington within the next week, the bill would ultimately be defeated even if its backers insisted on a fight to the death. (Johnson saw no point in mentioning that a number of the opponents of H.R. 3 also had to return home to campaign.)

Dirksen delivered Johnson's message and put Bennett on the spot. The senator from Utah made no commitment, but he did call the NAM and explain that to save the Senate from paralysis he might change his vote. As a former president of the NAM, a cosponsor of H.R. 3, a friend of Nixon, and a realistic legislator, Bennett was caught in a vise of cross-pressure. He knew the NAM was not about to let him off the hook with a smile, and eight years as a respected member of the Senate had made him wary of backing down from a promise, even for a good reason and after notice. On the other hand, Bennett, who had had some doubts about the wisdom of the policy of bringing H.R. 3 up as an amendment to another bill, especially when it had not had hearings in the Senate,† felt that the measure would not pass no matter what he did. If he voted against Carroll's

* The parliamentary situation was almost as complex as the political. A motion to recommit fails of passage on a tie vote. The Vice-President is under no obligation to vote on such an occasion, but, if he wishes, he may break the tie. Nixon seldom presided over the Senate, and it might have been wiser in terms of 1960 nomination strategy had he been out of the country or at least out of town at this time. Nixon, however, was in Washington, and Johnson had made sure that he was warned of a possible tie and that Senate Republicans were aware of that warning. Nixon strongly opposed H.R. 3, and it was expected that he would break the tie and kill the bill.

† Actually Bennett was wrong on this point. In 1956 the Judiciary Committee had held hearings on S. 373 and S. 3143, 84/2, which were companion measures to H.R. 3. See above, chap. 4, n. 51.

motion, Bennett feared that the liberal filibuster would probably strangle the Senate and H.R. 3 as well. If he did not vote, Bennett believed that Nixon would break the tie in favor of the liberals and in the process damage his political future. Without telling Dirksen or the NAM anything definite, Bennett decided not to decide until the last minute in the hope that he would not have to assume responsibility one way or the other.

When the clerk began calling the roll on Carroll's motion to recommit H.R. 3, the Majority leader was nervously pacing around the Senate chamber. He knew the vote was going to be close, and to add to the drama and suspense, Bennett was off the floor when his name was called. Then, to Johnson's dismay, Kerr of Oklahoma started onto the floor from the Democratic cloakroom. Johnson and Robert Baker came rushing over, grabbed Kerr's arms and propelled him back into the cloakroom, frantically pleading with him not to vote. Reluctantly, Kerr agreed; and when the clerk called his name—and Frear's, who was in the Marble Room where Thurmond and McClellan were not likely to be looking for him—Mike Mansfield, the Democratic whip, announced that the senator was absent on official business.

While the voting was going on, Bennett had come onto the floor and was counting the roll. After the pairs were announced and the last name ticked off, the count stood at 40–40. Nixon sat stoically behind the huge desk of the presiding officer as the clerk read Bennett's name again. In a steady voice the senator from Utah called out "Aye." H.R. 3 had gone down 41–40.[30]

THE COURT FOES OVERREACH THEMSELVES

The members of the anti-Court bloc had backed themselves into a double defeat. They had had the votes to pass S. 654 easily, but by pressing their cause too hard they had forced the Majority leader to fight them openly and bitterly. Not only were they outmatched by Lyndon Johnson's ability to muster votes, especially when backed by the AFL-CIO, but several southern leaders had grave doubts about H.R. 3. Because of pressure from their constituents they had to vote for the bill, but they would not use their influence to help persuade other senators to back H.R. 3.*

A third factor was important in this defeat. Furious at Johnson's snatching away victory Wednesday night and determined to force the issue Thursday, the anti-Court people had fallen into a neat but effective forensic trap. Hennings and Carroll had warned their group that during Thursday's debate no one was to mention the Nelson bill. H.R. 3 and only H.R. 3 was to be the target. Rising to the bait, the Thurmond-McClellan forces fought stubbornly on the pre-emption question, and when the vote was taken several senators[31] did not realize that both S. 654 and H.R. 3 were being buried.

THE COLE V. YOUNG BILL

With H.R. 3 taken care of, Johnson moved the senate on to other business, but the Court issue was still very much alive. Thursday morning the House and Senate conferees agreed on a bill to reverse *Cole* v. *Young*.[32] Olin D. Johnston protected the administration's provision making it discretionary rather than mandatory for an agency head to suspend a suspected security risk. But House Post Office and Civil Service Committee Chairman Tom Murray got the gist of the House bill extending summary suspension regulations to all federal jobs, sensitive and nonsensitive. Olin Johnston was not pleased with the final bill; but while he had been willing to go along with Murray, two of the Senate conferees, Frank Church and Joseph Clark, had refused to sign the conference report.

Clark went straight to Lyndon Johnson and asked him not to call up the report. If it were brought up, Clark warned, the liberals would insist on another debate, this one even more extended than on Mallory. The Majority leader promised to see what he could do.

* A number of political scientists who have tried to analyze legislative behavior by quantitative methods have been forced to rely on roll call votes as their basic raw material. But since voting is only one of the means by which a legislator can express his views, roll calls are precise measurements neither of intensity of feeling nor of the bargaining process which preceded the vote. Because most bills are strongly indorsed by only a minority of legislators and seriously opposed only by another minority, active recruitment of support from those colleagues who do not have—or perceive—an important stake in a given piece of legislation is frequently a far more accurate—though wholly immeasurable in precise mathematical terms—index of a legislator's position than the actual roll call.

The House approved the conference measure on Friday afternoon,[33] and Murray went over to the Senate to watch the progress of the bill there. Lyndon Johnson met Murray just as he was coming onto the Senate floor. Calling Olin Johnston over to join them, the Majority leader pulled a letter out of his pocket and let Murray read it. The three men talked together for a few more minutes and then shook hands. The Majority leader and Johnston went back on the floor, and Murray left the Senate. A conference report is privileged and can be called up immediately, usually by the Majority leader or the ranking member of the conference committee. But instead of seeking recognition Olin D. Johnston walked over to his desk and sat down, and Lyndon Johnson began chatting with some colleagues. The *Cole* v. *Young* bill was not mentioned again.

MALLORY RETURNS

Since the passport legislation and the proposal to redefine "organize" in the Smith Act had never come out of committee, there were only two more viable anti-Court measures left. In view of the immediacy of adjournment and the strength of liberal opposition—which had been reinforced by communications from a group of law school professors and a federal Court of Appeals judge blasting the Parker bill as being basically anti-Negro[34]—Johnson did not call up the habeas corpus proposal. *Mallory* posed problems which appeared less difficult. The House and Senate had passed bills differing only in the one key word "reasonable," and a conference had been appointed to iron out that difference.

The conferees met for the first time on Thursday, August 21. Led by Kenneth Keating, four of the five House members were pushing for a bill to revise as thoroughly as possible the *McNabb-Mallory* rule. The Senate delegation was divided. Eastland, and to a lesser extent Dirksen, favored the House version, but they had other urgent business to attend to and had given O'Mahoney their proxies in exchange for his promise to do his best to get workable legislation back to the Senate. Carroll, who had Wiley's proxy, wanted no change from the bill the Senate had passed.

Keating opened the meeting by suggesting that the Senate bill be approved but that a section be added defining "reasonable." Carroll and Emanuel Celler would have none of this and pleaded with O'Mahoney to reject the offer. As a result, the first day's conference broke up with no success and very little progress. The group met again on Friday, but with similar results. Carroll and O'Mahoney, supported by Celler, would not accept a twenty-two-word amendment proposed by Cramer of Florida. Cramer's amendment would have overturned the *McNabb-Mallory* doctrine and would have returned to the old common law rule that only "involuntary" confessions were inadmissible in evidence.

After this second meeting, hope for a solution faded. Celler stated publicly—and not too regretfully—that he saw no point in holding future sessions, and Keating announced plans to introduce a new bill in the Eighty-sixth Congress.[35] The liberals were jubilant. They had feared that O'Mahoney would succumb to the temptation to compromise. Indeed, without mentioning O'Mahoney by name, they had voiced this fear several times during Senate debate on *Mallory*.

But the celebration came too soon. On Saturday evening O'Mahoney yielded to persistent pressure to report some sort of a bill and called Carroll in for a surprise meeting with the House people. As soon as the conference got underway, O'Mahoney gave in to Keating's argument that failure to accept Cramer's amendment would mean no legislation for at least a year. The result was conference approval of a bill[36] stating: (1) that "reasonable delay" in arraignment would not of itself invalidate a confession obtained during such delay; (2) that no confession or statement would be admissible unless prior to interrogation the suspect had been advised of his right to silence and warned that anything he said might be used in evidence; (3) "that such delay is to be considered as an element in determining the voluntary or involuntary nature of such statements or confessions." Celler, Carroll, and Wiley refused to sign this conference report.

WAYNE MORSE DISSENTS

The House passed the measure Saturday night,[37] but the Senate road was rockier. When the Saturday evening conference broke up, Carroll was disheartened. He sought out Morse and told him they had been defeated. But Morse, the eternal maverick, was far from beaten.

"Johnny," he told Carroll, "if you've got the guts we can still win. All I need is for you to speak five hours out of every twenty, and I'll talk this thing to death."

Carroll was afraid to use the filibuster since he was one of the liberals who were planning to open the Eighty-sixth Congress with a fight to change the Senate rules regarding unlimited debate. He suggested instead that it might be possible to utilize a point of order. One of Javits' staff had reminded Carroll and Javits that Rule XXVII of the Senate Rules forbade a conference to add new material to a bill, and the Cramer amendment had not been in either the House or Senate version. If the point of order were sustained the bill was supposed to be recommitted to conference. On this, the last day of the session, such a move would bury the *Mallory* issue.

Morse agreed that the point of order was well taken, but he cautioned Carroll that being right on a mater of parliamentary procedure was not good enough to win that point; a tough approach with a mean weapon was also necessary. And a two-man filibuster was just such a weapon to bludgeon the opposition into accepting truth.

Carroll was still reluctant to filibuster, and he said he would talk to the other liberals and try to arrange a full debate which might have much the same effect. Morse conceded that would be an excellent strategy, but he warned Carroll that the other liberals would not go along. An hour later Carroll came back to Morse more disconsolate than ever. He had been able to persuade only Javits and Proxmire to co-operate, and they would pledge only about an hour of speeches apiece.

At this point Morse told Carroll he would go it alone. He was sure the bill could be talked to death, even by a one-man filibuster. He knew that Lyndon Johnson had to adjourn the Senate quickly. With the 1958 elections only two months away, senators and representatives had been leaving Washington all day. Johnson would have difficulty mustering a quorum on Sunday.

At 8:00 P.M. Morse walked onto the Senate floor wearing a red rose in his lapel, the Oregon senator's well-known warning of an impending filibuster. There were moans and a scattering of cheers at this storm signal; and as soon as he spotted the rose, the Majority leader came charging over, demanding to know what was up. "*Mallory* is up," Morse replied. Johnson began to argue that O'Mahoney was behind the bill, that it was good legislation, and that a filibuster might wreck the Senate. "Lyndon," Morse said, "I can't argue with you. I've got to conserve my strength. It's a bad bill, and I'm going to beat you. You might keep in mind that no Majority leader in history has ever kept the Senate in session on a Sunday, and you're losing your quorum by the minute. But there is a way you can save face. Talk to Carroll and Javits about a point of order they have under Rule XXVII."

Johnson said he had no authority to agree to a point of order against a bill that had been approved by a conference committee. To take any action, he would first have to call a meeting of the Democratic Policy committee. "Good," Morse said, "I'll be sleeping in the lounge. And, Lyndon, I feel fine."

The policy committee meeting was brief. Johnson laid down Morse's ultimatum to accept the point of order or be subjected to a filibuster. Senator Russell made a three-point statement: first, the liberals were probably right on the point of order; second, Morse was an eloquent speaker who would persuade everyone they were right anyway; and third, Morse was the meanest man in the Senate, and he would undoubtedly speak for twenty-four hours out of sheer orneriness, not to mention a desire to recapture the individual filibuster record from Thurmond. Russell concluded that there was nothing to do but surrender, and the committee agreed.

Johnson came back to the Senate lounge and woke Morse to tell him he had won. The parliamentarian had said that the point of order was valid, and when Carroll raised it the Vice-President would sustain him. "There'll have to be a few speeches, though," Johnson added. "The *Mallory* boys will have to go down fighting." Morse said that was all right; but if there were speeches for the bill and against the Court, they would have to be answered. Johnson agreed that was as it should be.

THE PHONY WAR

The Senate had been in continuous session from 10:00 A.M. Saturday when, early Sunday morning, O'Mahoney presented the conference report,[38] and the mock battle followed. Emotions had reached such a pitch, however, that although both sides realized that the outcome had already been decided, they debated in deadly earnest. Carroll and

Morse tried to block consideration of the report by refusing unanimous consent, but they were overruled by a majority vote. Then, after O'Mahoney had begun explaining the conference changes, Hennings asked his loaded questions and O'Mahoney obligingly answered:[39]

HENNINGS: "Mr. President, will the Senator from Wyoming yield?"

O'MAHONEY: "I yield."

HENNINGS: "I thank the distinguished Senator from Wyoming, my colleague on the Committee on the Judiciary."

"Let me ask him whether the language of the conference report which provides that 'such delay . . .' was in either the House version or the Senate version of the bill."

O'MAHONEY: "It was in neither."

HENNINGS: "Then that language is entirely new matter?"

O'MAHONEY: "It is entirely new matter."

Carroll waited until Hennings had finished his questioning and until Olin Johnston had also interrogated O'Mahoney. Then he struck:

"Mr. President, I rise to a point of order on the conference report. I point to Rule XXVII in support of the point of order."[40]

Caught in the trap, O'Mahoney, joined by Lausche, Ervin, and Russell Long of Louisiana, angrily fought back, but Carroll and Morse snapped shut the escape gate and each in turn read back the record of O'Mahoney's colloquy with Hennings. As the debate threatened to string out through the morning, Lyndon Johnson, tired of play-acting and bone-weary from eight long months of riding herd on ninety-five other strong-willed, egoistic, vinegary senators and sick to death of both the defenders and critics of the Warren Court, asked for a ruling from the chair. At ten minutes past 4:00 in the morning, the Vice-President played his role properly by sustaining Carroll's motion.

The Senate adjourned at 4:11 A.M., Sunday, August 24. The attack on the Warren Court which had come in with a thunderclap went out with a sham battle over a point of order.

10. THE CRISIS RESOLVED

The Eighty-fifth Congress adjourned in the cool, predawn hours of Sunday, August 24; and although the climax of the congressional attacks on the Warren Court had passed, there was to be no miraculous return to peaceful relations. In fact, on August 23, the Conference of State Chief Justices had approved by a 36–8 vote a document which David Lawrence described as a "scathing rebuke" of the High Bench. The Chief Justices' report read in part:

> We believe that in the fields with which we are concerned, and as to which we feel entitled to speak, the Supreme Court too often has tended to adopt the role of policy-maker without proper judicial restraint. . . . We are not alone in our view that the Court, in many cases arising under the Fourteenth Amendment, has assumed what seems to us primarily legislative powers. . . . We do not believe that either the framers of the original Constitution or the possibly somewhat less gifted draftsmen of the Fourteenth Amendment ever contemplated that the Supreme Court would, or should, have the almost unlimited policy-making powers which it now exercises. . . .
>
> It has long been an American boast that we have a government of

> laws and not of men. We believe that any study of recent decisions of the Supreme Court will raise at least considerable doubt as to the validity of that boast.[1]

Although the State Chief Justices' criticism was published in time to be included in the last pages of the *Congressional Record* for 1958, it came too late to have a real impact on the Eighty-fifth Congress. It served more as the opening gun of a fresh assault on the Warren Court than as the finale of the 1958 attack. David Lawrence's *U.S. News & World Report* exploited the dissatisfaction of many southern federal judges with the School Segregation cases by mailing a questionnaire to all district court and Court of Appeals judges asking if they agreed with the Chief Justices' report. Only 128 of the 351 jurists polled replied; but of those, 59 expressed agreement with the report, 50 disagreement, and 19 claimed no opinion.[2]

RE-ENTER THE BAR

The Chief Justices' report and the *U.S. News* poll evoked dissent. The Chief Justice of Pennsylvania charged that the report's criticism of the High Bench had been segregationist-inspired,[3] and the poll was called "brazen" and "improper" by a number of federal judges. Equally as controversial was the February, 1959, action of the American Bar Association's House of Delegates in approving the recommendations of its Committee on Communist Strategy, Tactics, and Objectives.[4] The committee chairman was Peter C. Brown, the attorney who had lost the Slochower case and a former member of the Subversive Activities Control Board whose decision on registration of the Communist party had been reversed by the Court in 1956. Among the other committee members was Louis Wyman, the losing lawyer in *Sweezy* v. *New Hampshire,* who had roundly condemned the Court before the National Association of Attorneys General in 1957.

The bar report, which accused the High Bench of handing down decisions "in such a manner as to encourage an increase in Communist activities in the United States," contained a number of specific recommendations to Congress, including a reversal of the Nelson case, a redefinition of "organize" in the Smith Act, as well as a striking-out of the distinction made by *Yates* between advocacy of and incitement to violent overthrow of the government. On the other hand, the bar committee reiterated disapproval of the Jenner bill; and, while praising the work of the House Un-American Activities Committee and the Senate Internal Security Subcommittee, the report suggested that Congress spell out with greater clarity the exact authority of investigating committees.

The House of Delegates officially approved only the recommendations of the committee, not its report; but the intention of a large segment of the ABA to wound the prestige of the Warren Court was quite evident. As Loyd Wright, former chairman of the President's Commission on Government Security, said in support of the committee's resolutions, "Isn't it time we told the Court to read the law and stop writing ideological opinions?"[5]

In general, southern congressmen and newspapers applauded the ABA's action, but there were strong adverse reactions from such liberal sources as the American Civil Liberties Union. And the association's stand was also rejected by the Philadelphia and New York City bars.[6] The Eisenhower administration became involved when, at the President's press conference on February 25, 1959, Laurence Burd of the *Chicago Tribune* asked Eisenhower if he agreed with the bar association that the Supreme Court had created gaps in the American security system. The President's answer was as whimsical as his earlier comments on the Jenner-Butler bill:

> Well, Mr. Burd, I am not lawyer enough to say where if any of these occur. They can be filled by legislation, and what other action would have to be taken, would be necessary. I do want to establish my position—that I have to take the law, and I want to repeat this again, I have to take the law as it's interpreted by the Supreme Court and that is the law of the land that I am called upon by oath to enforce. Now, just what can be done, let's say, in spite of or because of Supreme Court decisions by the Congress itself to change that law, I am just not enough of a lawyer to know.[7]

Warren Olney III, who had left the Justice Department to become director of the Administrative Office of U.S. Courts, was somewhat less evasive in his reactions. Following the ABA's February resolutions, Olney sent a letter of resignation to the association.* Although his letter gave no reason for his withdrawal, he frankly told reporters: "The action taken by the Board of Governors and the House of Delegates with reference to the Supreme Court is, in my opinion,

* Thus joining Earl Warren, who had resigned in 1957.

so discreditable to the association that I do not want to be identified with the organization any longer."[8]

Ross Malone, president of the ABA, was genuinely concerned by the furor the February resolutions had caused. In speeches at Pittsburgh and Syracuse, as well as in testimony before the Senate Internal Security Subcommittee, he valiantly but unconvincingly tried to explain that the lawyers had meant no criticism of the Supreme Court.[9] Despite Malone's protestations, the bar became even more deeply involved in the Court attacks at its next meeting in August, 1959. The association's Committee on Constitutional Rights submitted a report, drafted by Professor Arthur E. Sutherland of the Harvard Law School, which examined the same decisions as had the Communist Tactics Committee. The constitutional rights report concluded:

> On balance, this Committee is unable to see any indication that the security of the Nation or of the states has been impaired by the Supreme Court of the United States. . . . No matter what the sympathies of the Bar may be in specific instances of litigation, there should be no question of their sympathy with and their enthusiastic regard for the institution of a courageous and independent judiciary even though this necessarily means that from time to time decisions will be handed down disappointing the interest of someone.[10]

The anti-Court factions within the House of Delegates announced that they would oppose acceptance of this new report, and a lengthy floor fight resulted when Loyd Wright moved to table the report. In the face of charges of imposing a gag rule, the anti-Court delegates finally agreed to withdraw the tabling motion with the understanding that the report represented only the views of the committee and not of the association.[11] Since this was the ABA's rule for all reports, this wrangle pointed up the resentment within the association toward the High Bench.*

RACE RELATIONS: 1958 TERM

The Court's work went on. In August, 1958, four days after the Eighty-fifth Congress adjourned, the Justices were called back into

* In another action, the House of Delegates also reindorsed H.R. 3, although with the qualification that it be prospective and not retroactive in effect (*New York Times*, August 26, 1959, 30:1).

special session to hear a case concerning Little Rock's integration problems. The Court rejected pleas of the city school board to be permitted to "revert" to segregation until the public sentiment which Governor Faubus had so artfully aroused had calmed down.[12] In a unanimous opinion, Warren stated with force and clarity the authority of the Supreme Court in the American system of government:

> Article 6 of the Constitution makes the Constitution the "supreme Law of the Land." In 1803, Chief Justice Marshall, speaking for a unanimous Court, referring to the Constitution as "the fundamental and paramount law of the nation," declared in the notable case of Marbury v. Madison that "It is emphatically the province and duty of the judicial department to say what the law is." This decision declared the basic principle that the federal judiciary is supreme in the exposition of the law of the Constitution, and that principle has ever since been respected by this Court and the country as a permanent and indispensable feature of our constitutional system.

The Chief Justice was also able to insert dicta in his opinion which offset any inference that denial of review in the second Girard College case meant that the Court would approve a publicly supported "private" school scheme as a means of evading the School Segregation decisions. Warning that the Court would not countenance either ingenious or ingenuous efforts at nullification, Warren wrote: "State support of segregated schools through any arrangement, management, funds, or property cannot be squared with the [Fourteenth] Amendment's command that no State shall deny to any person within its jurisdiction the equal protection of the laws."

Later, Harlan, Warren, and Douglas made public speeches which supplied oblique answers to Court critics; Douglas, in particular, asserted that the High Bench "would not take a back seat." But in spite of the strong beginning in the Little Rock case, the Court's attitude toward segregation seemed less aggressive in the 1958 Term than in previous years.

On the one hand, the Court cut down a technical barrier protecting bus segregation,[13] again thwarted Alabama's efforts to drive the NAACP out of the state,[14] and reversed a contempt conviction growing out of a Virginia legislative investigation of the Negro organization.[15] On the other hand, the Justices unanimously affirmed a lower court decision that Alabama's pupil placement law[16]—a statute whose sponsors had openly boasted was designed to preserve segregation—was not unconstitutional on its face. The Court also refused to review an Arkansas Supreme Court decision requiring the NAACP to reveal to the state the names of its local officials and to surrender financial data.[17] A sixth decision delayed review of a Georgia contempt sentence against the NAACP until the state action had become "final."[18] In addition, with Warren, Douglas, and Brennan dissenting, the Court twice applied the doctrine of equitable abstention—that a federal court should not rule on the constitutionality of a doubtfully worded state statute until state courts had had an opportunity to interpret it—to uphold a refusal by a three-judge district court in Arkansas to pass on the constitutionality of state anti-NAACP laws[19] and to reverse a ruling by another special three-judge tribunal that Virginia's anti-NAACP regulations were invalid.[20]

BROKEN FIELD RUNNING: MORE COLD WAR CASES

The 1958 Term also presented a number of cases in the political offender field. By setting down *Scales* v. *United States* for re-reargument, the Justices for the third time ducked the hot question of the validity of the Smith Act's clause making membership in the Communist party a crime. In other decisions, however, the Warren Court could not avoid heatedly controversial issues.

Two cases came as startling withdrawals from the broad implications, if not the precise holdings, of *Watkins* v. *United States* and *Sweezy* v. *New Hampshire*. By a 5–4 vote, *Barenblatt* v. *United States* upheld the contempt conviction of a college professor for refusing to answer questions posed by the House Un-American Activities Committee concerning his own membership in the Communist party as well as his knowledge of Communist activities at the University of Michigan. For the majority, Harlan saw the Court's function as one of balancing the federal government's right to root out subversives against Barenblatt's right to silence, and in so doing Harlan did not accord a "preferred position" to First Amendment guaranties.

In striking the balance in favor of the government, Harlan made four main points. First, he explained that *Watkins* had not decided that the resolution setting out the authority of the Un-American Activities Committee was unconstitutionally vague. The sole basis of *Watkins* had been that the committee had failed to show the pertinency of questions asked Watkins. Second, Harlan denied that the pertinency point applied here because Barenblatt, unlike Watkins, had not invoked it; besides, he had been clearly informed both of the purpose of the investigation and of his own interrogation. Third, Harlan rejected the assertion that the investigation infringed on First Amendment rights. The investigation had had a valid legislative purpose, that of discerning the extent of Communist infiltration in colleges, and the Communist party's advocacy of violent revolution put it outside the category of a normal political party. "In the last analysis," Harlan wrote, the power to investigate communism "rests on the right of self-preservation."

Harlan's final point was that the Court would not look into the charge that the real purpose of the investigation had been exposure rather than legislation. "So long as Congress acts in pursuance of its constitutional power, the judiciary lacks authority to intervene on the basis of the motives which spurred the exercise of that power."

Black, joined by Warren, Douglas, and Brennan, dissented. Black took issue with Harlan's approach to the case. He denied that the Court's function was one of balancing rights. The First Amendment spoke in absolute terms: "Congress shall make no law. . . ." But, Black continued, if balancing were the proper function of the Court, Harlan had put the wrong weights on the scales. It was not Barenblatt's right to silence which should have been pitted against Congress' right to know, but "the interest of the people as a whole in being able to join organizations, advocate causes and make political 'mistakes' without later being subjected to governmental penalties for having dared to think for themselves."

Second, Black argued that the authorizing resolution of the Un-American Activities Committee was so vague that it was "inconceivable" that a Court would put a man in the position of having to guess, at peril of prison, what types of investigations and interrogations were possible under it. Last, Black countered the usual charge of judicial legislation with an indictment of legislative adjudication. The real purpose of the committee, he claimed, was to expose, try, and punish suspected Communists. This function the Constitution reserved to the courts.

Uphaus v. *Wyman* was decided the same day as *Barenblatt* and caused the same 5–4 division. Frankfurter, Harlan, Clark, Whittaker, and Potter Stewart—whom Eisenhower had promoted from the Court of Appeals to succeed Burton early in the 1958 Term—voted to sustain the contempt conviction of Willard Uphaus for refusing to surrender a guest list of a camp suspected by Wyman of being a meeting place for Communists. For the majority, Clark found that the interests of New Hampshire in discovering the presence of possible subversive persons outweighed any right to privacy which may have been involved. The investigation was justified "in the interest of self-preservation, 'the ultimate value of any society.' "

Brennan wrote a lengthy opinion for the four dissenters. Utilizing official records and reports of Wyman's investigations, Brennan hammered home time and again the basic point that the record "not only fails to reveal any interest of the State sufficient to subordinate appellant's constitutionally protected rights, but affirmatively shows that the investigatory objective was the impermissible one of exposure for exposure's sake."

As in the 1957 political offender cases, the votes of Frankfurter and Harlan were decisive. In *Watkins* Frankfurter and Harlan had joined in Warren's opinion of the Court, though Frankfurter had also filed a separate opinion stating his understanding of what the case held. In *Sweezy* the two Justices had taken a somewhat different but no less strong position than that of the Chief Justice. In 1959, however, neither Frankfurter nor Harlan repeated the eloquent defense of academic freedom or the brilliant exposition of the inescapable duties of the judicial function which had been set forth in their *Sweezy* opinion. Nor did they repeat their former insistence on "definiteness" of relevance and pertinency of questions asked witnesses. As if to direct attention to the Court's withdrawal, Frankfurter, as the senior majority judge, assigned the *Uphaus* opinion to Clark, the author of the dissenting opinions in *Sweezy* and *Watkins*.

In contrast to these two retreats, the Court unanimously reversed another contempt of Congress conviction[21] because of a faultily drawn indictment and also reversed three out of four contempt convictions involving Ohio's Little Un-American Activities Committee.[22] Then, late in the term, the Justices decided two Federal Loyalty-Security Program cases.[23]

William Vitarelli, an employee working in the Pacific Trust Islands under the Department of Interior, had been fired from his job in March, 1954, for security reasons. After exhausting his administrative remedies, Vitarelli resorted to the federal courts. While his case was pending, the Secretary of Interior sent him a second notice of dismissal, canceling the first order and firing him without giving any reason.

The district court and the Court of Appeals decided for the government; but by a 5–4 vote, Harlan joining Warren, Black, Douglas, and Brennan, the Supreme Court ordered Vitarelli's reinstatement, "subject, of course, to any lawful exercise of the Secretary's authority hereafter to dismiss him. . . ." Speaking for the majority, Harlan found the error to have been similar to that in *Service* v. *Dulles*. The Secretary of Interior, though he had power to fire Vitarelli without giving any reason, had chosen to follow the loyalty-security procedures which he had established for the department. And the record showed three violations of those procedures in Vitarelli's case. These errors voided the first dismissal. The second dismissal, Harlan held, was without legal effect; it was only an effort to moot Vitarelli's court action.

Frankfurter wrote a dissenting opinion for himself, Clark, Whittaker, and Stewart. He agreed that the 1954 dismissal was invalid for the same reasons as Harlan had listed but thought that the Secretary's first action did not taint the second dismissal. "I cannot join in an unreal interpretation which attributes to governmental action the empty measure of confetti throwing."

The Vitarelli case was decided on purely procedural grounds and put no real obstacle in the path of the loyalty-security program. In contrast, *Greene* v. *McElroy* dealt a body blow to the accepted methods of operating the security system and posed a further threat of a knockout. The case began in 1951 when the government revoked the security clearance of William L. Greene, a vice president of Engineering Research Corporation, a firm working on navy contracts. This revocation meant that ERCO had to give up its defense contracts or fire Greene. The company chose the latter course, and Greene started a long fight for reinstatement of his clearance.

During the entire course of the security proceedings Greene categorically denied all charges of sympathetic association with known Communists; he also called a number of witnesses who testified as to his loyalty and substantiated his accounts of events which the loyalty board thought suspicious. The government presented no witnesses or testimony at the open hearings but relied instead on confidential reports. Greene was not allowed to see these reports, nor was he permitted to confront and cross-examine the witnesses whose testimony comprised the reports. (The board members were allowed to read these reports, but they were apparently not given the opportunity to see and question the witnesses.)

After exhausting his administrative remedies, Greene took his case to the courts, asserting that the government had taken away his Fifth Amendment right to pursue his private profession and had done so in violation of his Sixth Amendment right to confront and cross-examine witnesses against him. These issues, though pertaining to private rather than public employment, paralleled the questions which in 1951 had divided the Vinson Court 4–4 in *Bailey* v. *Richardson* and which in 1955 the Warren Court had avoided in *Peters* v. *Hobby*. In 1959 Warren mustered Stewart along with Black, Douglas, and Brennan behind his opinion ordering Greene's reinstatement, but once again the Court did not meet the basic constitutional problem head-on.

Warren used the tactics which had become the trade-mark of his chief justiceship. First, he invoked the Constitution and held that the right to follow a private profession free from unreasonable governmental interference was guaranteed by the Fifth Amendment. Then he spoke warmly of the traditional safeguards of confrontation and cross-examination of hostile witnesses, rights which Greene had been denied. After this discussion, Warren announced it would not be necessary to decide whether the Industrial Security Program was a violation of the Fifth or Sixth Amendments because neither Congress nor the President had authorized the Secretary of Defense to dispense with the historic rights of the Sixth Amendment.

> Before we are asked to judge whether, in the context of security clearance cases, a person may be deprived of the right to follow his chosen profession without full hearings where accusers may be confronted, it must be made clear that the President or Congress, within their constitutional powers, specifically have decided that the imposed procedures are necessary and warranted and have author-

> ized their use. . . . Whether those procedures under the circumstances comport with the Constitution we do not decide. Nor do we decide whether the President has inherent authority to create such a program, whether congressional action is necessary, or what the limits on executive or legislative authority may be. We decide only that in the absence of explicit authorization from either the President or Congress the respondents were not empowered to deprive petitioner of his job in a proceeding in which he was not afforded the safeguards of confrontation and cross-examination.

Frankfurter, Harlan, and Whittaker concurred in the result, agreeing with Warren that neither presidential nor congressional authorization had been shown for the Secretary's refusal to allow cross-examination. Harlan appended a brief opinion in which he chided the Chief Justice for dwelling too heavily on the very issues which the Court claimed not to be deciding. Harlan then turned on Clark's dissent and scolded him for yielding to the temptation to pen literary phrases which were far more colorful than accurate.

Dissenting alone, Clark lashed out at the majority and even tacked on a footnote answering Harlan's criticism. In his opening pages Clark capsuled his disagreement with Warren: "To me this case is both clear and simple. . . . Surely one does not have a constitutional right to have access to the Government's military secrets. . . . What for anyone else would be considered a privilege at best has for Greene been enshrouded in constitutional protection. This sleight of hand is too much for me." Clark denied that the procedures of the security program were unfair and found no doubt that such procedures had been authorized both by Congress and the President.

APPLYING THE JENCKS STATUTE

A week before the term ended the Court decided a pair of cases under the new Jencks Act. In *Rosenberg* v. *United States,* an appeal from a fraud conviction, the Justices were unanimous in their belief that under the Jencks law the trial judge should have ordered the prosecution to give to the defendant certain documents which the government had in its possession. Frankfurter, Clark, Harlan, Whittaker, and Stewart, however, felt that the judge's error had been harmless. Warren, Black, Douglas, and Brennan disagreed.

The other case, *Palermo* v. *United States,* involved an income tax prosecution. All nine Justices agreed that a summary of a witness' statement, unsigned and otherwise unapproved by the witness, did not have to be given to the defendant; but the Court divided 5–4 in its reasoning. Frankfurter, in an opinion in which Clark, Harlan, Whittaker, and Stewart joined, explained the *Jencks* decision as having been based on the Supreme Court's power to prescribe, in the absence of congressional regulations, procedures for the administration of federal justice. Since Congress had adopted the Jencks law, that statute and not the *Jencks* decision governed such cases. Frankfurter then held that Congress had intended the Jencks Act to be the exclusive means for the production of witnesses' statements in the possession of the United States. Therefore, because the summary of the witness' statement here was neither signed nor approved by that witness, it could not be given to the defendant.

Brennan, speaking for Warren, Black, and Douglas as well, attacked Frankfurter's opinion as far too broad for the facts of the case. It was not necessary, Brennan said, to rule whether the Jencks Act was the sole procedural method open to a defendant who wished to secure a statement of a witness. Indeed, such an interpretation raised serious questions involving the Sixth Amendment. "It is true that our holding in Jencks was not put on constitutional grounds, for it did not have to be; but it would be idle to say that the commands of the Constitution were not close to the surface of the decision. . . ." Cases could conceivably arise in which the Sixth Amendment would require production of government reports not covered by the Jencks law. Therefore, Brennan believed, the Court should have restricted itself to ruling that the statement requested by the defendant in this situation fell neither within the terms of the Jencks statute nor under that category of documents which a trial judge might, at his discretion, order produced.

MORE STIRRINGS ON CAPITOL HILL

Once again the Court issue spilled over into the legislative process. Senator McClellan warned a New York audience that usurpation of legislative power by the High Bench "threatens the very foundations of our Republic."[24] And Eastland continued to deplore the "disastrous trend" of Supreme Court decisions. The chairman of the Judiciary Committee advised the Senate that "the Court is taking to itself powers, and exercising those powers, without any justification in statute or Constitution, without any reliance on recognized principles of law, without any basis whatever except its own naked thirst for power."[25]

Representative Francis Walter was ready to repair the security program with fresh legislation specifically denying employees' rights to confrontation and cross-examination of hostile informants.[26] His proposal was approved by the Un-American Activities Committee,[27] but it was not taken up by the House in the first session of the Eighty-sixth Congress.

There was some legislative action, however. Congress reversed *Guss* v. *Utah,* a 1957 decision which had applied the pre-emption doctrine in such a way as to deny a state the right to regulate interstate labor disputes even where the NLRB refused to take action;[28] but this reversal was part of the comprehensive design of labor control legislation, not a facet of a Court-curbing scheme. In another law, Congress reversed a 1959 decision[29] which had extended traditional state authority to tax firms engaged in interstate commerce.[30] This statute was out of the main stream of Court criticism, since it was the act of Congress and not the Court decision which took away state power.

These were the only pieces of legislation which could have been interpreted as aimed at the Court or Court doctrine to get through both houses in 1959. H.R. 3, the Mallory bill, the Nelson measure, a modified habeas corpus bill, and the proposal to broaden the definition of "organize" in the Smith Act were all dutifully repassed by the House,[31] but in the Senate the most these bills could do was to writhe a bit before dying in committee. Legislation to reverse *Cole* v. *Young* was buried in committee in both houses. The only plan to revoke Court jurisdiction which received anything like serious attention was a proposed constitutional amendment by Herman Talmadge[32] to give states exclusive authority to determine how public schools should be operated, and this resolution was tabled in subcommittee.

One of the most interesting aspects of the 1959 phase of Court-congressional relations involved the matter of passports. In September, the House Foreign Relations Committee reported a moderate measure[33] which would have allowed the Secretary of State to deny passports to persons who had been members or active supporters of the Communist party since 1951, providing that the Secretary found that the travel abroad of such persons would be "harmful to the security of the United States." Individual rights were protected by: (1) a requirement that no passport application be rejected except after an opportunity for a hearing; (2) a prohibition against a refusal to grant a passport "solely on the basis of membership in any organization or association with any individual or group"; and, most important, (3) persons refused passports were guaranteed a right of "judicial review *on the record.*"

This last requirement, in line with the theory behind the Supreme Court's 1959 ruling in *Greene* v. *McElroy*, would have forced the Secretary of State to reveal at least some of his sources of adverse information or issue a passport. During floor debate, Francis Walter and Alvin Bentley (Rep., Mich.) tried to amend this provision to permit use of confidential information, but each of their proposals was defeated. The bill then passed the House 371–18, but it was too late for the Senate to take action.[34]

THE CRITICS CONFOUNDED

The spark of 1958 was missing from the Court critics, and the temper of the Eighty-sixth Congress' first session was markedly different from that of the Eighty-fifth. The Court foes had reached a peak of excitement in the summer of 1958, and in spite of the additional ammunition supplied by the State Chief Justices and the American Bar Association, they could not achieve that fever pitch again the next year. The modified attitude of the Eighty-sixth Congress was also due in part to a change in personnel in both houses. In the Senate, for example, seven Republicans who had fought alongside the segregationists for one or more of the anti-Court bills had left Capitol Hill. Jenner and Knowland had retired; Bricker of Ohio, Thye of Minnesota, Watkins of Utah, and Revercomb and Hoblitzell of West Virginia had been defeated for re-election. Except in the case of the West Virginia senators,* it was unlikely that the Court

* Even in West Virginia the Court itself was not directly at issue. The United Mine Workers attacked Revercomb and Hoblitzell for "anti-union" attitudes, of which their support of H.R. 3 was supposedly one example.

bills had constituted a popular political issue. But the 1958 election results were generally interpreted as a return to liberalism; and relatively few leaders of either party were anxious to face the 1960 electorate with a record of having labored to curb the most liberal branch of the federal government, especially with the race issue bubbling so clearly beneath the surface. As Senator Kuchel of California —who had voted in support of H.R. 3 in 1958—said in reply to a speech by Eastland in March, 1959: Since the Court bills which had gone down to "well-deserved defeat" in the Eighty-fifth Congress had not had the support of the Senate or of the people, there was no reason to revive them.[35]

Two other events had helped sap the vigor of the Court attacks. First, *Barenblatt* had soothed some of the institutional anger generated by *Watkins,* and *Uphaus* had eased resentment among local officials by acknowledging broad state authority to deal with internal subversion against a state as contrasted with state authority to punish subversion against the United States. Increasing the critics' problems was the obvious fact that after several years of living with decisions like *Mallory, Nelson, Yates,* and *Cole* v. *Young,* a crisis in law enforcement had not developed, nor had packs of Communists descended on the country or infested government employment. In light of this failure of dire predictions, *Uphaus* and *Barenblatt* provided a ready means by which the Court foes could execute a face-saving retreat of their own. The *U.S. News & World Report* claimed victory in the 1958 Term: "In effect, a five-year trend toward limiting the powers of States and Congress is to be halted or reversed."[36] On a New York television program, "National Forum of the Air," Louis Wyman echoed this assertion, stating that "the Court is returning to the middle of the road."[37]

THE 1959 TERM AND THE EIGHTY-SIXTH CONGRESS' SECOND SESSION

In its 1959 Term, the Court continued to move slowly in the race relations field. The Justices were unanimous in striking down efforts of officials of Little Rock and North Little Rock, Arkansas, to use license tax ordinances to obtain the names of local NAACP members.[38] In *Wolfe* v. *North Carolina,* however, the Court divided 5–4 in upholding trespass convictions of Negroes who had used a segregated public golf course. The majority, speaking through Justice Stewart, agreed that segregation on the golf course was unconstitutional but reasoned that the convictions would have to stand because no federal question was presented by the case. Through "some quirk of inadvertence" the fact that a federal court injunction against continued segregation had been obtained after the arrest of the defendants had not been mentioned in appeal to the North Carolina Supreme Court, though this had been brought out at the trial. Warren, for himself, Black, Douglas, and Brennan, found the majority opinion to be poor technical law and worse substantive justice.

The majority was even more wary in the political offender field. A decision in *Scales* v. *United States,* which had first come to the Court in 1955, was postponed for the fourth time. This case challenged the validity of the provision in the Smith Act which makes it a crime to be a member of an organization which advocates the violent overthrow of the government.* Even more ticklish was the problem presented by *Abel* v. *United States,* reviewing the conviction of the Soviet spy Rudolph Ivanovich Abel.

FBI agents, suspecting Abel of espionage but lacking sufficient evidence to obtain a warrant, arranged with the Immigration and Naturalization Service for Abel, an alien, to be arrested for possible deportation. This procedure eliminated the necessity for a judicial warrant, since Congress had authorized the Immigration Service to use "administrative warrants" in deportation cases. When Immigration authorities went to arrest Abel, they were accompanied by FBI agents. After arresting him, Immigration officers searched the prisoner and his hotel room and found some evidence bearing on a possible espionage offense. After Abel had been taken away—the officers had him check out of his hotel—FBI agents, with the hotel's permission, conducted a further search of his room and found additional incriminating evidence.

For a five-judge majority, Frankfurter stated that the central issue was whether the federal officers had co-operated in bad faith to avoid the constitutional restraints of the Fourth Amendment. Finding no such bad faith, the majority sustained both searches. In separate

* The case was finally decided in 1961. By a 5–4 vote, Warren, Black, Douglas, and Brennan dissenting, the Court sustained this part of the statute. Justice Harlan wrote the opinion of the Court.

dissents, Douglas (joined by Black) and Brennan (joined by Warren, Black, and Douglas) claimed that the majority had misstated the fundamental question. Douglas wrote that "the issue is not whether the F. B. I. were in bad faith. Of course they were not. The question is how far zeal may be permitted to carry officials bent on law enforcement." Brennan added: "It is the individual's interest in privacy which the Amendment protects, and that would not appear to fluctuate with the 'intent' of the invading officers." Utilizing previous insistences by Justice Frankfurter on the necessity of procedural regularities in criminal trials, the dissenters charged that not only was a constitutional guaranty being undermined, but an important judicial check on executive authority was also being eroded.

Not as dramatic, but even more significant in terms of the Court's withdrawal, was the decision in *Nelson and Globe* v. *Los Angeles*. Two county employees, Thomas Nelson and Arthur Globe, had invoked the Fifth Amendment before a subcommittee of the House Un-American Activities Committee. Pursuant to a state statute which commanded that government employees answer questions about subversion posed by duly authorized state or federal investigating agencies, the two men were thereupon discharged from their jobs. Nelson was a permanent employee, and the Court divided 4–4 (Warren did not participate) on the constitutionality of his dismissal. But Globe had only a temporary status, and the Court held, 5–3, that his firing did not abridge due process.

There seemed to be a close parallel between this situation and that of the Slochower case in 1956, but Frankfurter, Harlan, Clark, Whittaker, and Stewart thought otherwise. Frankfurter, as the senior majority Justice, assigned the task of writing the opinion of the Court to Clark. Clark relied on *Beilan* and *Lerner* and distinguished the *Slochower* decision on the ground that whereas New York had discharged Slochower solely because he had invoked the Fifth Amendment, Los Angeles officials had fired Globe for insubordination. He had utilized the Fifth Amendment after having been warned that failure to answer the subcommittee's questions would result in dismissal.

The nicety of this distinction escaped the three dissenters. Brennan found Globe's case to be identical with that of Slochower: each had been summarily fired because each had claimed the Fifth Amendment before a congressional investigation.

> Accordingly there is presented here the very same arbitrary action—the drawing of an inference of unfitness for employment from the exercise of the privilege before another body, without opportunity to explain on the part of the employee, or duty on the part of the employing body to attempt to relate the employee's conduct specifically to his fitness for employment—as was involved in Slochower.

Black agreed (Douglas concurred in both dissents) and added that the action of the Los Angeles officials was also a violation of the national supremacy clause in that it penalized Globe for having exercised a federal constitutional privilege.

Many of the foes of the Warren Court were still not reconciled, but *Abel* and *Nelson and Globe* were not the kinds of decisions which could be used to rally a fresh congressional assault against the High Bench. There was, however, some old business which could be hashed over again. Unnoticed by House liberals, Representative Francis Walter of the House Un-American Activities Committee slipped onto the consent calendar his bill to overcome *Greene* v. *McElroy*, and the measure passed without debate on February 2, 1960.[39] Although the Senate took no action on Walter's proposal,[40] the Senate Judiciary Committee did report out[41] on June 30, 1960, a four-part internal security measure sponsored by Keating of New York and Dodd of Connecticut. The first two sections dealt with registration of foreign agents and with espionage. The third part broadened the definition of "organize" in the Smith Act, and the fourth authorized the Secretary of State to deny passports to Communists or to Communist sympathizers. This fourth section differed from the bill passed by the House in 1959 in its provisions allowing the Secretary to use confidential information which he would not have to reveal.

This omnibus bill immediately created a jurisdictional dispute. On July 1, Senator Fulbright of Arkansas, chairman of the Foreign Relations Committee, announced that his committee had been holding hearings on a passport bill and that he had twice informed Senator Eastland that passport legislation was properly a matter for the Foreign Relations Committee, not the judiciary group. Fulbright warned that if the bill came to the floor he would have to insist that it be referred to his committee for study.[42] But with national—and congressional—attention focused on the 1960 presidential campaign, neither the passport bill nor any other Court measure received floor consideration in the Senate.

IV CONCLUSION

11. CONGRESS AND THE COURT

During 1954–57, the Warren Court handed down decisions which had significant effects in shaping public policy in such vital areas as race relations, loyalty-security programs, conduct of congressional investigations, admission to the bar, and prosecution of subversives. Stirred sometimes by resentment against judicial policy-making, sometimes by pressures from interest groups and newspapers whose goals had been thwarted by the Court, sometimes by fear of the effects of the Court's decisions on national security or racial peace, and sometimes by a combination of these causes, many congressmen supported proposals to reverse various facets of judge-made policies and even to curb the Court's basic authority. Although only legislation to modify the future effects of the *Jencks* decision was adopted, the Court, as Bernard Schwartz observed, "remoulded its jurisprudence so as to render moot much of the criticism against it."[1]

The *New York Times* exaggerated when it editorialized in early 1960 that "what Senator Jenner was unable to achieve the Supreme Court has now virtually accomplished on its own,"[2] but there were visible changes in the Court's outlook. Raw statistics tell some of the story. During the 1956 Term, the year of *Jencks, Yates,* and *Watkins,* the Court rejected civil liberties claims in only 26 per cent of all cases decided by full opinion; during the next term, the Court rejected civil liberties claims in 41 per cent of such cases. The figure rose to 48.8 per cent during the 1958 Term.[3]

Close analysis of the cold war and race relations decisions is even more revealing. While there can be reasonable doubt as to how much, or even whether, the *Beilan* and *Lerner* cases in the 1957 Term represented a change in judicial policy, *Barenblatt* and *Uphaus* were obvious shifts. Four of the earlier six-judge majority in *Watkins* and *Sweezy* dissented. Clark, who had dissented from both *Watkins* and *Sweezy,* joined the new majority in *Barenblatt* and wrote the opinion for the Court in *Uphaus.* Then, two weeks later, Frankfurter's majority opinion in *Palermo* v. *United States* almost totally relinquished to congressional discretion questions as to when and under what circumstances FBI files could be made available to criminal defendants.

In the race relations field, the Court's refusal to strike down the Alabama pupil placement law, even though its supporters had openly boasted that it was designed to insure that "no brick will ever be removed from our [state's] segregation wall,"[4] indicated a go-slow attitude toward integration. This attitude was also reflected in the Court's refusal to sustain a lower federal court's decision declaring unconstitutional Virginia's anti-NAACP laws, and its reliance on a dubious technicality to uphold a trespass conviction of Negroes for using a segregated public golf course. These decisions took some of the strength from the Court's powerful opinion in the Little Rock case.

THE PATTERNS OF HISTORY

The retreat of the Warren Court was a tactical withdrawal, not a rout. None of the race cases showed evidence of a willingness to breathe new life into Jim Crow; nor did such decisions as *Vitarelli* v. *Seaton* or *Greene* v. *McElroy* support the view that the Justices had abdicated authority in the political offender field. While many civil libertarians were disappointed in the Court's refusal to stand its ground, there should have been no surprise, for the course of the Warren Court's conflict with Congress followed a well-worn pattern. First came decisions on important aspects of public policy. Historically these issues have varied from prosecutions under the Alien and Sedition statutes to those under the Smith Act; from congressional control over slavery in the territories to congressional control over wages, hours, and other conditions of employment; from a centralized banking system to paper money to income taxes—but the next step has been one of severe criticism of the Court coupled with threats of remedial and/or retaliatory legislative action.

The third step has usually been a judicial retreat. Marshall was ready to submit to congressional review of Court decisions, and while such a concession was never forced, his Court did pass up the opportunity to declare unconstitutional the peremptory removal of circuit judges by the Jeffersonians. Twenty years later, in the face of new attacks, the Court cut back into Marshall's earlier opinions and eased its restrictions on state authority. During Reconstruction, the judges at first courageously defended civil liberties against martial law and bills of attainder. When confronted with Radical threats, however, the Justices, as Gideon Welles said, "caved in."[5] Jeremiah Black was less kind in his comments: "The court stood still to be ravished and did not even hallo while the thing was being done."[6]

In the twentieth century, the pattern has been similar. For a dozen years after 1905, the Justices did not rigidly follow their earlier laissez faire line, though to what degree this policy can be ascribed to Progressive political pressure is difficult to determine. The Taft Court, perceiving the weakness and disorganization of its opponents, unashamedly established judicial supremacy. But, when the Hughes Court was challenged by Franklin D. Roosevelt, the Justices executed the most dramatic and important reversal in Court history, one far beyond the scope of the Warren Court's retreat.

There were also peculiarities in the conflict over the Warren Court. Except for the Reconstruction period, most major attacks against the Court had been occasioned by decisions defending property rather than civil or political rights. Jeffersonian anger had been stirred by judicial refusal to invalidate the Alien and Sedition Acts and by fear that the bench would dominate the federal and state governments. Later conflicts involved Court protection of creditors against debtors; of corporations against workers, farmers, or consumers; of hard money interests against soft money; or, as in *Dred Scott,* of property rights of masters against human rights of slaves. The Justices could expect, and they did receive, stout support from conservative forces when they defended business against government regulation or extended judicial control over labor. They could not reasonably have expected similar support when they protected rights of defeated rebels to trial by jury as in the 1860's, or, as in the 1950's, rights of Communists to free speech or fair trial, rights of supposedly disloyal persons to procedural justice, or rights of Negroes to cross caste lines and destroy white supremacy.[7] While attitude studies indicate that people from professional and managerial groups are likely to be more tolerant on civil liberties matters than are workers,[8] "tolerance" and positive support have vastly different political effects. And it is probable that the economic decisions of the Warren Court (and the Court generally since 1937) had alienated a good part of what little positive support for the political offender decisions might have been forthcoming from the business community. Indeed, the NAM and the Chamber of Commerce were more than willing to take advantage of the attack on the Court to get H.R. 3 through Congress.

The method of attack on the Warren Court was also different from the historical model. Some of the bills would have required extraordinary majorities to invalidate a statute; several others proposed constitutional amendments to reverse the school decisions; still others threatened the jurisdiction of the federal courts; and there was even talk of impeachment. But, aside from the Jenner-Butler measure, none of these kinds of proposals received serious consideration. Nor, in light of the impact on Court policy of the appointment of Warren, Brennan, and even Harlan, was there any effort to increase the number of Justices, though several plans were introduced to require "previous judicial experience" for future Supreme Court nominees.[9]

Southern foes of the Court relied on resistance at the state level (a venerable practice) to fight the School Segregation cases; but at the national level they attacked the racial decisions mainly in speeches and joined with northern conservatives in concentrating on reversing the Court on cold war issues. The principal tactic of this coalition was that of remedial legislation, the tactic which business groups had perfected during the previous decade. Use of this approach was made easier, of course, by the Court's own frequent reliance on statutory rather than on constitutional interpretation.

In a sense, Lyndon Johnson's role in the battle over the Warren Court was unique. Johnson fully understood the ethic of the Senate. He knew how to advise without becoming patronizing; how to warn without seeming boorish; how to bargain without appearing to bribe or promising more than he could deliver; how to appeal to personal honor, party unity, Senate loyalty, or national welfare without becoming unctuous. Moreover, Johnson knew where each of his colleagues in both parties stood—or wavered—and what each wanted or feared. At the same time, he cleverly camouflaged his own position; few people knew what Johnson really wanted, other than to come out on the winning side. Perhaps most important, his tactical genius and marvelous ability to dissemble were geared to a restless energy and a burning personal ambition. There were many factors which played a part in the defeat of the anti-Court bills; but without Johnson's leadership, even though it was only warily accepted by the more ardent of the Court defenders, more legislation would certainly have been passed and much of it signed into law.

In a broader sense, this element of dynamic leadership was not altogether without parallel in previous Court conflicts, though it was more usually found on the side of the Court foes. The character of earlier Court fights had been largely shaped by the political style of men like Jefferson, Thaddeus Stevens, the two Roosevelts, and, despite his disorganized following, Robert La Follette. In defense of the Court, Wheeler, O'Mahoney, and Borah in 1937 had displayed skills which, though different from, were equally if not more effective than those of Johnson in 1958.

There was no real parallel, however, for the frankness with which the majority and minority Justices of the Warren Court viewed judicial power. Holmes, Brandeis, Stone, and Cardozo had tried to demonstrate the speciousness of the Court's claim to Jovian aloofness and, instead, to place much of the responsibility for constitutional decisions on the personal reactions of the judges to the demands of conflicting forces within society. But even in defeat in 1937 the conservative judges clung to the old myth that the judicial process involved only an exercise of judgment and not of the will. In contrast, no member of the Warren Court believed that judicial review was an exact science. Clark's dissents showed no sign of accepting or appealing to the will-judgment dichotomy; and, before coming to the bench, Frankfurter on the one hand and Douglas on the other had both been members of the realist school of jurisprudence, a school whose chief contribution to legal theory had been the continuation of Holmes's efforts "to wash the law in cynical acid."

Less academically oriented though he was, Black's early career on the Court indicated acceptance of the realist critique of the judicial myth. Indeed, Charles Curtis noted that after Black's first term "most of the bar regarded him as if he were filled with new wine; others . . . as one who had fed on wild honey."[10] During his third year as Chief Justice, Earl Warren had stated that judges were "not monks or scientists, but participants in the living stream of our national life"[11]—something few Justices who sat on the bench prior to 1937 would have said, and even fewer truly believed, at least as far as "sound" judges like themselves were concerned.

Nevertheless, the struggle among the members of the Warren Court was not fought in the candidly sophisticated manner of a learned law journal debate among realists. Both sides took occasional refuge in the judicial myth by criticizing the other for giving in to personal predilections rather than following the ineluctable commands of the Constitution.[12] This allusion to the old formulas of Hamilton, Marshall, Sutherland, and Roberts indicated understanding of the limits of rational persuasion. It also pointed up the fact that the realism of both the Black-Douglas and Frankfurter wings of the Court has been part of the perennial "search for objectivity in constitutional law."[13] These judges had expounded on the personal element in decision-making not to justify their own prejudices but to control them by exposing them to rational scrutiny.[14]

There has been no set pattern for the role of the Chief Justice in the third or retrograde phase of a Court crisis. Voting last in conference, the Chief Justice knows which way the decision will go before he fully commits himself.* He thus has a greater degree of flexibility than his associates, especially when there is a close division within the Court. The Chief Justice may lead his colleagues in retreat; or, even if originally opposed to a withdrawal, he may use his flexibility to cast his lot with the new majority. In such instances he may justify stifling his personal feelings either: (1) to protect the Court's prestige by securing as large a majority as possible; (2) to foster his personal reputation outside the Court as a leader of his associates; or (3) to retain his prerogative when with the majority of

* Since the Justices give their views in order of seniority, the Chief Justice usually has indicated his general position before the vote is taken.

assigning responsibility for writing the opinion of the Court, and thus keeping some measure of control over the Court's new course.[15]

Chase and Hughes were part of the majority which voted to disengage the Court from its political conflict, and to a lesser extent so was Marshall. At least insofar as Marshall and Hughes[16] were concerned, joining the retreat meant a change from the views expressed in previous votes. On the other hand, Warren, like Taney, refused to retreat. Taney dissented vigorously in the Prize Cases and drafted opinions declaring unconstitutional other war policies of the federal government. It would be difficult to imagine him writing or even acquiescing in Chase's opinion in the McCardle case. Warren, too, stood fast. He apparently was willing to forego any possible advantages to himself, to his policies, or to the Court which might have been gained by joining the new majority.*

GROUP CONFLICT

Court-congressional relations can be partly explained in terms of the judiciary's involvement in the struggle among competing groups to influence public policy. Groups which cannot achieve their goals in the legislative or administrative processes can often do so through the judicial process. Groups whose interests have been frustrated by the courts can likewise seek redress from legislators or executive officials.[17] This sort of group action has played an important role in most Court attacks, and it also played a significant part in the attacks on the Warren Court, though because of the presence of ideological as well as economic questions this role was not always clear-cut.

* Not only did Warren dissent in each of the cold war retreats (except *Nelson and Globe,* in which he did not participate), but in the 1957 Term he cast 30 dissenting votes in the 119 cases decided by full opinion, 26 dissenting votes in the 1958 Term out of 112 full opinion cases, and 23 dissenting votes in the 115 full opinion cases of the 1959 Term. In the 1953 Term Warren had dissented in only 8 of 101 full opinion cases; in 6 of 87 full opinion cases in the 1954 Term; in 13 out of 111 in the 1955 Term; and in 12 of the 115 in the 1956 Term. By way of contrast, in his first nine full terms as Chief Justice (1930–38), Charles Evans Hughes cast a total of only 23 dissenting votes in some 1,382 full opinion decisions. (These statistics will vary slightly depending on the method of classification. For Hughes I have depended on the computations of Felix Frankfurter, James M. Landis, and Henry M. Hart in their annual *Harvard Law Review* articles on the Court during the 1930's. For Warren's dissents I have classified "full opinion" decisions as contrasted with "memorandum" dispositions in the same way as the Lawyers' Edition of the Supreme Court Reports. I have counted opinions rather than cases. That is, if one opinion for the Court covered several pieces of litigation, I have counted this as only one case.)

CONCLUSION

The lobbying of three groups was especially successful in 1957–58: that of the FBI, the NAM, and the AFL-CIO. The Chamber of Commerce and the NAACP were also effective, although to a lesser extent. Each of these five had a tangible and immediate stake in one or more aspects of the Court proposals; each was well organized and skilfully led; and each devoted considerable time—if not money—to a lobbying campaign.* The size of the memberships involved varied from the millions of the AFL-CIO to the few thousand, at most, of the FBI. Numbers, of course, are not always an accurate measure of political strength. Prestige, money, personal contacts, access to mass media of communication, and ability to dramatize and popularize aims are often as significant as sheer size.[18] Indeed, of all these groups the FBI was the most effective and the NAM a close second, while the AFL-CIO was able only at the very last minute to help swing the few votes needed to bury H.R. 3.

Other groups went on record for or against the Court legislation, but they were hardly prime forces in the conflict. The American Civil Liberties Union, the Americans for Democratic Action, and the American Veterans Committee, for instance, lacked the numbers to offer a ballot-box sanction and the social status or governmental position to exert the kind of pressure the FBI could. The American Farm Bureau Federation lobbied for H.R. 3; but, because there was no bread-and-butter interest of farmers involved, this activity was widely discounted as just another example of the alliance between the leaders of the Farm Bureau and the NAM. Similarly, what lobbying the AFL-CIO did against proposals other than H.R. 3 was also discounted on the grounds that it represented the desires of labor leadership rather than an interest of the rank and file.†

The American Legion has real influence where veterans' legislation is concerned, but, at least with uncommitted legislators, its views on ideological issues carry far less weight. Besides, the Legion made

* The White Citizens Councils were also influential in many respects, but because of their geographical concentration and their general identification with the racial views of the majority of southern voters rather than because of any attempts at lobbying. A group which does not even have to announce its position to have it respected and to some extent followed is, clearly, a most powerful organization—though the councils' influence was restricted to one area of the nation.

† One of the functions of leadership is to be informed and interested in matters of which the membership is ignorant; but a sophisticated legislator could have doubted the ability of labor leaders to rally their followers on the political offender issues on the grounds that workers would be among the least sympathetic to the civil liberties the Court had protected.

no concerted effort to lobby for any of the Court bills. Opposition of the International Association of Police Chiefs to the *Mallory* decision was important, but as a means of reasonable persuasion rather than political pressure. On the other hand, members of the Governors' Conference, the National Association of Attorneys General, or the Conference of State Chief Justices could apply heavy pressure on members of Congress; yet they could do so because of their personal power in individual states rather than because of their status as a group, though without a doubt speaking collectively created a greater public impact. Poor timing, however, took away some of the possible public effect of their pronouncements. The governors indorsed states' rights legislation in 1956, almost two years before the peak of the congressional attack, and the Chief Justices' criticism of the Court came a few days too late to affect the fate of the bills in the Eighty-fifth Congress.

There were also broader fractions of the public which were concerned about the Court decisions. White people in the South, despite all their other differences, could find common interest in preserving their caste system. Although not identifiable by skin pigment, the ultra-security-conscious also approved of congressional action against the political offender decisions. To this company could be added those citizens who believed that sterner police methods were a necessary part of any campaign against increasing crime rates.

Nor were all the Court defenders represented by a few organizations. Law school and college professors denounced the attacks, and a considerable number of citizens who felt that some phases of loyalty-security programs and congressional investigations had gone beyond what was reasonably necessary did not sympathize with the Court bills. Nor did all white southerners wish to retaliate against the Court. The riots at Clinton, Tennessee, Tuscaloosa, Alabama, and Little Rock, Arkansas, and the scattered bombings of churches and synagogues throughout the South had brought home to many people the harsh fact that anarchy and mob rule would be the eventual price of white supremacy.

How a legislator gauged the direction and force of these currents of opinion—organized and unorganized—depended on his understanding of his own constituency. It also depended on his ambitions, his sense of security, his courage, his skill, and his concept of his own role. As David Truman has said, "the legislature is not just a sounding board or passive registering device for the demands of organized political interest groups."[19] Congress usually refracts as well as reflects public opinion, and the Warren Court struggle was no exception.

In sizing up his constituency's views on a bill, a legislator has to consider such factors as the amount of publicity and the extent of public awareness of the issues as well as the complexity of those issues and the depth of public understanding. In spite of initial widespread publicity accorded the political offender decisions, newspaper attention quickly faded. The civil rights bill overshadowed the Jencks maneuvering in 1957, and the Lebanon crisis kept the Court controversy out of the headlines in the summer of 1958. In addition, the political offender decisions had been based on narrow legal technicalities, and the remedial legislation was usually esoteric. There was no simple question like "Court-packing"; nor were there presidential addresses to inform and persuade the electorate. In late August, 1958, public view was further obscured by a legislative situation so muddled as even to confuse some veteran senators.

Moreover, a legislator cannot accept at face value the asserted opposition or support of a pressure group. The AFL-CIO does not include in its membership all or even most workers; nor do a majority of American lawyers belong to the American Bar Association. The American Legion has only a minority of veterans in its ranks, and the NAM and Chamber of Commerce together do not represent all businessmen. And, as has already been indicated, there is often doubt as to the competency of a group's leadership to speak for its actual membership.

One of the most important limitations on a leader's ability is that of overlapping memberships and cross-pressures.[20] A member of the AFL-CIO might have followed the views of the American Legion (to which he also belonged) rather than his union representatives, just as a Jewish businessman might have preferred to see H.R. 3 beaten because of his approval of the libertarian decisions of the Warren Court.[21] Nor are cross-pressures limited to groups to which the voter is actually or presently a member. A determining influence may be exerted by a group to which a voter aspires to be a member. For example, a worker with white-collar ambitions might vote with management rather than with his union, or a corporation lawyer who hopes to become a professor might follow the general attitude of law school deans rather than that of his business associates.

Working within an institutional framework, such cross-pressures can produce the sort of schizophrenic contortions which characterized the actions of the ABA's leadership during 1957–59. A sophisticated legislator would have had little trouble explaining his voting for or against any or all of the Court bills, even the Jenner-Butler proposal and H.R. 3, as really in line with the ABA's announced principles.*

The Catholic church, with its militant opposition to communism and all forms of Communist activity, had a large stake in the possible effects of the cold war decisions. As with the ABA, however, there were cross-pressures at work, not the least being the church's official belief in racial equality and consequent support by the hierarchy (though by no means of all Catholic laymen or clergy) of the School Segregation cases. A legislator who wished to please either the Catholic clergy or laity would have had a difficult time if he had had to depend on public statements. *Commonweal* had praised the political offender decisions; *America* had been more reserved; the Holy Name Societies of the diocese of Rockville Center, N.Y., had supported the Jenner bill. And the American diocesan press, supposedly the voice of the Catholic bishops, devoted relatively little attention to the political offender decisions of June, 1957, or to congressional reactions—though decisions upholding state and federal obscenity statutes were given front page headlines. For example, the *Boston Pilot,* Cardinal Cushing's newspaper, the *Michigan Catholic,* authorized by Cardinal Mooney, and the *Pittsburgh Catholic,* Bishop Dearden's publication, said nothing at all about the cold war cases. Cardinal Spellman's *Catholic News* did not even report the 1957 political offender decisions as news, though two weeks later it did

*For the ABA's specific pronouncements see above, chaps. 7 and 10. The ABA's statement on S. 2646 was equivocal enough, but it covered only the original bill. The association's opposition to the Jenner proposal as reported out of committee was stated in 1958 in a letter from the ABA's president, Charles S. Rhyne, asserting that "in my view" the opposition to S. 2646 also applied "in principle" to Butler's amendments (Senate Report No. 1586, 85/2, p. 62). When H.R. 3 was being debated in the House, Rhyne also wrote Celler declaring that the ABA had indorsed a somewhat different version of the proposal so that "it is not correct to say that the association has approved the pending bill" (104 *Congressional Record* 13849). After 1959, a legislator who voted against any of the more specific bills which the ABA's committees had approved could have relied on the report of the Committee on Constitutional Rights. Before 1959, he could have cited the ABA's repudiation of S. 2646 and reasonably claimed that, under the particular circumstances of the legislative situation, these other bills were different in form rather than intent from Jenner's proposal. To bolster this argument, he could have quoted from the very first of the ABA's Canons of Professional Ethics: "Judges, not being wholly free to defend themselves, are peculiarly entitled to the support of the Bar against unjust criticism and clamor."

comment critically that these decisions were "difficult and hard to grasp."[22] While advocating legislation in August, 1957, to "unshackle the FBI,"[23] the *News* did not devote further space to the Court attacks either in straight reporting or editorializing.[24]

In fact, of six leading diocesan papers examined, only the *Tidings*, the official publication of Cardinal McIntyre's archdiocese of Los Angeles, had extensive news coverage of the cold war cases and the resulting criticism of the Court. *Jencks* was singled out for special attention under a column heading "Supreme Court Scuttles the FBI."[25] But while the *Tidings* reprinted statements by Louis Wyman and the ABA's Communist Strategy Committee and played up a critical column by Rev. John B. Sheerin,[26] its own editorials were quite moderate, conceding the difficulties in reconciling liberty and authority in complex constitutional cases.[27] When the counterattack was in full force in 1958, the *Tidings* refrained from comment; and Sheerin's column shifted its line, declaring that although some of the bills "to close loopholes exposed by the court's decisions are worthy of serious consideration," proposals like Jenner-Butler were dangerous meddling.[28]

POWER AND PRUDENCE: A LEGISLATIVE VIEW

While no politician is ever completely free, such factors as lack of public understanding of pending issues or of legislative maneuvers, cross-pressures on individuals or organizations, and differences in outlook between group leaders and their followers can operate to increase the scope of a legislator's freedom of choice. In addition, an experienced politician can turn the influence of a group to further his own ends, just as several southern senators utilized the lobbying of the NAM to reinforce their own attack on the Court. A legislator can also arouse one group to counter the pressures of another organization. If such a group struggle already exists, he can play off one against the other.[29] Furthermore, a legislator can assist in the metamorphosis of an incipient or potential group into an active, organized pressure group—southern state legislators and the White Citizens Councils being the most obvious case in point.

Because of the make-up of their constituencies, some legislators have very little leeway on certain questions. When the Jenner-Butler bill came up, every southern senator had to vote for the measure and against the Court; but few southern senators felt it necessary to try to bargain with undecided colleagues in order to gain new recruits for the bill. A favorable vote and a stump speech against the Court were thought to be sufficient for fence-mending purposes.

The Jencks bill was one Court issue that was widely simplified and dramatized as a matter of saving the FBI from destruction. Despite the spotlight on the civil rights debate, few senators or representatives dared oppose *any* Jencks bill. But the bill quickly became so enmeshed in technical discussion that it was quite easy for thoughtful members of Congress to work to soften any possible blow to the Court's prestige and to get the kind of equitable legislation that was finally adopted. The point is that however a legislator's alternatives may seem to be limited by group pressures, he will usually have a meaningful measure of discretion. In the case of the Warren Court fight, this discretion was both relatively wide in scope and important in effect.

There is yet another kind of group interest whose pressure a legislator feels, an interest in which he has a direct, personal stake; that is, a legislator has an interest as a member of the legislature. If he is serious about getting his policy aims enacted into law, a prudent legislator must act with a view not merely toward getting re-elected but also toward his long-range power in terms of his place within the legislative structure. If he sees his political career as tied to the legislative branch, he must also act with an eye toward the legislature's place in the political system.

Court-congressional conflicts have developed only over important issues of public policy; but something more than an important issue must have been involved, otherwise political crises would have become almost weekly occurrences. Historically, the policy over which conflict has developed has also been one on which constitutional language is unclear and one on which public sentiment has been largely unsettled. Second, the policy has been one in which powerful groups—either organized or incipient—have had immediate interests at stake which they—or at least their leadership—have perceived as vital. Third, on the issue of public policy the Court has made what congressmen have considered to be a threat, direct or indirect, to legislative authority; and a sufficient number of congressmen have estimated that it was feasible as well as wise to counter that threat under existing circumstances.*

The Warren Court did not deny congressional authority in the same way, for instance, that *Dred Scott, Ex parte Milligan,* the Income Tax Cases, or the New Deal decisions had. In fact, the Warren Court's decisions had been more cautionary than forbidding. They had warned Congress that fundamental constitutional rights were being endangered by the exercise of legislative and administrative powers; they had not denied the authority of Congress to cope with problems of internal security. But many congressmen still saw the Court as invading fields of legislative prerogative, though admittedly in a more subtle and stealthy fashion than had earlier tribunals. And it was undeniable that the Justices were playing an important role in shaping public policy—and shaping policy in a direction which many members of Congress either questioned or disapproved.

This institutional interest of legislators can express itself in complex ways, especially in the Senate where its adherents have almost transformed it into a mystique.[30] While jealous considerations of the authority of the Senate in formulating public policy caused many senators to resent the Warren Court decisions, it also caused some of those same senators to play for lower stakes than the sort of onslaught against the judiciary which Jenner-Butler attempted. This institutional interest also helps explain one of the most intriguing mysteries of the fight over the Warren Court: the strong southern support of Lyndon Johnson's adjournment motion on that crucial Wednesday night after the Majority leader had been beaten in his first effort to shelve H.R. 3.

It was evident to all who had followed the maneuvering that if the adjournment motion carried and Johnson got a twelve-hour breather

* At first glance, Jefferson's attack on the Court might be considered an exception to this third criterion in that he criticized the Justices for not declaring the Alien and Sedition Acts and, in his later years, the Bank of the United States unconstitutional. But Jefferson understood that the work of the Court is twofold: it can shape policy both by negating and by approving acts of other departments of government. This positive function provided one of the causes for Jefferson's attacks; but he was also angered by the speeches of Federalist judges against his party and policies, as well as by such threats of negative action as the show-cause order in *Marbury* v. *Madison* and Marshall's subpoena during the Burr trial. Jefferson expressed these fears when he wrote to Dickinson in 1801: "The Federalists have retired into the judiciary as a stronghold . . . and from that battery all the works of republicanism are to be beaten down and erased" (*Writings,* X, 302). In his later years Jefferson could see that in cases like *Cohens* v. *Virginia* and *McCulloch* v. *Maryland* Marshall was helping to create a climate of opinion which would consider national supremacy as beyond question.

to persuade people to change sides, H.R. 3 would probably be defeated. Backing the Majority leader on procedural points is customary, yet there was more to the matter: a fear, felt by a number of institutionally oriented senators, that in approving a bill as drastic as H.R. 3 the Senate might be upsetting not only the federal-state political balance, but also what might be described as the balance of power among the three branches of the federal government.

Tension among the three branches of the federal government is inevitable, a tribute to the skill of the Framers. But, "the twentieth century," as one commentator has said, "has been hard on national legislatures."[31] Especially since 1933, executive power in the United States has dramatically increased, and this increase has been accompanied by a parallel loss in legislative authority.[32] William S. White[33] has interpreted the history of the Senate—and, one might add, that of the House of Representatives, though admittedly to a lesser extent—since 1945 as a dedicated effort to recover the prestige and initiative lost during FDR's first term. A case could also be made for back-dating White's thesis to the period 1937–41. Senate refusal to adopt the Court-packing scheme, Roosevelt's failure to get any major New Deal reform legislation passed after 1937 except for the Fair Labor Standards Act, the continued domestic deadlock under Truman, the 1951 attempts to control presidential discretion to send American troops overseas, and the fight over the Bricker Amendment could be as much a syndrome of institutional nostalgia for lost power, at least as much as symptoms of the effects of opposing vectors of group pressure.

On the surface, it might have seemed that Eisenhower's administration would have soothed senatorial jealousy, especially since Taft in 1953 took command of the Senate. In fact, Louis Koenig has described Eisenhower's concept of the Presidency as "the greatest retreat in the national experience since the first battle of Bull Run."[34] But Taft died within six months, and later Little Rock and Lebanon showed that Eisenhower could act just as swiftly, and perhaps even as impetuously, as Truman. More fundamentally, these decisions demonstrated that the power of the Presidency was still very much alive, although it had probably been kept alive as much by the day-to-day decision-making of men like Sherman Adams, John Foster Dulles, George Humphrey, or his successor, Robert Anderson, as by Eisenhower's episodic and unpredictable utilizations of plenary authority. This meant that continued growth of executive power—and shrinkage of legislative power—remained a very real possibility, especially since the Twenty-second Amendment would cause a change in presidents on January 20, 1961. And it took a senatorial memory only as long as the Steel Seizure case to recall that the Court could check executive prerogative.[35]

Many senators must also have realized that legislators can use court decisions as defenses against presidential pressure to pass certain legislation as well as against constituent pressure. To cite a striking example of the second use, which, though it took place after the failure of the attacks on the Warren Court, is not atypical: when federal aid to parochial schools was being discussed in 1961, Supreme Court pronouncements about "the wall of separation" between church and state became godsends to harried senators and congressmen who did not wish to offend Catholic, Protestant, Jewish, or agnostic voters. By wrecking the prestige of the Court, legislators would have had to confess a fuller degree of responsibility for their actions when controversial constitutional issues arose in the future.

Furthermore, most of the Court foes considered themselves to be conservatives. They might well have calculated that traditionally the Supreme Court has been the most conservative of the three branches of the federal government and that the period since 1937 was only a temporary aberration which would eventually be corrected by the appointment of "sound" judges. Conservative senators could thus have doubted that curbing the Court, however tempting in the short run, would be expedient over the long haul. Then, too, the history of Court-congressional conflicts in general, and that of 1937 in particular, had shown that *passage* of a Court curb was not necessary to effect a change in the judicial mind. The mere threat of congressional action could work wonders in shuffling alignments on the High Bench.

When the adjournment vote came, some senators supported Lyndon Johnson because they were opposed to H.R. 3; some because it had been a long day and they wanted to go home; some because it was the custom to side with the Majority leader on such questions; some because they neither understood nor cared about the issue; some because they thought that the liberals could prevent a vote on the merits anyway; but some southern senators went along because, in current military parlance, they preferred limited war against the Court to massive retaliation. Their votes and speeches on the merits of H.R. 3 and Jenner-Butler would clear them with their constituents, and they could hope that the adoption of one or two less drastic measures like the Nelson, habeas corpus, or Mallory bills would frighten the Court into retreat. They did not want to strike down a current foe who might someday be a needed ally. They put into practice the admonition which the Russian diplomat Count Ruminiatzov once gave to John Quincy Adams: Always love your friend as though one day he might become your enemy; and always hate your enemy as though one day he might become your friend.[36]

In 1937 there had been a similar reluctance among members of Congress to pay for removing the judicial check on their own authority by giving up the judicial check on executive power. The leading opponents of the Court-packing bill, after all, were hardly friends of the judiciary. Borah had been one of the chief critics of the Taft Court during the 1920's, and Wheeler had run in 1924 as La Follette's vice-presidential candidate. Like O'Mahoney, both men were unalterably opposed to judicial supremacy; each wanted to reverse recent Court decisions and to curb judicial power.[37] But each was also opposed to presidential supremacy. During Roosevelt's first administration, the White House became, as it had not been at least since Woodrow Wilson, the dynamic center of government; and Congress was frequently charged—sometimes with considerable justification—with being no more than a rubber stamp.

FDR's failure to consult with party leaders on Capitol Hill in preparing his Court bill was another affront to congressional pride. As irritating as this snub was, many members of Congress saw the issue as more basic. They could sense what Thomas Corcoran put into words: "If the President wins the court fight, everything will fall into his basket."[38] In rejecting compromise on the Court-packing bill, Senator Wheeler summed up this fear of executive domination: "We must teach that man in the White House a lesson. We must show him that the United States Senate has to be consulted and is going to have something to say about how the Government is run."[39]

It may not be possible to ascertain to what extent in earlier Court fights this fear of worsening the power distribution within the federal government affected either legislators or Presidents and their advisers. But it is typical of previous Court conflicts that the President and Congress never joined together to press a serious assault on judicial power. The one notable exception was the passage of the judiciary acts of 1802 turning out the circuit judges and postponing the next session of the Supreme Court. Yet shortly thereafter Jefferson's party broke ranks during Chase's impeachment trial, and the threatened wholesale removal of Federalist judges never came about. It is also significant that the only other attack, aside from the Eleventh Amendment, which was successful in securing legislation directly imposing an important curb on judicial power,* was made by the Radical Republicans as part of their efforts to cripple both the Presidency and the judiciary in order to establish unchecked legislative supremacy.[40]

POWER AND PRUDENCE: A JUDICIAL VIEW

As a participant in public policy-making who has only limited power, a Justice of the Supreme Court, like a legislator, must weigh considerations of political prudence. American constitutional law, as Robert McCloskey has noted, "though not simply the creature of the popular will nevertheless [has] had always to reckon with it. . . ."[41] A judge must weigh questions of power and prudence on a different scale and accord them different values than does a legislator or an executive official; but a judge who wishes to do good, or evil for that matter, must act with a view toward his influence within the Court[42] as well as toward the role, actual and potential,

* I have not classified such legislation as the acts of 1910 (36 Stat. 1162; 22 U.S.C.A. § 2281) and 1937 (50 Stat. 751; 28 U.S.C.A. §§ 2282, 2284), requiring three-judge district courts to enjoin enforcement of state and federal laws, as major attacks. One might reasonably classify the Norris–La Guardia Act as a major attack on judicial power. Even so, the statement as to the absence of presidential-congressional co-operation to curb the Court is unaffected since Hoover opposed the measure (see Swisher, *American Constitutional Development*, pp. 811–12, and literature cited).

The Eleventh Amendment poses more subtle problems of taxonomy. Professor Alpheus T. Mason has suggested to me that the peculiar wording of the Amendment ("The Judicial Power of the United States shall not be construed to extend . . ."), although specifically curtailing the jurisdiction of federal courts, might well be interpreted as an implicit congressional acceptance of the authority of the Court to construe the Constitution—at least insofar as Art. III was concerned. Furthermore, the resort to a constitutional amendment rather than a simpler form of legislative action indicated the very great authority which was accorded a Supreme Court construction of the Constitution.

of the Court in the political system.[43] As Max Weber put the matter, a political decision-maker "works with the striving for power as an unavoidable means. Therefore, 'power instinct,' as is usually said, belongs indeed to his normal qualities."[44]

If a judge wishes, for example, to protect constitutional rights rather than write libertarian tracts, he must try to visualize the possible reactions of other branches of government to any decision. It is often better, both from the viewpoint of the group whose rights are involved (though not perhaps of the individual litigant) and of the Court as an institution, that a decision not be made than that it be made and then reversed by an angry Congress. If a number of such reversals on important issues were to come at the same time, or if such reversals were to become commonplace, the prestige of the High Bench would suffer a blow which would gravely impair its ability to protect other rights. In 1812 Chancellor Waties of South Carolina stated this consideration in its most extreme form: "The interference of the judiciary with legislative Acts, if frequent or on dubious ground, might occasion so great a jealousy of this power and so generally a prejudice against it as to lead to measures ending in the total overthrow of the independence of the judges, and so of the best preservative of the constitution."[45]

Yet to maintain judicial prestige a judge cannot act so timidly as to lose public or professional respect. This means that he must possess or develop an ability to distinguish between abusive criticism which only flays without threatening serious injury, and the potential attack which might well cripple judicial power. He must also have the courage to recognize the occasions when he cannot retreat without irretrievable loss of constitutional principles and the wisdom to judge whether such a loss justifies risking judicial power itself.

The difficulty, of course, lies in finding some means of correctly analyzing each set of circumstances. No precise calibrators are available to judges any more than to other public officials. In fact, judges have even fewer aids. Unlike legislators they cannot—or at least, should not—consult their mail; nor do they have influential constituents whose advice they may seek. Judges, however, do not have to flounder helplessly in crosscurrents of popular opinion. They can read newspapers, the *Congressional Record,* and professional journals. Moreover, most Justices have had wide experience in practical politics; and from this past experience, if not from their present contacts, they can estimate what courses of action congressmen or executive officials are most apt to pursue. And they also have an almost unlimited number of technicalities which they can use to delay a decision on the merits of an issue until they have either made up their minds or until times are more propitious for judicial action.[46]

Modern judges have an additional advantage in assessing public opinion. Pollsters, while hardly infallible and probably not nearly as scientific as they themselves claim, can shed valuable light on public views. There were no polls published by any recognized national agency which dealt directly with legislation aimed at the Warren Court,[47] but a number of surveys by Gallup's American Institute of Public Opinion bore indirectly on the Court's problems. First, beginning in the summer of 1954, AIPO took periodic soundings of reactions to the School Segregation cases. While the exact degree of support varied, all of these polls recorded approval by well over a majority of the nation.[48]

Second, in late 1955 Gallup conducted four polls among Republicans and Independents asking their preferences for a presidential nominee in 1956 if Eisenhower chose not to run again. Among Republicans Earl Warren led in three[49] out of these four polls and Richard Nixon in one.[50] Among Independents the Chief Justice led in all four; in one of the four he received more than twice Nixon's Independent support,[51] and in another almost three times as much.[52] A fifth poll,[53] this one putting the question whether the respondent would like to see Warren run for the Presidency, reported that 50 per cent answered yes, 25 per cent no, and 25 per cent were undecided. AIPO also ran two "trial heats" with Warren as a "candidate." In the first,[54] the Chief Justice and Adlai Stevenson received equal support (47 per cent each); and in the second Warren led Averell Harriman 59 per cent to 37 per cent.[55]

Third, in July, 1957, Gallup announced[56] that a national sample asked "Which do you have the greater respect for—Congress or the Supreme Court?" divided almost evenly. Thirty per cent said the Supreme Court, 29 per cent said Congress, 23 per cent declared equal respect, and 18 per cent expressed no opinion. In answering the question, "Has your attitude toward the Supreme Court changed in recent years?" 20 per cent said yes, and three-quarters of these stated that at the time they held an unfavorable opinion. Not surprisingly, among those reporting a change in opinion, more than twice as many were from the South as from any other region; and an overwhelming majority (better than six to one) of these southern informants reported that their opinion had changed for the worse.

This 1957 prestige sampling is in marked contrast to a 1953 AIPO release on the popularity of J. Edgar Hoover. Replying to a question as to a favorable or unfavorable opinion of the FBI chief, 78 per cent reported a favorable opinion and only 2 per cent unfavorable; 20 per cent were undecided.[57]

These polls, if consulted, could have warned the Court that any decision adverse to the FBI would have to be justified on the firmest of legal grounds—though certainly no poll should have been needed to arrive at this conclusion. On the other hand, these surveys also indicated, though they did not conclusively prove, that the School Segregation decisions had solid and widespread public support and that the Chief Justice was still one of the best-known and most popular national figures. These polls also indicated that the Court's prestige, while probably not at an all time high, was nevertheless superior to that of Congress outside the South, even after the controversial decisions of June, 1957.*

Many judges, like many other public officials, probably believe that Congress is more accurate than poll reports as a gauge of the kind of public opinion which will be translated into public policy; and each judge weighs this evidence in light of his own experience, fears, hopes, skills, and concept of his role.[58] It was Frankfurter and Harlan who were primarily responsible for the Warren Court's shift in direction. Singly or together they had often been a necessary part of the majority coalition, and it was clear that they had played important roles in shaping opinions. Harlan, in fact, had written the Court's official opinion in such cases as *Cole* v. *Young, Service* v. *Dulles,* and *Yates* v. *United States.* The phrase "with all deliberate speed," used as the implementing formula of the School Segregation decisions, was one Frankfurter had previously employed on several

* The 1957 Gallup poll which posed the most pertinent question on the Court issue was not published. In July, 1957, AIPO asked the question: "Some people say that the Supreme Court has too much power these days. Do you agree or disagree?" Only the results of the first five hundred interviews were tabulated. They showed: 28.2 per cent agreed with the statement that the Court had too much power and 51.8 per cent disagreed; 18.6 per cent expressed no opinion and 1.4 per cent did not answer this question (AIPO Files, Set 586K, Q. 6, July 16, 1957). This support of the Court makes an interesting comparison with Gallup's 1937 findings. See above, p. 61 n.

occasions,[59] and the Warren Court's resort to technicalities rather than to the Constitution itself was a sign of the influence of Frankfurter's (and apparently Harlan's) preference for decisions on procedural grounds wherever possible.

It would have been predictable that in case of a Court-Congress crisis, a coalition which included Black and Douglas as well as Frankfurter and Harlan would become highly unstable.[60] The Frankfurter-Harlan theories of self-restraint were much more deferential to Congress—on the constitutional issues raised by the political offender cases—than were the Black-Douglas self-restraint theories. But Harlan and Frankfurter could not have brought about a change by themselves. Even with Clark they would have formed only a three-judge minority had not Whittaker and Stewart joined them in the new political offender decisions.*

RETREAT IN RETROSPECT

The majority of the Warren Court can be charged with having made several important mistakes. The first was poor craftsmanship in cases like *Nelson, Jencks, Watkins,* and *Sweezy,* though this was by no means a peculiar failing of recent Court appointees;[61] a second was to take on too many powerful enemies at one time. While from any point of view the first of these alleged errors was unfortunate, the second was not necessarily an unmixed evil. It is true that the legislative attacks against the Court were initiated by conservative Republicans and Southern Democrats and, as the roll call votes show,

* It might also be anticipated that the differences among their views on civil liberties will make any Frankfurter-Harlan-Clark coalition as unstable as the differences on self-restraint among Black, Douglas, Frankfurter, and Harlan made the earlier alliance. Professor Harry Kalven has noted that "the impression will not down that the cases [*Watkins* and *Barenblatt*] are really deeply inconsistent, and that it might have been better to say so candidly and overrule *Watkins*. . . . Yet it is also possible that the future may not read *Barenblatt* as overruling *Watkins*. We may see instead two powerful precedents so close on their facts that future courts will for all practical purposes be free to choose between them and to decide that it is the one and not the other precedent that today controls the case before it" ("Mr. Alexander Meiklejohn and the Barenblatt Opinion," 27 *U. Chi. L. Rev.* 315, 321–22 [1960]). Events since Kalven's prediction have supported his interpretation. Compare *Braden* v. *United States* (1961) and *Wilkinson* v. *United States* (1961) with *Deutch* v. *United States* (1961). By a 5–4 vote, *Braden* and *Wilkinson* affirmed contempt of Congress convictions; by a 5–4 vote *Deutch* reversed such a conviction. *Braden* and *Wilkinson* followed *Barenblatt;* the *Deutch* opinion followed *Watkins,* though the case was ultimately disposed of on a different but closely related point of law. Justice Stewart was the swing-man in these decisions.

strongly supported by this coalition. Yet it is at least open to doubt whether northern liberals of either party would have been able to put up the sort of defense they did if the Warren Court had not become identified as the grand protector of Negro rights. If the issue had been only national security against individual liberty, it may be argued, the attack on the Court would have been less bitter, but it might have also been more effective in producing legislation.[62]

It is also possible that some members of the Warren Court made a mistake in their decision to execute a withdrawal. Before Chase's acquittal, Marshall had faced disaster; so had the Court after the Civil War; and continuing to impose laissez faire on an unwilling nation after 1937 would doubtless have led to a Court-curb, though not necessarily the one Roosevelt had proposed. But the Warren Court's position was different. It retreated after the attack against it had been broken. With an all-out effort, the Court foes in the Eighty-sixth Congress might have mounted a more dangerous threat than they actually did, but it is improbable that any such attack could have even approached the vigor of that in the Eighty-fifth Congress.

There is an alternative explanation for the Court's retreat. In the minds of some of the Justices, the withdrawal may have been planned rather than forced. It is conceivable that some of the Justices could have acted on a theory that the Court, having reminded the other branches of government as well as the general public of the commands of the Constitution, could best protect civil liberties by allowing non-judicial officials to exercise responsibility for achieving the most satisfactory reconciliations between conflicting and competing rights. This has long been the ideal of judicial restraint. Whether, or to what extent, it was the aim here will probably never be known with absolute certitude. Nor, even if intended or its intention accepted as a working hypothesis, would its results be subject to precise measurement since public policy is usually an ongoing series of adjustments to changing situations rather than a neatly finished final product.

Because self-restraint is a compound of policy and power, separation of these two elements is possible only in the realm of logical analysis. Consistent with the basic tenets of self-restraint, the Justices could have acted to quiet the attacks against them by passing back much of the burden of solving the disputed problems to legislators and executive officials, believing that fuller authority to make decisions affecting civil liberties might inculcate a more responsible attitude among many of these office-holders. While such an attitude in the long run would constitute a sturdier defense for libertarian values than would judicial prohibitions, one unanswered question is whether such a protective attitude would take firm root in a society accustomed to look—admittedly often in vain—to judges for protection of civil rights.[63]

A second unanswered question is whether the timing of this maneuver—assuming it was planned rather than forced—did not destroy much of its value by leaving the widespread impression that the Justices had backed down under pressure. Whether true or false, such an impression does not help the cause of civil liberties, nor, as Justice Grier protested in the McCardle case, does such an imputation increase the prestige of the Court.

THE STRUGGLE FOR POLITICAL POWER

Through adjustments made in both the legislative and judicial processes, the crisis in the Warren Court's relations with Congress passed without serious injury to the prestige or power of either institution; but finality, as Disraeli said, "is not the language of politics." Before leaving the executive department, Robert H. Jackson wrote that conflict among the branches of the federal government is inherent in the Constitution.[64] Such conflict is also inherent in the nature of American politics. With three broad avenues—and dozens of narrower alleys—of access to national power open, interest groups will always exploit that path which offers the greatest opportunities and try to shut off the influence of those which provide the greatest threats.

In such struggles the Court will constantly be called on to participate in formulating public policy; and experience from Marshall to Warren indicates that the chances are slim that a majority of the Justices will habitually subordinate other values to those of self-restraint. Recognizing the potential threat to their own policy aims which the authority of the High Bench poses, members of Congress and executive officials will continue to view judicial power with a suspicion which will turn to hostility whenever they themselves or articulate segments of their constituencies disapprove of specific decisions, or when those officials fear that their own policy-making prerogatives are being threatened. The issues generating conflict may change, but the Court in the future is likely to remain as it has been in the past—a focal point in the struggle for political power.

NOTES

PREFACE

1. C. Herman Pritchett, *The Roosevelt Court: A Study in Judicial Politics and Values, 1937–1947* (New York: Macmillan Co., 1948).
2. Glendon A. Schubert, Jr., *Quantitative Analysis of Judicial Behavior* (Glencoe, Ill.: Free Press, 1960).
3. Stephen K. Bailey, *Congress Makes a Law: The Story behind the Employment Act of 1946* (New York: Columbia University Press, 1950), p. ix.
4. C. Herman Pritchett, *The Political Offender and the Warren Court* (Boston: Boston University Press, 1958), p. 74.

1. INTRODUCTION

1. Joseph Alsop and Turner Catledge, *The 168 Days* (New York: Doubleday & Co., Inc., 1938), p. 135.
2. William Howard Taft to Charles Warren, October 28, 1922. Taft Papers, Library of Congress.
3. "Law and the Court," *Speeches of Oliver Wendell Holmes* (Boston: Little, Brown & Co., 1918), p. 98.

2. MARSHALL, TANEY, AND THE DEMOCRACY

1. See especially Charles G. Haines, *The Role of the Supreme Court in American Government and Politics, 1789–1835* (Berkeley: University of California Press, 1944), chaps. 4–5; Charles Warren, *The Supreme Court in United States History* (rev. ed.; Boston: Little, Brown & Co., 1926), I, chaps. 1–3. Despite his many obvious personal biases and his often uncritical defense of the Court, Warren's two volumes are still the most valuable work on Supreme Court history.

While I have often disagreed with his interpretations and sometimes with his statements of fact, chapters 2 and 3 of this book owe a great debt to Warren's researches—as does the work of Haines, whose principal purpose was to rebut the interpretations of "Federalist" historians like Warren. Consult Haines, "Histories of the Supreme Court of the United States Written from a Federalist Point of View," 4 *Southwestern Pol. and Soc. Sci. Q.* 1 (1923).

Hereafter bibliography will be cited only to indicate specific debits, but among the other broad historical studies found most useful were: Carl B. Swisher, *American Constitutional Development* (Boston: Houghton Mifflin Co., 1943, 1954) (I have used and cited the 1943 edition); Benjamin F. Wright, *The Growth of American Constitutional Law* (Boston: Houghton Mifflin Co., 1942); Alfred H. Kelly and Winfred A. Harbison, *The American Constitution* (New York: W. W. Norton & Co., Inc., 1948); and Alan H. Monroe, "The Supreme Court and the Constitution," 18 *Am. Pol. Sci. Rev.* 737 (1924).

2. For details consult Robert McKay, "Georgia versus the United States Supreme Court," 4 *J. of Pub. L.* 285 (1955), and Warren, *op. cit.,* I, 91–102.

3. For example, *Hayburn's Case* (1792); *United States* v. *Yale Todd* (1794); *Hylton* v. *United States* (1796); cf. *Calder* v. *Bull* (1798).

4. *Ware* v. *Hylton* (1797).

5. Quoted in Albert J. Beveridge, *The Life of John Marshall* (Boston: Houghton Mifflin Co., 1919), III, 22.

6. Paul L. Ford (ed.), *The Works of Thomas Jefferson* (New York: G. P. Putnam's Sons, 1905), IX, 247 (hereinafter cited as *Works*).

7. Nathan Schachner, *Thomas Jefferson: A Biography* (New York: Thomas Yoseloff, Inc., 1951), p. 672.

8. *Works,* IX, 248.

9. For details see Warren, *op. cit.,* I, 195.

10. Quoted in *ibid.,* I, 204.

11. *Annals of Congress,* 7th Cong., 1st sess., p. 38.

12. *Ibid.,* p. 47.

13. *Ibid.,* pp. 59, 61, 63.

14. *Ibid.,* p. 179.

15. *Ibid.,* p. 181.

16. For a full account see Beveridge, *op. cit.,* III, 122; Warren, *op. cit.,* I, 269–73.

17. Beveridge, *op. cit.,* III, 75.

18. Warren, *op. cit.,* I, 231–32.

19. *Ibid.,* I, 276–77; Claude Bowers, *Jefferson in Power* (Boston: Houghton Mifflin Co., 1936), pp. 273–74.

20. Quoted in Warren, *op. cit.,* I, 228–29.

21. Quoted in Beveridge, *op. cit.,* III, 166–67.

22. This is the position taken by most scholars. Bowers, however, seems to doubt that Jefferson had such an intention. Rather, Bowers implies, Jefferson merely wanted to get Chase off the bench and force the judges to abandon their party partisanship. Bowers, *op. cit.,* chap. 13.

23. Quoted in Beveridge, *op. cit.,* III, 173.

24. *Ibid.,* III, 83.

25. *Works,* X, 403 n.

26. Beveridge, *op. cit.,* III, 186 n.

27. Quoted in *ibid.,* III, 177.

28. A shorthand record of Chase's impeachment trial was made by Charles Evans and published as: *Report of the Trial of the Hon. Samuel Chase* (Baltimore: Butler and Keatinge, 1805). For analyses consult: Bowers, *op. cit.,* p. 291; Haines, *op. cit.,* p. 263; Henry Adams, *John Randolph* (Boston: Houghton Mifflin Co., 1883), pp. 140 ff.; Gerald W. Johnson, *Randolph of Roanoke: A Political Fantastic* (New York: Minton, Balch, 1929), pp. 140–44; William C. Bruce, *John Randolph of Roanoke, 1773–1833* (New York: G. P. Putnam's Sons, 1922), I, 206; Wilfred Binkley, *American Political Parties: Their Natural History* (3d ed.; New York: Alfred A. Knopf, Inc., 1959), p. 88.

29. Noble E. Cunningham, *The Jeffersonian Republicans: The Formation of Party Organization* (Chapel Hill: University of North Carolina Press, 1957), has a systematic analysis of the complex political maneuvers among various regional groups which led to the formation of the Jeffersonian party.

30. While the usual view is that of Schachner, *op. cit.,* p. 779, that Chase's acquittal was a "stunning blow" to the President, Bowers, *op. cit.,* pp. 292–93, and Haines, *op. cit.,* p. 264, argue that the real victory was Jefferson's in that Chase's defenders had been forced to concede the impropriety of the Justice's conduct, and that thereafter no federal judge dared behave in such an openly partisan manner. But, if removal of the Federalist judges were really Jefferson's aim, as Bowers and Haines seem to doubt, then he certainly suffered a defeat.

31. *Ex parte Bollman* (1807).

32. The trial is reported *sub nom. United States* v. *Burr* (1807). For lengthy accounts and for congressional reactions see Beveridge, *op. cit.,* III, chaps. 7–9, and Warren, *op. cit.,* I, 301–15.

33. Henry Adams, *History of the United States of America* (New York: Charles Scribner's Sons, 1889–91), IV, 442.

34. Jefferson to Hay, *Works,* X, 407 n. Ford, *ibid.,* X, 406 n., is not sure that this letter was ever sent. Beveridge, *op. cit.,* III, 518–19, assumes that it was. Certainly Jefferson would not have submitted to any efforts to enforce the subpoena. See below, notes 73, 74, and also Jefferson to Jarvis, September 28, 1820, *Works,* XII, 161–64; Jefferson to Hay, June 2, 1807, *ibid.,* X, 396–97.

35. Jefferson to Wilkinson, September 20, 1807, *Works,* X, 499–500.

36. Beveridge, *op. cit.,* IV, 480.

37. Jefferson to Tyler, May 26, 1810, in Andrew A. Lipscomb (ed.), *The Writings of Thomas Jefferson* (Washington: The Thomas Jefferson Memorial Association, 1903), XII, 392 (hereafter cited as *Writings*).

38. Quoted in Warren, *op. cit.,* I, 558 n.

39. Jefferson to Ritchie, December 25, 1820, *Writings,* XV, 297; also *Autobiography, Writings,* I, 121.

40. Jefferson to Roane, March 9, 1821, *Writings,* XV, 326.

41. August 18, 1821, *Writings,* XV, 331–32.

42. Jefferson to Coray, October 31, 1823, *Writings,* XV, 487.

43. *Autobiography, Writings,* I, 120–22; Jefferson to Barry, July 2, 1822, *ibid.,* XV, 389–90; Jefferson to Kercheval, July 12, 1816, *ibid.,* XV, 34; Jefferson to Coray, October 31, 1823, *ibid.,* XV, 486–87; Jefferson to Livingston, March 25, 1825, *ibid.,* XVI, 113–14. Although Jefferson frequently referred to impeachment as a "scarecrow," he advocated its use as late as 1821. Jefferson to Macon, August 19, 1821, *Works,* XII, 206 ff.

44. At one point Jefferson made the suggestion that judges in Virginia should be elected to office. Jefferson to Kercheval, July 12, 1816, *Writings,* XV, 36.

45. Jefferson to Livingston, March 25, 1825, *Writings,* XVI, 114.

46. Jefferson to Justice Johnson, March 4, 1823, *Writings,* XV, 421–22; Jefferson to Ritchie, December 25, 1820, *ibid.,* XV, 297–98.

47. Herman V. Ames (ed.), *State Documents on Federal Relations* (Philadelphia: Department of History, University of Pennsylvania, 1900), p. 49. Warren has a full account of the Pennsylvania affair, *op. cit.,* I, 366–89. See also William O. Douglas, "Interposition and the Peters Case," 9 *Stan. L. Rev.* 3 (1956).

48. Charles Warren, "Legislative and Judicial Attacks on the Supreme Court of the United States," 47 *Am. L. Rev.* 1, 4 (1913).

49. *Supreme Court in U.S. History,* I, 444 ff.

50. See Bray Hammond, *Banks and Politics in America from the Revolution to the Civil War* (Princeton: Princeton University Press, 1957), pp. 266 ff.

51. Quoted in Warren, "Legislative Attacks on the Supreme Court," p. 13.

52. Quoted in *ibid.,* pp. 13–14.

53. Jefferson to Roane, September 6, 1819, *Works,* XII, 135–40.

54. Beveridge, *op. cit.,* IV, 318–23.

55. The exact amount is disputed. I have used Hammond's figures, *op. cit.,* p. 267.

56. Haines, *op. cit.,* p. 486.

57. *Annals of Congress,* 17th Cong., 1st sess., p. 75.

58. *Ibid.*

59. Jefferson to Pleasants, December 26, 1821, *Works,* XII, 214–15.

60. Story to Jeremiah Mason, January 10, 1822, William Story (ed.), *The Life and Letters of Joseph Story* (Boston: Little, Brown & Co., 1851), I, 411.

61. Warren, *Supreme Court in U.S. History,* I, 446, concedes that the Fairfax case was apparently decided by a minority but thinks that the popularly held view about the Green case was probably wrong. *Ibid.,* I, 640, 640–41 n., 790 n., and "Legislative Attacks on the Supreme Court," p. 23. For comments on the belief about the Green case see Haines, *op. cit.,* pp. 467–68.

62. *Annals of Congress,* 18th Cong., 1st sess., p. 38. A similar resolution had been tabled earlier: *ibid.,* pp. 28, 32.

63. *Ibid.,* pp. 336–37.

64. Warren's article, "Legislative Attacks on the Supreme Court," is still the best summary of the efforts to repeal or amend sec. 25.

65. *Annals of Congress,* 18th Cong., 1st sess., p. 915.

66. *Register of Debates in Congress,* 21st Cong., 2d sess., Appendix, p. lxxix.

67. *Ibid.,* p. lxxxii.

68. Quoted in Warren, *Supreme Court in U.S. History,* I, 727.

69. Story to Ticknor, January 22, 1831, Story, *op. cit.,* II, 48.

70. Donald G. Morgan, *Justice William Johnson: The First Dissenter* (Columbia: University of South Carolina Press, 1954), p. 266.

71. *Register of Debates,* 21st Cong., 2d sess., pp. 532–35.

72. *Ibid.,* p. 542. The day before this vote, the House refused, 115–61, to consider a proposal by Representative LeCompte of Kentucky to amend the Constitution in order to set six-year terms for federal judges. *Ibid.,* p. 540.

73. *Writings,* VII, 309.

74. *Writings,* XI, 50. Compare the portion of Jefferson's message to Congress of December 8, 1801, which he deleted at the last moment (reprinted in Beveridge, *op. cit.,* III, Appendix A), and also the opinion of the Attorney General of June 25, 1802 (*Opinions of the Attorney General,* I, 119).

75. See McKay's article, cited above, note 2.

76. Ames, *op. cit.*, p. 128.

77. "Andrew Jackson and the Judiciary," 71 *Pol. Sci. Q.* 341 (1956).

78. Jackson to Coffee, April 7, 1832, John S. Bassett (ed.), *The Correspondence of Andrew Jackson* (Washington: Carnegie Institute, 1926–35), IV, 430. Marquis James remarks: "This poor plea deceived no one. As much as any man living, Andrew Jackson could give strength to the arm of the government when he chose to do so." *Andrew Jackson: Portrait of a President* (Indianapolis: Bobbs-Merrill Co., 1937), p. 305.

79. James D. Richardson (ed.), *Messages and Papers of the Presidents* (Washington: Government Printing Office, 1896), II, 582. Hammond, *op. cit.*, p. 405, calls the veto message "a famous state paper. It is legalistic, demagogic, and full of sham. Its economic reasoning was said by Professor Catteral, over fifty years ago, to be beneath contempt. Its level is now no higher." But whatever the value of his economic reasoning, Jackson's constitutional logic had a strong basis, though not one accepted by the Supreme Court. For Taney's role in drafting the message consult Carl B. Swisher, *Roger B. Taney* (New York: Macmillan Co., 1935), pp. 194–97. Warren, *Supreme Court in U.S. History*, I, 762–64, accepts the interpretation offered by Taney in 1860 that Jackson had not meant to deny responsibility to execute a court decision but only to claim the privilege of determining for himself the constitutionality of a bill presented to him for his signature. Haines, *op. cit.*, p. 607 n., questions this. Longaker, *op. cit.*, pp. 352–53, suggests that perhaps neither Jackson nor Taney had had a clear concept of the doctrine they were putting forth in the veto message. This is possible, but I cannot accept Warren's interpretation. For additional comments by Taney when he was Attorney General on the effect of a Supreme Court decision on the other branches of government (comments which closely parallel those of Lincoln on *Dred Scott*, discussed below) see Swisher, "Mr. Chief Justice Taney," in Allison Dunham and Philip B. Kurland (eds.), *Mr. Justice* (Chicago: University of Chicago Press, 1956), p. 212.

80. Beveridge, *op. cit.*, IV, chap. 9, especially pp. 480 ff., 512–14, 585; Haines, *op. cit.*, pp. 579 ff.; Warren is less candid, *Supreme Court in U.S. History*, I, chap. 20. Compare the thesis of W. W. Crosskey, "Mr. Chief Justice Marshall," in Dunham and Kurland, *op. cit.*

81. *Bank of the United States* v. *Dandridge*.

82. Beveridge, *op. cit.*, IV, 514.

83. Charles G. Haines and Foster H. Sherwood, *The Role of the Supreme Court in American Government and Politics, 1835–1864* (Berkeley: University of California Press, 1957), p. 504. Swisher, *Taney*, pp. 584–86, sees Taney as more fundamentally opposed to Marshall's policies than perhaps do Haines and Sherwood, but Taney's personal views did not always prevail on the Court. It would be an error, nevertheless, to conclude that there were no important changes in constitutional law, especially in the field of state control over corporations. For a balanced evaluation consult Robert G. McCloskey, *The American Supreme Court* (Chicago: University of Chicago Press, 1960), pp. 28, 82–85, 99–100.

84. "Chief Justice Taney," 10 *Vand. L. Rev.* 227, 257 (1957).

85. For details see Haines and Sherwood, *op. cit.*, chap. 4.

86. *United States* v. *The Amistad* (1841).

87. *Prigg* v. *Pennsylvania* (1842).

88. *Jones* v. *Van Zandt* (1847).

89. *Moore* v. *Illinois* (1852).

90. For an excellent recent study of the abolitionists see Louis Filler, *The Crusade against Slavery 1830–1860* (New York: Harper & Bros., 1960). Chap. 9, especially p. 205, has some details on the abolitionists' attitude toward the Court and the Constitution. For an analysis of the abolitionists' arguments that slavery was unconstitutional see Jacobus tenBroek, *The Antislavery Origins of the Fourteenth Amendment* (Berkeley: University of California Press, 1951), Parts I, II.

91. Warren, *Supreme Court in U.S. History,* II, 208–17.

92. *Congressional Globe,* 31st Cong., 1st sess., Appendix, p. 1058.

93. *Ibid.,* Appendix, pp. 474, 477–78.

94. The background of the Dred Scott case can be found in Swisher, *Taney,* pp. 496–500; Vincent C. Hopkins, *Dred Scott's Case* (New York: Fordham University Press, 1951), chap. 5.

95. Richardson, *op. cit.,* V, 431.

96. Quoted in Swisher, *Taney,* p. 502.

97. Warren has collected a number of editorial comments, *Supreme Court in U.S. History,* II, 304 ff.

98. Roy P. Basler (ed.), *The Collected Works of Abraham Lincoln* (New Brunswick: Rutgers University Press, 1953–55), II, 494–96 (hereafter cited as *Collected Works*).

99. The adverse report is at: *Congressional Globe,* 35th Cong., 1st sess., p. 2348. See Warren, *The Supreme Court in U.S. History,* II, 333.

100. *American Constitutional Development,* p. 251. For a defense of the decision see Hopkins, *op. cit.,* p. vi; and Wallace Mendelson, *Capitalism, Democracy, and the Supreme Court* (New York: Appleton-Century-Crofts, Inc., 1960), p. 51.

101. Quoted in David Silver, *Lincoln's Supreme Court,* Illinois Studies in the Social Sciences, XXXVIII (1956), 42.

102. *Congressional Globe,* 37th Cong., 2d sess., p. 8.

103. *Ibid.,* p. 28.

104. *Ibid.,* p. 37.

105. *Ibid.,* p. 155.

106. *Collected Works,* IV, 268.

107. James G. Randall's *Constitutional Problems under Lincoln* (New York: Appleton-Century-Crofts, Inc., 1926) is still basic. Haines and Sherwood, Swisher's biography of Taney, and Charles Fairman, *Mr. Justice Miller and the Supreme Court 1862–1890* (Cambridge, Mass.: Harvard University Press, 1939) all have valuable sections on the Court during the Civil War. The best single book, however, is that by David Silver, cited above, note 101.

108. *Ex parte Merryman* (1861).

109. Quoted in Warren, *Supreme Court in U.S. History,* II, 369.

110. Quoted in Silver, *op. cit.,* p. 32.

111. *Collected Works,* IV, 430.

112. Quoted in Warren, *Supreme Court in U.S. History,* II, 393–94.

113. Quoted in *ibid.,* II, 390.

114. Quoted in Silver, *op. cit.,* p. 187.

3. THE STRUGGLE FOR POLITICAL SUPREMACY

1. Quoted in Charles Warren, *Supreme Court in U.S. History,* II, 430, 432.
2. "Milligan's Case," 1 *Am. L. Rev.* 572, 573 (1867).
3. *Congressional Globe,* 39th Cong., 2d sess., p. 251.
4. *Ibid.,* p. 502.
5. *Cummings* v. *Missouri* (1867); *Ex parte Garland* (1867).
6. Quoted in Warren, *op. cit.,* II, 459.
7. *Mississippi* v. *Johnson* (1867).
8. *Georgia* v. *Stanton* (1868).
9. *Ex parte McCardle* (1868).
10. *Congressional Globe,* 40th Cong., 2d sess., pp. 477–89, 506.
11. Warren, *op. cit.,* II, 471.
12. See the discussion in Fawn M. Brodie, *Thaddeus Stevens: Scourge of the South* (New York: W. W. Norton & Co., 1959), p. 322.
13. For details see Warren, *op. cit.,* II, 474–80.
14. *Congressional Globe,* 40th Cong., 2d sess., p. 2117.
15. *Ibid.,* p. 2168.
16. *Ibid.,* p. 2128.
17. *Ibid.,* p. 2170.
18. This opinion was not published in the official U.S. Reports. It is, however, quoted from contemporary newspaper accounts by Warren, *op. cit.,* II, 482.
19. *Ex parte McCardle* (1869).
20. *Ex parte Yerger* (1869). For details consult Warren, *op. cit.,* II, 491–96, and Charles Fairman, *Mr. Justice Miller,* pp. 142–44.
21. Senate Report No. 280: introduced, December 6, 1869, *Congressional Globe,* 41st Cong., 2d sess., p. 3; reported December 9, 1869, *ibid.,* p. 45; text as amended and explained, *ibid.,* pp. 167 ff. The bill was passed over twice, April 22, 1870, *ibid.,* p. 2895, and June 10, 1870, *ibid.,* p. 4305.
22. Senate Report No. 274: introduced December 6, 1869, *Congressional Globe,* 41st Cong., 2d sess., p. 2; explained December 13, 1869, *ibid.,* pp. 86 ff.; adversely reported February 14, 1870, *ibid.,* p. 1250.
23. Senate Report No. 341: introduced December 16, 1869, *Congressional Globe,* 41st Cong., 2d sess., pp. 164, 2895–96; reported and indefinitely postponed, July 7, 1870, *ibid.,* p. 5314.
24. One of the most detailed and best accounts of this crisis is Sidney Ratner, "Was the Supreme Court Packed by President Grant?" 50 *Pol. Sci. Q.* 343 (1935). See also Warren, *op. cit.,* chap. 31; Fairman, "The Retirement of Federal Judges," 51 *Harv. L. Rev.* 397, 416–19 (1938); Fairman, *Mr. Justice Miller,* chap. 7; and Fairman, "Mr. Justice Bradley's Appointment to the Supreme Court and the Legal Tender Cases," 54 *Harv. L. Rev.* 977–1034, 1128–1155 (1941).
25. *Knox* v. *Lee* (1871).
26. The Compromise of 1877 was, of course, far more complex. The best account is C. Vann Woodward, *Reunion and Reaction* (2d ed.; New York: Doubleday & Co., Inc., 1956).
27. These cases are listed and discussed in Eugene Gressman, "The Unhappy History of Civil Rights Legislation," 50 *Mich. L. Rev.* 1323 (1952). The leading decisions were: *United States* v. *Cruikshank* (1876); *United States* v. *Reese*

(1876); *Virginia* v. *Rives* (1880); and *United States* v. *Harris (*1883). Much of the groundwork had been laid in the Slaughter-House Cases (1873).

28. Vann Woodward comments: "The decision constituted a sort of validation of the Compromise of 1877, and it was appropriate that it should have been written by Justice Joseph P. Bradley, the 'Fifth Judge' of the Electoral Commission [which decided that the contested state elections had all gone for Hayes in 1876]." *Op. cit.,* p. 266.

29. *Munn* v. *Illinois* (1877).

30. For discussions of the individual cases see Bruce Trimble, *Chief Justice Waite: Defender of the Public Interest* (Princeton: Princeton University Press, 1938), chap. 13.

31. Benjamin R. Twiss, *Lawyers and the Constitution* (Princeton: Princeton University Press, 1942) traces the early aims, efforts, and influences of the American Bar Association.

32. For a detailed account see Clyde E. Jacobs, *Law Writers and the Courts* (Berkeley: University of California Press, 1954).

33. See Fairman, *Mr. Justice Miller,* chap. 9, and Alan F. Westin, "The Supreme Court, the Populist Movement, and the Campaign of 1896," 15 *J. of Pols.* 3 (1953).

34. *Chicago, Milwaukee & St. Paul Ry.* v. *Minnesota* (1890); *Smyth* v. *Ames* (1898).

35. The best account of the reading of laissez faire into the Constitution is Edward S. Corwin, *Liberty against Government* (Baton Rouge: Louisiana State University Press, 1948). Fairman's *Mr. Justice Miller,* chaps. 14–16, has some valuable insights, as does Carl B. Swisher, *Stephen J. Field: Craftsman of the Law* (Washington: The Brookings Institution, 1930). See also Robert G. McCloskey, *The American Supreme Court,* chap. 5, and the annotated bibliography at pp. 245–47.

36. Alfred H. Kelly and Winfred Harbison, *The American Constitution,* p. 552.

37. For details consult: Roy and Gladys Blakey, *The Federal Income Tax* (New York: Longmans, Green & Co., 1940), chap. 1; Swisher, *Stephen J. Field,* chap. 15; Swisher, *American Constitutional Development,* chap. 20, and literature cited; Westin, *op. cit.;* and Charles Evans Hughes, *The Supreme Court of the United States* (New York: Columbia University Press, 1928), pp. 53–54. For general background see John D. Hicks, *The Populist Revolt* (Minneapolis: University of Minnesota Press, 1931).

38. *Hylton* v. *United States.*

39. *Springer* v. *United States.*

40. James B. Weaver, *A Call to Action* (Des Moines: Iowa Publishing Co., 1892), p. 133.

41. Westin, *op. cit.,* p. 24.

42. 29 *Am. L. Rev.* 293, 306 (1895).

43. Quoted in Westin, *op. cit.,* p. 29.

44. "The Income Tax Decision, and the Power of the Supreme Court to Nullify Acts of Congress," 29 *Am. L. Rev.* 550, 558 (1895).

45. Quoted in Westin, *op. cit.,* p. 32.

46. Kirk H. Porter, *National Party Platforms* (New York: Macmillan Co., 1924), pp. 184–85.

47. See Westin, *op. cit.,* p. 36.

48. For details consult Kelly and Harbison, *op. cit.*, pp. 612–16; Swisher, *American Constitutional Development*, pp. 530–36.

49. *Flint* v. *Stone Tracy Co.* (1911); cf. *Knowlton* v. *Moore* (1900).

50. *Loewe* v. *Lawlor* (1908).

51. *Adair* v. *United States* (1908); *Coppage* v. *Kansas* (1915).

52. *Standard Oil Co.* v. *United States* (1911); *United States* v. *American Tobacco Co.* (1911).

53. *United States* v. *Trans-Missouri Freight Ass'n* (1897); *United States* v. *Joint Traffic Ass'n* (1898).

54. See Justice Harlan's dissenting opinion in *Standard Oil* v. *United States* (1911), and the citations in Representative Frear's speech, 64 *Congressional Record* 2607–15.

55. For a full study see Harding C. Noblitt, "The Supreme Court and the Progressive Era, 1902–1921," unpublished Ph.D. thesis, University of Chicago, 1955. See also McCloskey, *op. cit.*, pp. 136–39.

56. Oregon: *Muller* v. *Oregon* (1908); Massachusetts: *Riley* v. *Massachusetts* (1914); California: *Miller* v. *Wilson* (1915), *Bosley* v. *McLaughlin* (1915); Arizona: *Dominion Hotel* v. *Arizona* (1919).

57. *Northern Securities Co.* v. *United States* (1904).

58. *Hipolite Egg Co.* v. *United States* (1911).

59. *McCray* v. *United States* (1904).

60. *Champion* v. *Ames* (1903).

61. *United States* v. *Doremus* (1919).

62. *Hoke* v. *United States* (1913).

63. *Wilson* v. *New* (1917).

64. Roosevelt explained his position in "Judges and Progress," 100 *Outlook* 40 (January 6, 1912); see also Walter F. Dodd, "Social Legislation and the Courts," 28 *Pol. Sci. Q.* 1 (1913); Gilbert E. Roe, *Our Judicial Oligarchy* (New York: Huebsch, 1912); Louis B. Boudin, "Government by Judiciary," 26 *Pol. Sci. Q.* 238 (1911).

65. Taft to Elihu Root, December 21, 1922, Taft Papers.

66. This section is based in part on an examination of the Taft Papers in the Library of Congress. The best published account of Taft's chief justiceship is that in Alpheus T. Mason, *The Supreme Court from Taft to Warren* (Baton Rouge: Louisiana State University Press, 1958), chap. 2; see also Henry F. Pringle, *The Life and Times of William Howard Taft* (New York: Farrar & Rinehart, 1939), II, chaps. 50–56; and Walter F. Murphy, "In His Own Image: Chief Justice Taft and Supreme Court Appointments," *1961 Supreme Court Review*.

67. For speculation concerning Brandeis' position see Alexander Bickel, *The Unpublished Opinions of Mr. Justice Brandeis* (Cambridge, Mass.: Harvard University Press, 1957), chap. 1.

68. WHT to Horace Taft, May 15, 1922.

69. For later history of this litigation see Edward Berman, *Labor and the Sherman Act* (New York: Harper & Bros., 1930), pp. 126 ff. Taft was quite pleased with his opinion in this case, and he received several congratulatory letters from friends. For Brandeis' reaction consult Bickel, *op. cit.*, chap. 5.

70. *New York Times*, May 16, 1923, 21:5.

71. Telegram from W. G. Lee, president of the Brotherhood of Railroad Trainmen, to WHT, June 23, 1922.

72. Quoted in 64 *Congressional Record* 2614.

73. McSwain: 62 *Congressional Record* 860 (January 6, 1922); Borah: 64 *ibid.* 3004 (February 5, 1923). Representative Carl Hayden of Arizona had introduced a similar resolution (H.J. Res. 15) in 1921. 61 *ibid.* 100.

74. The speech is reprinted in full at 62 *Congressional Record* 9076–82. The quoted remarks are at p. 9077.

75. 64 *ibid.* 2607–15.

76. 64 *ibid.* 2615, 3173.

77. "Public Opinion Defends the Court," 8 *Constitutional Review* 119 (1924), has a collection of statements by various bar associations. "Proposals for Curbing the Supreme Court in Its Jurisdiction and Judicial Power," 2 *Congressional Digest* 271 (1923), contains an excellent debate between pro- and anti-Court writers.

78. "Judicial Veto Wholly without Authority in the Constitution," 28 *Am. Federationist* 723 (1921). See Clark's earlier articles: "Where Does the Governing Power Reside?" 52 *Am. L. Rev.* 687 (1918), and "Back to the Constitution," 50 *ibid.* 1 (1916). Also see a reply to Clark by Preston A. Shinn, reprinted at 62 *Congressional Record* 10292.

79. "Judicial Power To Declare Legislation Unconstitutional," 9 *A.B.A.J.* 689 (1923).

80. Porter, *op. cit.*, pp. 519–20.

81. WHT to Pierce Butler, December 5, 1922.

82. WHT to the Chief Justice of New Jersey, April 12, 1922.

83. WHT to Calvin Cobb, March 8, 1923.

84. WHT to Horace Taft, December 28, 1922.

85. *Ibid.*, April 4, 1923.

86. WHT to Robert Taft, July 29, 1922; WHT to Van Devanter, August 19, 1922.

87. WHT to Robert Taft, April 16, 1923.

88. September 10, 1922.

89. WHT to Charles P. Taft, September 10, 1922. This analysis of the Progressives was also made in Taft's letter to Sutherland of the same date. The Progressives themselves recognized their lack of party discipline as one of their chief weaknesses. See the discussion in A. M. Schlesinger, Jr., *The Politics of Upheaval* (Boston: Houghton Mifflin Co., 1960), p. 413.

90. John D. Hicks, *The Republican Ascendancy, 1921–1933* (New York: Harper & Bros., 1960), p. 109.

91. WHT to Horace Taft, September 29, 1923.

92. Quoted in Swisher, *American Constitutional Development,* p. 773.

93. Hicks, *op. cit.*, p. 102.

94. Brandeis to WHT, December 23, 1922; *Burns Baking Co.* v. *Bryan* (1924), dissenting opinion.

95. WHT to Van Devanter, August 19, 1922.

96. Benjamin F. Wright, *The Growth of American Constitutional Law,* p. 113. For general discussions of the work of the Court during this period consult Mason, *op. cit.*, chap. 2; Kelly and Harbison, *op. cit.*, chap. 26; Swisher, *American Constitutional Development,* chaps. 31–33.

97. *Duplex Printing Co.* v. *Deering* (1921); *American Steel* v. *Tri-City Central Trades Council* (1921); *United States* v. *Brims* (1926); *Bedford Cut Stone Co.* v. *Journeymen Stone Cutters* (1927).

98. For example, *Railroad Commission* v. *Chicago, Burlington & Quincy Railroad* (1922); *Stafford* v. *Wallace* (1922); *Dayton-Goose Creek Railway* v. *United*

States (1924); *Brooks* v. *United States* (1925). *Board of Trade* v. *Olsen* (1923) sustained a statute regulating trading in grain futures which had been redrafted along lines suggested by Taft's opinion for the Court in *Hill* v. *Wallace* (1922), invalidating an earlier act.

99. Brandeis to WHT, December 23, 1922. For a discussion of specific cases see Kelly and Harbison, *op. cit.*, pp. 711–14, and Carl McFarland, *Judicial Control of the Federal Trade Commission and the Interstate Commerce Commission 1920–1930* (Cambridge, Mass.: Harvard University Press, 1933).

100. Merlo Pusey, *Charles Evans Hughes* (New York: Macmillan Co., 1951), II, 733.

101. Alpheus T. Mason, "The Supreme Court: Temple and Forum," 48 *Yale Rev.* 524, 527 (1959).

102. *Home Building and Loan Ass'n* v. *Blaisdell.*

103. *Norman* v. *B. & O. Railroad* (1935); *Perry* v. *United States* (1935).

104. *Railroad Retirement Board* v. *Alton* (1935). *Panama Refining Co.* v. *Ryan* (1935) might be considered as the logical beginning of the Court's war with the New Deal, but there were special circumstances involved. For one thing, no copy of the administrative order regulating oil production had been available to the oil companies.

105. *Schechter Poultry Co.* v. *United States* (1935).

106. *Louisville Bank* v. *Radford* (1935).

107. *Humphrey's Executor* v. *United States* (1935). In 1958, Frankfurter's opinion for the Court in *Wiener* v. *United States* finally admitted the basis of FDR's asserted authority was supported by Taft's opinion.

108. *Myers* v. *United States* (1926).

109. Quoted in Schlesinger, *op. cit.*, p. 280.

110. FDR's comments are printed in Samuel I. Rosenman (ed.), *The Public Papers and Addresses of Franklin D. Roosevelt* (New York: Random House, 1938 ff.), IV, 200–222. For evaluations see Schlesinger, *op. cit.*, pp. 285–87, and James M. Burns, *Roosevelt: The Lion and the Fox* (New York: Harcourt, Brace & Co., Inc., 1956), pp. 222–23.

111. Robert H. Jackson, *The Struggle for Judicial Supremacy* (New York: Alfred A. Knopf, Inc., 1941), p. 140.

112. Alpheus T. Mason, *Harlan Fiske Stone: Pillar of the Law* (New York: Viking Press, Inc., 1956), p. 408 n.

113. *Rickert Rice Mills* v. *Fontenot* (1936).

114. *Ashwander* v. *TVA* (1936).

115. *Carter* v. *Carter Coal Co.* (1936).

116. *Ashton* v. *Cameron County* (1936).

117. See, however, *Colgate* v. *Harvey* (1935).

118. C. Herman Pritchett, *The Roosevelt Court: A Study in Judicial Politics and Values, 1937–1947* (New York: Macmillan Co., 1948), p. 6.

119. Quoted in Mason, *Stone,* p. 426.

120. *Ibid.*, pp. 438–39.

121. Raoul Desvernine, *Democratic Despotism* (New York: Dodd, Mead & Co., Inc., 1936), pp. 175, 182.

122. Quoted in Jackson, *op. cit.*, p. 174 (italics supplied).

123. There are numerous accounts of the New Deal fight. I have relied primarily on: Mason, *Stone,* chaps. 26–29; Alsop and Catledge, *The 168 Days;* Burns, *op. cit.*, chap. 15; and Jackson, *op. cit.* The first 200 pages of the second

volume of *The Secret Diary of Harold L. Ickes* (New York: Simon & Schuster, Inc., 1954) contain a number of pungent "inside" comments.

124. Hughes's statement is discussed at length in Mason, *Stone*, pp. 450–55; Pusey, *op. cit.*, II, 754–57; and Samuel Hendel, *Charles Evans Hughes* (New York: King's Crown Press, 1951), pp. 250–52.

125. *Wright* v. *Vinton Branch* (1937).

126. *Virginian Railway* v. *Federation* (1937).

127. *Sonzinsky* v. *United States* (1937).

128. *NLRB* v. *Jones & Laughlin* (1937); *NLRB* v. *Fruehauf Trailer Co.* (1937); *NLRB* v. *Friedman, Harry Marks Clothing Co.* (1937).

129. Edward S. Corwin, *Constitutional Revolution, Ltd.* (Claremont, Calif.: The Claremont Colleges, 1941), pp. 64–65.

130. *Carmichael* v. *Southern Coal Co.* (1937); *Steward Machine Co.* v. *Davis* (1937).

131. Senate Report No. 711, 75th Cong., 1st sess.

132. Quoted in Burns, *op. cit.*, p. 315.

133. *Ibid.*

4. JUDICIAL RESTRAINT FROM STONE TO WARREN

1. *Currin* v. *Wallace* (1939); *Mulford* v. *Smith* (1939); *United States* v. *Rock Royal* (1939).

2. *United States* v. *Carolene Products* (1938).

3. *United States* v. *Appalachian Electric Power Co.* (1940); *Oklahoma* v. *Atkinson* (1941).

4. See, for an extreme example, *Martino* v. *Michigan Window Cleaning Co.* (1946).

5. *Wickard* v. *Filburn* (1942).

6. *United States* v. *Darby Lumber Co.* (1941).

7. *Williamson* v. *Lee Optical* (1955).

8. For detailed analyses of divisions within the Court over general judicial theory as well as specific issues see: Pritchett, *The Roosevelt Court;* Mason, *Harlan Fiske Stone*, Part VI, and *The Supreme Court from Taft to Warren*, chap. 4; Walter F. Murphy, "Mr. Justice Jackson, Free Speech, and the Judicial Function," 12 *Vand. L. Rev.* 1019 (1959); Helen Shirley Thomas, *Felix Frankfurter: Scholar on the Bench* (Baltimore: Johns Hopkins University Press, 1960).

9. See especially the famous footnote 4 in *United States* v. *Carolene Products* (1938), and the discussion in Mason's books cited above, note 8.

10. *Ullmann* v. *United States* (1956), concurring opinion.

11. *West Virginia* v. *Barnette* (1943).

12. For discussions of these cases see: Pritchett, *The Roosevelt Court*, chaps. 5–6, and *Civil Liberties and the Vinson Court* (Chicago: University of Chicago Press, 1953), chaps. 7–8; Murphy, "Desegregation in Education," 15 *Md. L. Rev.* 221 (1955), and "The South Counterattacks," 12 *West. Pol. Q.* 371 (1959).

13. *Tot* v. *United States* (1943); *United States* v. *Lovett* (1946); and *United States* v. *Cardiff* (1952).

14. S.J. Res. 167, 79/2.

15. *Sipuel* v. *Oklahoma* (1948).

16. Quoted in Anna Rothe (ed.), *Current Biography 1949* (New York: H. W. Wilson Co., 1950), p. 185.

17. *Shelley* v. *Kraemer* (1948), and *Hurd* v. *Hodge* (1948).

18. 94 *Congressional Record* 5256.

19. There is no single full discussion of this congressional activity during the postwar decade, although Alan F. Westin is preparing one for the Fund for the Republic. For a general survey see note, "Congressional Reversal of Supreme Court Decisions: 1945–57," 71 *Harv. L. Rev.* 1324 (1958). For more specific studies consult: S. S. Surrey, "The Congress and the Tax Lobbyist—How Special Provisions Get Enacted," 70 *Harv. L. Rev.* 1150 (1957); Phillip L. Sirotkin, "An Analysis of Congressional Attitudes toward the Supreme Court," unpublished Ph.D. thesis, University of Chicago, 1951; E. R. Bartley, *The Tidelands Oil Controversy* (Austin: University of Texas Press, 1953); and Lucius Barker, "The Offshore Oil Controversy since 1953," 1958 *Wisc. L. Rev.* 107.

20. *Hirabayashi* v. *United States* (1943); *Korematsu* v. *United States* (1944).

21. *Garner* v. *Board* (1951); *Wieman* v. *Updegraff* (1952).

22. This analysis of the Vinson Court follows the interpretation in Pritchett, *Civil Liberties and the Vinson Court,* chaps. 3–6, 12–13.

23. *American Communications Association* v. *Douds* (1950); *Osman* v. *Douds* (1950).

24. *Joint Anti-Fascist Refugee Committee* v. *McGrath* (1951).

25. *Dennis* v. *United States* (1951).

26. Pritchett, *Civil Liberties and the Vinson Court,* p. 239.

27. Fred Rodell, *Nine Men* (New York: Random House, 1955), p. 304.

28. *Youngstown Sheet & Tube Co.* v. *Sawyer* (1952). For discussions see: Edward S. Corwin, "The Steel Seizure Case: A Judicial Brick without Straw," 53 *Col. L. Rev.* 53 (1953); Glendon A. Schubert, Jr., "The Steel Case," 6 *West. Pol. Q.* 66 (1953); and Alan F. Westin, *The Anatomy of a Constitutional Law Case* (New York: Macmillan Co., 1958).

29. 98 *Congressional Record* 6278.

30. S.J. Res. 44, 83/2, 100 *Congressional Record* 6347.

31. Senator John McClellan (Dem., Ark.), *Southern School News* (September, 1956), p. 15; Senator Eastland, 101 *Congressional Record* 7120; Rep. L. Mendel Rivers (Dem., S.C.), *Southern School News* (April, 1956), p. 12.

32. 102 *Congressional Record* 4460.

33. For detailed accounts of the first years of the Warren Court see: C. Herman Pritchett, *The Political Offender and the Warren Court* (Boston: Boston University Press, 1958), and Clyde Jacobs, "The Warren Court—After Three Terms," 9 *West. Pol. Q.* 937 (1956).

34. For an elaboration of this general tendency among freshman Justices consult E. C. Snyder, "The Supreme Court as a Small Group," 36 *Social Forces* 232 (1958).

35. See, for instance, Earl Latham, "The Supreme Court and the Supreme People," 16 *J. of Pols.* 207 (1954).

36. *Toth* v. *Quarles* (1955).

37. 102 *Congressional Record* 7341.

38. *Ibid.,* p. 6384.

39. The quotations are at *ibid.,* pp. 6384–86.

40. *Ibid.,* p. 10173.

41. *Ibid.,* pp. 6063–64.

42. *Ibid.,* p. 6064.

43. Internal Security Subcommittee, "Hearings on S. 3603 and S. 3617" (May 11, 1956), 84/2. These hearings were not printed; they can be found in Vol. XXXVII of the subcommittee's unprinted hearings, pp. 2510–11.

44. Internal Security Subcommittee, "Hearings on S. 4050, S. 4051, and S. 4047" (June 26, 1956), 84/2, Vol. LVIII of unprinted hearings, pp. 3345–48.

45. *Lincoln Federal Labor Union* v. *Northwestern Iron and Metal Co.* (1949); *American Federation of Labor* v. *American Sash & Door Co.* (1949).

46. *Hill v. Florida* (1945); *Bethlehem Steel* v. *New York* (1947); *International Union* v. *O'Brien* (1950); *Amalgamated Association* v. *Wisconsin* (1951).

47. *United Mine Workers* v. *Arkansas Oak Flooring Co.* (1956).

48. See the testimony of Douglas Berman of the Texas state legislature, Subcommittee #1, House Committee on the Judiciary, *Hearings on H.R. 3* (Serial 9, July 12, 1955), 84/1, Part I, pp. 75–76.

49. *Ibid.*

50. *Ibid.* (Serial 9, April 20, 1956), 84/2, Part II.

51. Senate Committee on the Judiciary, *Hearings on S. 373 and S. 3143* (May 18, 1956), 84/2.

52. Senate *Hearings,* p. 25.

53. House *Hearings,* II, 161.

54. 41 *A.B.A.J.* 1075 (1955); the text of the bar committee's report is at Senate *Hearings,* pp. 63 ff.

55. *Proceedings of the Conference of the National Association of Attorneys General 1955* (Chicago: Council of State Governments, 1956), p. 169.

56. House *Hearings,* II, pp. 140–41.

57. House Report No. 2576, 84/2.

58. Some of the early background of H.R. 3 was related by Howard Smith in testimony reprinted at: House Committee on the Judiciary, *Hearings on H.R. 3* (Serial 16, May 13, 1958), 85/2, pp. 20–21.

59. *Time,* June 25, 1956, p. 16.

60. "Recent Attacks upon the Supreme Court: A Statement by Members of the Bar," 42 *A.B.A.J.* 1128 (1956).

61. *Southern School News* (October, 1956), p. 14.

62. *1956 Proceedings of the Governors' Conference* (Chicago: Conference of State Governors, 1956), pp. 188–89.

5. THE RESURGENCE OF JUDICIAL POWER

1. P. 50.

2. H. Res. 174 (adopted February 22, 1957), 2 *Race Rel. L. Rep.* 485.

3. See Snyder, "The Supreme Court as a Small Group," 36 *Social Forces* 232 (1958).

4. *Mesarosh* v. *United States* (1956).

5. *Fujimoto* v. *United States* (1958).

6. *Service* v. *Dulles* (1957).

7. "Constitutional Law in 1956–57," 52 *Am. Pol. Sci. Rev.* 140, 145 (1958).

8. *West Virginia* v. *Barnette* (1943).

9. *United States* v. *Du Pont de Nemours* (1957).

10. *Pennsylvania* v. *Board* (1957).

11. For a brilliant exposition and defense of the McNabb-Mallory Rule, consult James E. Hogan and Joseph M. Snee, "The McNabb-Mallory Rule: Its Rise, Rationale and Rescue," 47 *Geo. L. J.* 1 (1958).

12. Robert G. McCloskey, "Useful Toil or Paths of Glory? Civil Liberties in the 1956 Term of the Supreme Court," 43 *Va. L. Rev.* 803, 830 (1957). This was the second part of an excellent trilogy by McCloskey: "The Supreme Court Finds a Role: Civil Liberties in the 1955 Term," 42 *ibid.* 735 (1956); "Tools, Stumbling Blocks, and Stepping Stones: Civil Liberties in the 1957 Term of the Court," 44 *ibid.* 1029 (1958).

13. For a perceptive analysis of the tactics of the Warren Court see William M. Beaney, "Civil Liberties and Statutory Interpretation," 8 *J. of Pub. L.* 66 (1959).

14. Except where otherwise noted the following editorial comments are reprinted either in 103 *Congressional Record* (and indexed under Supreme Court) or in the *New York Times,* June 19, 1957, p. 19. For other highly critical evaluations of the Court's work see: L. Brent Bozell, "Blueprint for Judicial Chaos," 4 *National Rev.* 80 (1957); editorials, 4 *ibid.* 77, 245; James Burnham, "Why Not Investigate the Court?" 4 *ibid.* 83 (1957); Forrest Davis, "The Supreme Court Reaches for Total Power," 4 *ibid.* 33 (1957); Paulson Spense, "Get the Supreme Court out of Politics," 85 *Am. Mercury* 23 (October, 1957); and editorials in *U.S. News and World Report* throughout the summer of 1957.

15. Quoted at 103 *Congressional Record* 11423.

16. June 19, 1957.

17. *Daily Worker,* August 5, 1957.

18. June 10, 1944; the case was *Hartzel* v. *United States* (1944).

19. June 20, 1957.

20. June 5, 1957. The *Washington Post & Times-Herald* strongly supported the Du Pont decision in an editorial on June 6, 1957. See also Bruce Bromley, "Business's Views of the Du Pont–General Motors Decision," 46 *Geo. L. J.* 646 (1958); William G. McGovern, "The Power and the Glory: The Du Pont–GM Decision," 46 *ibid.* 655 (1958).

21. June 5, 1957.

22. June 18, 1957, 32:1–2.

23. 97 *America* 418 (July 20, 1957).

24. 66 *Commonweal* 339 (July 6, 1957).

25. July, 1957, p. 3.

26. 103 *Congressional Record* 10296.

27. *New York Times,* July 8, 1957, 15:5.

28. *Ibid.,* July 3, 1957, 6:3.

29. *Ibid.,* June 19, 1957, 18:3.

30. 103 *Congressional Record* 15972.

31. *Ibid.,* p. 10471.

32. *Ibid.,* p. 10123.

33. *Philadelphia Inquirer,* June 25, 1957.

34. For a summary of these proposals, see: Shelden D. Elliott, "Court Curbing Proposals in Congress," 33 *N. D. Lawyer* 597 (1958); Robert J. Steamer, "Statesmanship or Craftsmanship: Current Conflict over the Supreme Court," 11 *West. Pol. Q.* 265 (1958).

35. H.R. 692, 85/1, introduced by Representative Huddleston of Alabama.

36. Quoted in *New York Times,* July 1, 1957, 1:3.
37. H.R. 8600, H.R. 8867, H.R. 8341.
38. S. 2377.
39. *New York Times,* June 20, 1957, 18:2.
40. *Ibid.,* June 27, 1957, 10:5.
41. Wyman's speech is reprinted in *Proceedings of the Conference of The National Association of Attorneys General 1957* (Chicago: Council of State Governments, 1958), pp. 33 ff. See also the accounts of the meetings in the *New York Times,* June 25, 1957, 1:7, 18:3–5; June 26, 1957, 63:4; June 27, 1957, 18:3; and *Philadelphia Inquirer,* June 25, 1957.
42. 82 *Reports of the ABA* 120 (1957).
43. *Ibid.,* pp. 179–80, 328. See also the *New York Times,* July 26, 1957, 1:1, 8:5.
44. *Washington Post & Times-Herald,* July 31, 1957.
45. *New York Times,* July 16, 1957, 14:3; September 21, 1957, 12:4; September 22, 1957, 59:3–4.
46. *Proceedings of the 9th Annual Meeting of the Conference of Chief Justices* (Chicago: Council of State Governments, mimeo., 1957), p. 64. *New York Times,* July 14, 1957, 48:4–5.
47. *1957 Proceedings of the Governors' Conference,* pp. 218–19.
48. *New York Times,* October 6, 1957, 62:3–5.
49. House Document 303, 85/2, Res. 18 (1957).
50. Consult the statistics in Fellman, "Constitutional Law in 1956–57," 52 *Am. Pol. Sci. Rev.* 140 (1958).
51. See, for example, the comments in: McCloskey, "Useful Toil or Paths of Glory?"; Edmond Cahn, "A Dangerous Myth in the School Segregation Cases," 30 *N.Y.U.L. Rev.* 150 (1955); Bernard Schwartz, "The Warren Court—An Opinion," *New York Times Magazine,* June 30, 1957, pp. 10 ff.; Pritchett, *The Political Offender and the Warren Court,* p. 27 *et passim;* Herbert Wechsler, "Toward Neutral Principles of Constitutional Law," 73 *Harv. L. Rev.* 1 (1959); Henry M. Hart, "The Time Chart of the Justices," *ibid.,* p. 84; Alan F. Westin, "The Supreme Court Decisions—A New Balance on Civil Liberties," *New Leader,* August 5, 1957, p. 5; Alpheus T. Mason, "The Supreme Court: Temple and Forum," 48 *Yale Rev.* 524 (1959). The Warren Court has not been without critics who have asserted that even its decisions of the 1956 Term did not go far enough or fast enough to protect civil liberties: Arthur J. Keeffe, "Comments on the Supreme Court's Treatment of the Bill of Rights in the October 1956 Term," 26 *Fordham L. Rev.* 468 (1957); Harold W. Chase, "The Warren Court and Congress," 44 *Minn. L. Rev.* 595 (1960).
52. Brennan's error was picked up and exploited by several harsh critics of the Court: George Sokolsky, *Washington Post & Times-Herald,* August 5, 1957; and L. Brent Bozell, "Blueprint for Judicial Chaos," 4 *National Rev.* 80 (1957).
53. I interpret the major cold war cases of the 1956 Term as: *Schware* v. *New Mexico, Jencks* v. *United States, Yates* v. *United States, Watkins* v. *United States, Sweezy* v. *New Hampshire, Service* v. *Dulles,* and *Konigsberg* v. *California.* Frankfurter was with the majority in all except the last decision. In the 1957 Term Warren did not assign the opinion of the Court to Frankfurter in any of the fourteen civil liberties cases in which they voted together. See S. Sidney Ulmer, "Supreme Court Behavior and Civil Rights," 13 *West. Pol. Q.* 288, 293 (1960).

6. THE JENCKS BILLS

1. The Senate Subcommittee on Improvements in the Federal Criminal Code subscribed to a clipping service which collected editorial reaction to the Jencks case and the Jencks bill. Many of these editorials were reprinted in 103 *Congressional Record;* the remainder can be found in the National Archives in the subcommittee's 1957 files, Sen. 85–A–F11, Box 16 (hereafter cited as subcommittee files).

2. June 17, 1957, p. 19.

3. June 5, 1957.

4. See especially the editorial of July 19, 1957. The judge, incidentally, held the agent in contempt and fined him $1,000.

5. June 20, 1957, pp. 2863, 2884.

6. *New York Journal-American,* June 16, 1957.

7. *Ibid.,* June 11, 1957.

8. 103 *Congressional Record* 8290.

9. *Ibid.,* p. 15972.

10. *Ibid.,* p. 10741.

11. *Ibid.,* p. 11291.

12. Quoted in Carlsbad (New Mexico) *Current Argus,* June 9, 1957.

13. 103 *Congressional Record* 10526.

14. *Public Papers of the Presidents: Dwight D. Eisenhower, 1957* (Washington: Government Printing Office, 1958), p. 469.

15. *New York Times,* June 5, 1957, 21:2.

16. H.R. 8341; S. 2377.

17. *New York Times,* June 28, 1957, 1:8, 24:3–6.

18. 103 *Congressional Record* 10624; the *Washington Star,* June 30, 1957, had printed Potter's remarks the day before he made his speech, and the memorandum was written in reference to the newspaper story.

19. Subcommittee files, Box 8, July 1, 1957.

20. Neither the Senate nor House hearings were printed. The text of both witnesses' statements, however, are reprinted in Senate Report No. 981, 85/1.

21. Senate Report No. 569. The text of the bill is also at 103 *Congressional Record* 10120.

22. S. 2379.

23. House Report No. 700.

24. 103 *Congressional Record* 10878.

25. *Ibid.,* p. 10877.

26. July 8, 1957.

27. Subcommittee files, Boxes 8, 16.

28. 103 *Congressional Record* 10984.

29. Memorandum of July 2, 1957, subcommittee files, Box 8.

30. 103 *Congressional Record* 10984.

31. *Ibid.,* p. 11645.

32. *Ibid.,* p. 10986.

33. *Ibid.,* p. 15369.

34. Correspondence in subcommittee files, Box 16. Emanuel Celler brought out some of the FBI lobbying at 103 *Congressional Record* 16119–20, confirming a story by Drew Pearson, *Washington Post & Times-Herald,* July 3, 1957. My

sources of information gave a more detailed account of FBI pressures than either Celler or Pearson.

35. *Public Papers of the Presidents: Dwight D. Eisenhower, 1957,* p. 552.
36. *New York Times,* July 29, 1957, 12:2.
37. 103 *Congressional Record* A6638. As printed, the letter was undated. It appeared in the *Record* for August 13, 1957.
38. *Ibid.,* p. 14457.
39. Senate Report No. 569 withdrawn and Senate Report No. 981 substituted.
40. 103 *Congressional Record* 14913.
41. Subcommittee files, Box 8.
42. *Washington Post & Times-Herald,* August 15, 1957.
43. The text of the bill is at 103 *Congressional Record* 15787.
44. *Ibid.,* p. 15782.
45. *Ibid.,* p. 15806.
46. *Ibid.,* pp. 15930, 15935.
47. *Ibid.,* pp. 15935–36.
48. *Ibid.,* p. 15938.
49. H. Res. 411; House Report No. 1244.
50. 103 *Congressional Record* 16114.
51. *Ibid.,* pp. 16118–19.
52. *Ibid.,* p. 16113.
53. *Ibid.,* p. 16128.
54. *Ibid.,* p. 16121.
55. *Ibid.,* pp. 16122–23.
56. *Ibid.,* p. 16121.
57. *Ibid.,* p. 16129.
58. *Ibid.,* p. 16130.
59. Conference Report (House Report No. 1271); 103 *Congressional Record* 16737–39.
60. *Ibid.,* p. 16489.
61. *Ibid.,* p. 16742.
62. For comments on the final Jencks law see: McCloskey, "Useful Toil or Paths of Glory?" 43 *Va. L. Rev.* 803, 830 n. (1957); David Fellman, "Constitutional Law in 1956–57," 52 *Am. Pol. Sci. Rev.* 140, 159 (1958); Note, "The Jencks Legislation: Problems in Prospect," 67 *Yale L. J.* 674 (1958).
63. Pub. L. 85–269; 71 Stat. 595.
64. August 31, 1957.
65. August 31, 1957.
66. August 31, 1957.
67. September 1, 1957.
68. September 2, 1957, pp. 1, 8.
69. September 3, 1957.
70. 66 *America* 606 (1957).

7. THE ATTACK GAINS MOMENTUM

1. 103 *Congressional Record* 12806–10.
2. 96 *ibid.* 14914; 97 *ibid.* 3619.

3. Internal Security Subcommittee, *Hearings on S. 2646* (August 7, 1957), 85/1, Part I.

4. *Ibid.* (February 19–21, 25–28, March 4–5, 1958), 85/2, Part II. Unless otherwise indicated, the following testimony will be found in these hearings.

5. *New York Times,* March 16, 1958, 10E:6.

6. February 24, 1958.

7. The relevant portions of the ABA proceedings are reprinted in *Hearings on S. 2646,* II, 370 ff.

8. S. 3386.

9. The Casswell hearings were not printed. See *New York Times,* March 27, 1958, 17:1–3.

10. *Washington Post & Times-Herald,* April 2, 1958.

11. 104 *Congressional Record* 6096–98.

12. At least so Butler told the Senate. *Ibid.,* pp. 18665–66.

13. The final committee report, Senate Report No. 1586, pp. 6–7, asserted that this provision would not allow a committee to exceed its jurisdiction since a court could always rule against the committee chairman's decision. If true, this would seem to have been little more than a codification of the decision—though not the opinion—in *Watkins* v. *United States.*

14. Senate Report No. 1586.

15. Published as *The Bill of Rights* (Cambridge, Mass.: Harvard University Press, 1958).

16. *Washington Star,* April 25, 1958.

17. *Public Papers of the Presidents: Dwight D. Eisenhower, 1958,* p. 337.

18. S.J. Res. 169.

19. Committee on the Judiciary, *Internal Security Annual Report for 1957,* Senate Report No. 1477 (April 28, 1958), 85/2, pp. 210, 218.

20. 104 *Congressional Record* 2011.

21. *Ibid.,* p. 1240.

22. *Ibid.,* p. 2330.

23. House Committee on the Judiciary, *Hearings on H.R. 3* (Serial 16, May 13, 20, 1958).

24. Part of this background was brought out in a discussion between Smith and Representative Clarence Brown (Rep., Ohio). 104 *Congressional Record* 4670–71.

25. House Report No. 1878.

26. See notes 40, 43, 44, chap. 4.

27. Consult: House Committee on the Post Office and Civil Service, *Hearings on H.R. 8322, H.R. 981, etc.* (July 16, 17, 19, 23, 1957), 85/1.

28. Senate Report No. 686, 85/1.

29. 103 *Congressional Record* 14033–34.

30. House Report No. 1201, 85/1.

31. H.R. 8361. In the Eighty-fourth Congress the same bill was numbered H.R. 5649. For a critical discussion of the bill's probable effects, see: Louis H. Pollak, "Proposals to Curtail Federal Habeas Corpus for State Prisoners: Collateral Attack on the Great Writ," 66 *Yale L. J.* 50 (1956).

32. Quoted in: Subcommittee #3, House Committee on the Judiciary, *Hearings on H.R. 5649* (Serial 6, June 7, 24, 1955), 84/1, p. 32. The 1953 report of the Chief Justices' special committee on habeas corpus is reprinted at *ibid.,* pp. 92 ff.

33. Concurring opinion of Chief Judge Clark, *United States* v. *Murphy* (1955).
34. House Report No. 1200, 84/1.
35. House Report No. 1293, 85/2.
36. Special Subcommittee To Study Decisions of the Supreme Court, House Committee on the Judiciary, *Hearings on Mallory v. United States* (Serial 12, July 19, 25, August 1, 2, 22, October 28, 1957), 85/2, Part I. Unless otherwise indicated, the following testimony can be found in these hearings.
37. House Report No. 1815.
38. Constitutional Rights Subcommittee, *Hearings on Confessions and Police Detention* (March 7, 11, 1958), 85/2. Unless otherwise indicated, the following testimony can be found in these hearings.
39. H.R. 8867 (Keating, Rep., N.Y.); H.R. 8925 (Cramer, Rep., Fla.); H.R. 13272 (Walter, Dem., Pa.); H.R. 13491 (Colmer, Dem., Miss.).
40. See above, note 36, pp. 191 ff., *et passim.*
41. House Report No. 2495.
42. 104 *Congressional Record* 4675.
43. *Ibid.,* pp. 12940–41.
44. *Ibid.,* p. 13416.
45. *Ibid.,* p. 14162.
46. *Ibid.,* p. 17171.

8. OCTOBER TERM, 1957

1. For examples of decisions protecting aliens see: *United States* v. *Minker* (1956); *United States* v. *Zucca* (1956); *Brownell* v. *Tom We Shung* (1956); *United States* v. *Witkovich* (1957). On the other hand, there were a number of cases holding against aliens; *Jay* v. *Boyd* (1956); *Lehmann* v. *United States* (1957); *United States ex. rel. Hintopoulos* v. *Shaughnessy* (1957); *Mulcahey* v. *Catalanottee* (1957).
2. *Johannessen* v. *United States* (1912); *Tutun* v. *United States* (1926); *Baumgartner* v. *United States* (1944); *Knauer* v. *United States* (1946).
3. *Nowak* v. *United States* (1958); *Maisenberg* v. *United States* (1958).
4. The other two cases were *Toth* v. *Quarles* (1955) and *Reid* v. *Covert* (1957).
5. *Kent* v. *Dulles* (1958); *Dayton* v. *Dulles* (1958).
6. The case referred to was *Perkins* v. *Elg* (1939).
7. *Speiser* v. *Randall* (1958); *First Unitarian Church* v. *Los Angeles* (1958).
8. The author was present in the courtroom during the exchange. It was evident that Warren and Frankfurter were quite irked with one another.
9. The first incident occurred on October 16, 1957, during the argument in *Green* v. *United States* (1958), and is described in John Osborne, "One Supreme Court," *Life,* June 16, 1958, p. 93. The third incident took place during the announcement of the decision in *Caritativo* v. *California* on June 30, 1958, and is reported in the *New York Times,* July 2, 1958, 19:2.
10. *Pennsylvania* v. *Board* (1958).
11. 104 *Congressional Record* 14089.
12. *Ibid.,* p. 13406.
13. H.R. 13760, 85/2. The bill was reported by the House Foreign Relations Committee (House Report No. 2684) on August 21, 1958, and debated and passed on August 23 (104 *Congressional Record* 19653–59).

9. SHOWDOWN IN THE SENATE

1. Except where otherwise noted this chapter is largely based on interviews. The daily reports of the *New York Times,* the *Washington Post & Times-Herald,* and the *New York Herald Tribune* were also extremely helpful, especially the material in Anthony Lewis' columns in the *New York Times.* After this chapter was in draft form my attention was directed to an excellent unsigned article, by Jamison Cain, in the *Columbia* (South Carolina) *State,* August 24, 1958. Joseph Rauh published a fine article, "The Truth about Congress and the Court," 22 *Progressive* 30 (November, 1958). Although I have made use of Rauh and Cain, my account differs both in matters of fact and interpretation from each of theirs, and, as far as I can judge, from any other published material.

2. William S. White, *Citadel: The Story of the United States Senate* (New York: Harper & Bros., 1956), p. 2. For another recent and illuminating study of the Senate see Donald R. Matthews, *U.S. Senators and Their World* (Chapel Hill: University of North Carolina Press, 1960).

3. 104 *Congressional Record* 15418.

4. *Ibid.,* p. 16127. There was no written report submitted at the time.

5. Senate Report No. 2228.

6. Senate Report No. 2230.

7. For details of the bill see Senate Report No. 2252.

8. *Ibid.,* pp. 32–33.

9. For Johnson's role in the Senate consult: Arthur Krock's column in *New York Times,* July 13, 1956, 18:5; the letter of Wayne Morse to Johnson, *ibid.,* September 5, 1959, 11:3; *Congressional Q. W.,* Supplement to October 30, 1959, Weekly Report, pp. 3–4; Cabell Phillips, "The Way Lyndon Johnson Does It," *New York Times Magazine,* July 26, 1959, p. 9; articles by William S. White reprinted at 104 *Congressional Record* 3089, 12000, and White, *Citadel, passim,* especially p. 105.

10. 104 *Congressional Record* 18691.

11. National Chamber, "Intervention in State and Local Affairs," *Special Report,* July 23, 1958. See also: National Chamber, *Congressional Action,* Vol. II, nos. 28, 29, 31 (July 25, 30, and August 8, 1958), and *Washington Report,* Vol. I, no. 42 (August 1, 1958).

12. Quoted in Rauh, "The Truth about Congress and the Court."

13. For details on the functioning of the policy committees see Hugh A. Bone, "An Introduction to the Senate Policy Committees," 50 *Am. Pol. Sci. Rev.* 339 (1956); and David Truman, *The Congressional Party: A Case Study* (New York: John Wiley & Sons, Inc., 1959), especially chap. iv. The members of the Senate Democratic Policy Committee in 1958 were: Johnson (chairman), Mansfield (Mont.), Green (R.I.), Hill (Ala.), Kerr (Okla.), Russell (Ga.), Murray (Mont.), Hayden (Ariz.), and Hennings (Mo.).

14. *New York Times,* August 17, 1958, 42:1–3.

15. Department of Justice press release, August 18, 1958.

16. 104 *Congressional Record* 18511.

17. *Ibid.,* p. 18521.

18. H.R. 6789.

19. 104 *Congressional Record* 18687.

20. *Ibid.,* p. 18688.

21. *Ibid.*, p. 18693.
22. *Ibid.*, p. 18698.
23. *Ibid.*, p. 18730.
24. *Ibid.*, pp. 18732 ff.
25. *Ibid.*, p. 18748.
26. *Ibid.*, p. 18750.
27. *Ibid.*
28. In debate, Kuchel had indicated his desire to have S. 654 pass and had declared his opposition to any amendments (*ibid.*, pp. 18919–20). Since S. 654 and H.R. 3 (or rather S. 337, the Senate counterpart of H.R. 3) were considered collectively in the Senate, it is impossible to test these statements against roll call votes.
29. Lausche had second thoughts about his change; and in a colloquy, which to outsiders seemed obscure, managed to convey to Lyndon Johnson that he felt duped by the Majority leader's tactics. *Ibid.*, pp. 19058–59.
30. *Ibid.*, p. 18928.
31. Kuchel was an exception. See his remarks at *ibid.*, p. 18920.
32. Conference Report (House Report No. 2687).
33. 104 *Congressional Record* 19178.
34. *Ibid.*, pp. 19340–42. The letter from Circuit Judge William Denman had actually been sent to Senator Kilgore in 1956, but its being printed in the *Record* —at the request of Senator Morse—at this time gave the liberals moral support. Morse also inserted statements from the American Civil Liberties Union and the AFL-CIO.
35. *Washington Post & Times-Herald*, August 23, 1958.
36. Conference Report (House Report No. 2702).
37. 104 *Congressional Record* 19664.
38. *Ibid.*, p. 19557.
39. *Ibid.*, p. 19568.
40. *Ibid.*, p. 19576.

10. THE CRISIS RESOLVED

1. *Report of the Chief Justices' Committee on Federal-State Relationships* (Chicago: Council of State Governments, 1958), pp. 27–28. This report was approved by the conference. *Resolutions Adopted at the 10th Annual Meeting of the Conference of Chief Justices* (Chicago: Council of State Governments, 1958), p. 1.
2. October 24, 1958, pp. 36–37.
3. *Harv. L. Rec.*, October 23, 1958. Chief Justice Frederick W. Brune of Maryland, chairman of the committee which drafted the report, denied that any attack on the School cases had been intended (*New York Times*, January 8, 1959, 30:1).
4. *New York Times*, February 22, 1959, 1:3; February 25, 1959, 25:1–5. The report is reprinted at 105 *Congressional Record* 3007 ff. (daily ed.).
5. Quoted in John Nolan, "The Supreme Court versus the ABA," 70 *Commonweal* 179 (May 15, 1959).
6. See *New York Times*, April 19, 1959, 1:3; March 4, 1959, 18:4–6; March 11, 1959, 15:1; June 14, 1959, 1:7.

7. *Washington Post & Times-Herald,* February 26, 1959.

8. *New York Times,* April 9, 1959, 17:3.

9. *Washington Post & Times-Herald,* March 2, 1959; *New York Times,* March 12, 1959, 22:7, and April 28, 1959, 20:2.

10. *Washington Post & Times-Herald,* August 13, 1959. For a bibliography on this phase of the ABA's activities see Fellman, "Constitutional Law in 1958–59," 54 *Am. Pol. Sci. Rev.* 167, 171–72 (1960).

11. *New York Times,* August 26, 1959, 30:1.

12. *Cooper* v. *Aaron* (1958).

13. *Evers* v. *Dwyer* (1958).

14. *NAACP* v. *Patterson* (1959).

15. *Scull* v. *Virginia* (1959).

16. *Shuttlesworth* v. *Board* (1958).

17. *NAACP* v. *Arkansas* (1959).

18. *NAACP* v. *Williams* (1959).

19. *NAACP* v. *Bennett* (1959).

20. *Harrison* v. *NAACP* (1959).

21. *Flaxer* v. *United States* (1958).

22. *Raley* v. *Ohio* (1959).

23. *Vitarelli* v. *Seaton* (1959) and *Greene* v. *McElroy* (1959).

24. *New York Times,* March 10, 1959, 24:3.

25. 105 *Congressional Record* 3023 (daily ed.).

26. H.R. 8121, 86/1. A number of related bills were introduced in the Senate in the Eighty-sixth Congress, 1st sess., but received no action: S. 776 (Butler, Rep., Md.), S. 2392 (Johnston, Dem., S.C.), S. 2416 (Keating, Rep., N.Y.).

27. House Report No. 1122 (September 2, 1959).

28. Pub. L. 86–257, Sec. 701; 73 Stat. 541, amending 29 U.S.C. 164.

29. *Northwestern Portland Cement Co.* v. *Minnesota* (1959).

30. Pub. L. 86–272; 73 Stat. 555.

31. H.R. 3 was debated on June 22, 23, 24, 1959, and passed on June 24 by a 225–192 vote. 105 *Congressional Record* 10448–71, 10564–606, 10718–37 (daily ed.).

The Mallory bill, H.R. 4957, was debated and passed on July 7, 1959. 105 *Congressional Record* 11623–50 (daily ed.).

The "organize" redefinition, H.R. 2369, was passed without debate on March 2, 1959. 105 *Congressional Record* 2838 (daily ed.).

The habeas corpus proposal, H.R. 3216, was taken up and passed on July 29, 1959. 105 *Congressional Record* 13358–65 (daily ed.).

The Nelson measure, H.R. 2368, was reported by the Judiciary Committee, House Report No. 432, 105 *Congressional Record* 8798 (daily ed.), but since sec. 2 of the 1959 version of H.R. 3 contained an almost identical provision, there was no necessity for further House action.

32. S.J. Res. 32, 86/1.

33. H.R. 9069, House Report No. 1151.

34. The bill was debated on September 7 and 8, 1959, and passed on September 8. 105 *Congressional Record* 16932–43, 17066–80 (daily ed.).

35. 105 *Congressional Record* 3024 (daily ed.).

36. June 22, 1959, p. 48.

37. The program was televised on Channel WNEW, New York, N.Y., July 12, 1959. I watched the program, and the quotation is from my notes.

38. *Bates* v. *Little Rock* (1960).
39. 106 *Congressional Record* 1628–29 (daily ed.); see above, note 27, for the committee report.
40. Nor did the Senate take any action on three similar bills: S. 2314, S. 2392, and S. 2416.
41. S. 2652, Senate Report 1811, 106 *Congressional Record* 13989 (daily ed.).
42. 106 *Congressional Record* 14416 (daily ed.).

11. CONGRESS AND THE COURT

1. "The Supreme Court—October 1958 Term," 58 *Mich. L. Rev.* 165 (1959).
2. March 2, 1960, 36:1.
3. The statistics are taken from S. Sidney Ulmer, "The Analysis of Behavior Patterns on the United States Supreme Court," 22 *J. of Politics* 629, 631 (1960).
4. Quoted in *Southern School News,* February, 1957, p. 2. The statement was made in 1955 when the Alabama pupil placement law was being debated in the state legislature.
5. Howard K. Beale (ed.), *Diary of Gideon Welles* (New York: W. W. Norton & Co., Inc., 1960), III, 320, entry for March 23, 1868.
6. Quoted in Fawn Brodie, *Thaddeus Stevens,* p. 322.
7. For discussions of this problem, consult: Wallace Mendelson, "Mr. Justice Frankfurter—Law and Choice," 10 *Vand. L. Rev.* 333 (1957); and C. Herman Pritchett, *The Political Offender and the Warren Court,* pp. 70–74.
8. S. M. Lipset, *Political Man* (New York: Doubleday & Co., Inc., 1959), chap. 4, especially pp. 101–14, and literature cited.
9. Mr. Justice Frankfurter replied to the suggested requirement of previous judicial experience in his article: "The Supreme Court in the Mirror of the Justices," 105 *U. Pa. L. Rev.* 781 (1957).
10. Charles P. Curtis, Jr., *Lions under the Throne* (Boston: Houghton Mifflin Co., 1947), p. 192.
11. "Law and the Future," 52 *Fortune* 106 (November, 1955).
12. See, for example, the opinion of the Court in *Cooper* v. *Aaron* (1958), the opinions of Warren and Frankfurter in *Trop* v. *Dulles* (1958), Black's brilliant James Madison Lecture, "The Bill of Rights," 35 *N.Y.U. L. Rev.* 865 (1960), and Douglas, "On Misconception of the Judicial Function and the Responsibility of the Bar," 59 *Col. L. Rev.* 227 (1959).
13. George Braden's article, "The Search for Objectivity in Constitutional Law," 57 *Yale L. J.* 571 (1948), is an excellent critique of the efforts of Stone, Frankfurter, and Black to depersonalize their decision-making.
14. Frankfurter has been the most voluble in this attempt. See especially his separate opinion in *Public Utilities Commission* v. *Pollak* (1952), and his articles: "The Judicial Process and the Supreme Court," 98 *Proceedings of the American Philosophic Society* 233 (1954), and "The Reading of Statutes," 47 *Col. L. Rev.* 527 (1947). But I believe that this statement is no less true of Black, Douglas, Brennan, or Warren.
15. David Danelski has a thoughtful analysis of the power of the Chief Justice within the Court: "The Influence of the Chief Justice in the Decision-making Process of the Supreme Court," paper delivered at the 1960 Annual Meeting of the American Political Science Association. A shorter version of this paper is pub-

lished in Walter F. Murphy and C. Herman Pritchett, *Courts, Judges, and Politics* (New York: Random House, 1961).

16. Whether or to what extent Hughes switched his position has been heatedly debated. Merlo Pusey, *Charles Evans Hughes,* II, chaps. 69–71, especially pp. 770–72, feels that Hughes did not change. Alpheus T. Mason, "Charles Evans Hughes: An Appeal to the Bar of History," 6 *Vand. L. Rev.* 1 (1952), demolishes Pusey's argument. Although less outspoken than Mason, Samuel Hendel, *Charles Evans Hughes and the Supreme Court* (New York: King's Crown Press, 1951), p. 279, tends to agree: "When the pressure for innovation became great, and the risks to the nation and to the Court itself apparent, reluctantly at first, but increasingly he went along with change. Having sedulously sought to protect the precedents of the Court, sometimes at the risk of offending logic, he witnessed and often participated in the shattering of one precedent after another. He stood thus as a kind of heroic and, in a sense, tragic figure, torn between the old and the new, seeking at first to stem the tide but then relentlessly caught up and moving with it."

17. See Murphy and Pritchett, *op. cit.,* chap. 8. The literature on the group basis of politics is enormous. Among the more important works are: A. F. Bentley, *The Process of Government* (Chicago: University of Chicago Press, 1908); David B. Truman, *The Governmental Process* (New York: Alfred A. Knopf, Inc., 1951); Lipset, *op. cit.;* Angus Campbell *et al., The American Voter* (New York: John Wiley & Sons, Inc., 1960), especially chaps. 12–17, 20; Earl Latham, *The Group Basis of Politics* (Ithaca, N.Y.: Cornell University Press, 1952); see also the recent symposium "Bentley Revisited," by R. E. Dowling, Myron Q. Hale, and Robert T. Golembiewski in the December, 1960, issue of the *Am. Pol. Sci. Rev.*

For material specifically related to the courts consult: Jack W. Peltason, *Federal Courts in the Political Process* (New York: Random House, 1955); Victor Rosenblum, *Law as a Political Instrument* (New York: Random House, 1955); Note, "Private Attorneys General," 58 *Yale L. J.* 574 (1949); Fowler Harper and Edwin D. Etherington, "Lobbyists before the Court," 101 *U. Pa. L. Rev.* 1172 (1953); Walter F. Murphy, "The South Counterattacks: The Anti-NAACP Laws,"12 *West. Pol. Q.* 371 (1959), and book review, 73 *Harv. L. Rev.* 1236 (1960); Clement E. Vose, *Caucasians Only* (Berkeley: University of California Press, 1959), "The National Consumers' League and the Brandeis Brief," 1 *Midw. J. of Pol. Sci.* 267 (1957), and "Litigation as a Form of Pressure Group Activity," 319 *Annals* 20 (1958).

18. Compare, for example, the effectiveness of the American Medical Association: Stanley Kelley, Jr., *Professional Public Relations and Political Power* (Baltimore: Johns Hopkins University Press, 1956), chap. 3.

19. *Op. cit.,* p. 350. Cf. Julius Turner, *Party and Constituency: Pressures on Congress,* Johns Hopkins University Studies in History and Political Science, Series LXIX, No. 1 (1951).

20. In addition to the literature listed above in note 17 see Bernard R. Berelson, Paul F. Lazarsfeld, and William N. McPhee, *Voting: A Study of Opinion Formation in a Presidential Campaign* (Chicago: University of Chicago Press, 1954), and the material cited in Lipset, *op. cit.,* pp. 88–89 n.

21. For discussions of the general political attitudes and values of American Jews see: Lawrence Fuchs, *The Political Behavior of American Jews* (Glencoe, Ill.: Free Press, 1956); Wesley and Beverly Allinsmith, "Religious Affiliation and

Politico-economic Attitude," 12 *Pub. Op. Q.* 377 (1948); and Lipset, *op. cit.* pp. 243–44, 288–90, and literature cited.

22. June 29, 1957.

23. August 24, 1957.

24. Columnists Louis Budenz and John B. Sheerin did include some information about the Court.

25. June 7, 1957.

26. July 5, 1957.

27. July 19, 1957.

28. The quotations were taken from Sheerin's column in the *Michigan Catholic,* February 13, 1958, and in the *Pittsburgh Catholic,* April 3, 1958. This column is syndicated and appears in some twenty Catholic periodicals.

29. Donald R. Matthews, *U.S. Senators and Their World* (Chapel Hill: University of North Carolina Press, 1960), chaps. 8–9, has some interesting discussion of the relations between senators on the one hand and lobbyists and reporters on the other.

30. William S. White, *The Taft Story* (New York: Harper & Bros., 1954), chap. 16, and *Citadel, passim;* Matthews, *op. cit.,* chaps. 4–5; Richard S. Rovere, *Affairs of State: The Eisenhower Years* (New York: Farrar, Straus, & Cudahy, 1956), p. 225; David B. Truman, *The Congressional Party* (New York: John Wiley & Sons, Inc., 1959), p. 314.

31. Truman, *The Congressional Party,* p. 1.

32. For two recent and rather extreme statements on this matter consult: James Burnham, *Congress and the American Tradition* (Chicago: Henry Regnery Co., 1959); and C. Wright Mills, *The Power Elite* (New York: Oxford University Press, 1956), especially chap. 11.

33. White, *Citadel,* pp. 98–99.

34. Louis Koenig, *The Invisible Presidency* (New York: Holt, Rinehart & Winston, Inc., 1960), p. 339. For similar observations see: Jack Bell, *The Splendid Misery: The Story of the Presidency and Power Politics at Close Range* (New York: Doubleday & Co., Inc., 1960); Walter Johnson, *1600 Pennsylvania Avenue* (Boston: Little, Brown & Co., 1960). Cf. Richard Neustadt, *Presidential Power* (New York: John Wiley & Sons, Inc., 1960), particularly chap. 7. On Eisenhower's ideas about his administrative machinery and his efforts to reorganize the executive department consult: Robert J. Donovan, *Eisenhower: The Inside Story* (New York: Harper & Bros., 1956), particularly chap. 5; John L. Steele, "The New-Model Cabinet," *Life,* October 8, 1956, p. 89; Sydney Hyman, "The Cabinet Job as Eisenhower Sees It," *New York Times Magazine,* July 20, 1958, p. 7; House and Senate Committees on Government Operations, *Joint Hearings on Reorganization Plan #1 of 1953,* 83/1; Richard Neustadt, "Presidency and Legislation: The Growth of Central Clearance," 48 *Am. Pol. Sci. Rev.* 641 (1954); and Richard F. Fenno, *The President's Cabinet* (Cambridge, Mass.: Harvard University Press, 1959).

35. Glendon A. Schubert, Jr., *The Presidency in the Courts* (Minneapolis: University of Minnesota Press, 1957), p. 347, argues that "the most significant aspect of judicial review of presidential orders is its ineffectiveness." While it may be true that such cases as *Little* v. *Barreme* (1804) and the Steel Seizure case of 1952 are rare exceptions, they are still important ones. Congressmen may also use the Court as a prop to deny legislation to a popular President. Rather than fight the President on the merits of a proposal, recalcitrant members of Congress

can and have opposed a bill on the grounds that the Supreme Court would declare it unconstitutional.

36. Quoted in Samuel Flagg Bemis, *John Quincy Adams and the Foundations of American Foreign Policy* (New York: Alfred A. Knopf, Inc., 1949), p. 188.

37. Wheeler had introduced a bill, S.J. Res. 80, 75/1, proposing a constitutional amendment providing that if the Supreme Court declared an act of Congress invalid, Congress, after an intervening election, might repass the statute by a two-thirds vote and so reverse the Court's decision as to the law's constitutionality. O'Mahoney had proposed a constitutional amendment, S.J. Res. 98, 75/1, requiring a two-thirds majority of the Court—with each Justice writing his own opinion—to invalidate a state or federal law.

38. Quoted in Koenig, *op. cit.*, p. 286.

39. *Ickes Diaries,* II, 172.

40. Brodie, *op. cit.*, pp. 254, 293, 322.

41. McCloskey, *The American Supreme Court,* p. 15.

42. Harlan Stone once wrote to a friend explaining one of his opinions: "I should have preferred to have written your opinion than the one which will actually appear on the books. Had I done so I should have been in a minority of two or three, instead of a majority of six. . . . I proceed upon the theory . . . that the large objectives should be kept constantly in mind and reached by whatever road is open, provided only that untenable distinctions are not taken, and that I am not, in the process, committed incidentally to the doctrine of which I disapprove or which would hinder the Court's coming out ultimately in the right place. All of this proves that the university professor is the only free man who can develop legal doctrine in his own way and travel the road he chooses in accounting for his conclusions." Quoted in Mason, *Harlan Fiske Stone,* p. 308.

43. One of the most interesting analyses of this doctrine is John P. Roche, "Judicial Self-Restraint," 49 *Am. Pol. Sci. Rev.* 762 (1955). On the Court, the late Robert H. Jackson emphasized this aspect of self-restraint more than Frankfurter. See his remarks in the preface to his book, *The Struggle for Judicial Supremacy,* and the analysis in Walter F. Murphy, "Mr. Justice Jackson, Free Speech, and the Judicial Function," 12 *Vand. L. Rev.* 1019 (1959). Some of Jackson's private comments are reported in Mason, *op. cit.*, pp. 614–16, 674.

44. "Politics as a Vocation," in H. H. Gerth and C. Wright Mills (eds.), *From Max Weber: Essays in Sociology* (New York: Oxford University Press, 1946), p. 116.

45. *Administrators of Byrnes* v. *Administrators of Stewart* (1812).

46. Possible delaying tactics are spelled out in Roche, *op. cit.*, and in Loren Beth, "Technical and Doctrinal Aids to Constitutional Interpretation," 18 *U. Pitts. L. Rev.* 108 (1956).

47. I consulted the files of the American Institute of Public Opinion, Princeton, N.J., and also corresponded with the Roper Public Opinion Research Center at Williams College. The latter has a large file of national public opinion polls (as well as local samplings) other than those conducted by the Roper organization.

48. See especially the AIPO press releases of January 13, 1957, August 14, 1957, September 24, 1958, October 15, 1958, July 7, 1959. The January 13, 1957, and the July 3, 1959, releases have lengthy summaries of the results of previous polls.

49. AIPO press releases, April 13, 1955, November 6, 1955, and December 23, 1955.

50. October 9, 1955.
51. October 9, 1955.
52. April 13, 1955.
53. November 14, 1955.
54. AIPO release, April 15, 1955.
55. AIPO release, October 17, 1955.
56. AIPO release, July 28, 1957. According to AIPO's files, the poll was taken from June 26 to July 3, 1957.
57. AIPO release, December 26, 1953.
58. Neustadt, *Presidential Power,* chap. 4, has a valuable discussion of this problem as it relates to the Presidency.
59. *Addison* v. *Holly Hill* (1944); *Chrysler Corp.* v. *United States* (1942); *Radio Station WOW* v. *Johnson* (1945); *Sutton* v. *Lieb* (1952).
60. See especially Helen Shirley Thomas, *Felix Frankfurter: Scholar on the Bench* (Baltimore: Johns Hopkins University Press, 1960), chap. 12; Louis L. Jaffe, "The Judicial Universe of Mr. Justice Frankfurter," 62 *Harv. L. Rev.* 357 (1949), and Mendelson, *op. cit.*
61. Marshall's penchant for using dicta to speak on issues not actually before the Court may have been wise statesmanship, but it is a dangerous model of craftsmanship. Jefferson once commented to Justice Johnson: "This practice of Judge Marshall, of travelling out of his case to prescribe what the law would be in a moot case not before the court, is very irregular and very censurable." June 12, 1823, *Writings,* XV, 447. The *American Law Review*'s criticism of the Milligan case was quoted in chapter 3. Justice Harlan in dissent, and numerous commentators since, have emphasized Fuller's "error" in the Standard Oil case (1911). To support reading "the rule of reason" into the Sherman Act, Fuller had cited several cases which had specifically rejected such an assertion. The Court under Taft and Hughes was subjected to severe criticism, much of which came from within the Court itself. For trenchant outside criticism of the work of the Hughes Court see in particular: Thomas Reed Powell, "Commerce, Pensions, and Codes," 49 *Harv. L. Rev.* 1–43, 193–238 (1935), and "Some Aspects of American Constitutional Law," 53 *ibid.* 529, especially pp. 549–53 (1940); Felix Frankfurter and Henry M. Hart, Jr., "The Business of the Supreme Court at the October Term, 1934," 49 *ibid.* 68, 101–7 (1935); Henry M. Hart, Jr., "The Gold Clause in United States Bonds," 48 *ibid.* 1057 (1935); and Jackson, *op. cit.,* chap. 4.
62. C. Herman Pritchett goes even further and states that the segregation issue "guaranteed the defeat of the attack" against the Court. *Congress versus the Supreme Court* (Minneapolis: University of Minnesota Press, 1961), p. 120.
63. The results in the very short run do not appear at all hopeless for the cause of civil liberties. See the text of Executive Order 10865, 25 Fed. Reg. 1583 (1960), setting up new procedures for an industrial security program as a result of *Greene* v. *McElroy*. This order is discussed by Anthony Lewis in the *New York Times,* February 21, 1960, E7:4–8.
64. *Op. cit.,* p. viii.

CASE INDEX

CASE INDEX

CASE INDEX

SUBJECT INDEX

SUBJECT INDEX

SUBJECT INDEX